IMMIGRANTS IN A CHANGING LABOR MARKET:
Responding to Economic Needs

By Michael Fix,
Demetrios G. Papademetriou,
and Madeleine Sumption

Migration Policy Institute

March 2013

© 2013 Migration Policy Institute
All Rights Reserved.

No part of this publication may be reproduced or transmitted in any form by any means, electronic or mechanical, including photocopy, or any information storage and retrieval system, without permission from the Migration Policy Institute. Permission for reproducing excerpts from this volume should be directed to: Permissions Department, Migration Policy Institute, 1400 16th Street, NW, Suite 300, Washington, DC 20036, or by contacting communications@migrationpolicy.org or visiting www.migrationpolicy.org/about/copy.php.

Library of Congress Cataloging-in-Publication Data

Immigrants in a changing labor market : responding to economic needs / edited by Michael Fix, Demetrios G. Papademetriou, and Madeleine Sumption.
    pages cm
 ISBN 978-0-9831591-0-0
1. Foreign workers--United States--Government policy. 2. United States--Emigration and immigration--Government policy. 3. Labor market--United States. 4. Manpower policy--United States. I. Fix, Michael. II. Papademetriou, Demetrios G. III. Sumption, Madeleine.
  HD6300.I446 2013
  331.6'20973--dc23
                  2012050068

Cover Photo: "worker inside modern building in silhouette" by Rui Vale de Sousa, (29675341)
www.shutterstock.com
Cover Design: April Siruno, MPI
Typesetting: Erin Perkins, LeafDev

Suggested citation: Fix, Michael, Demetrios G. Papademetriou, and Madeleine Sumption, eds. 2013. *Immigrants in a Changing Labor Market: Responding to Economic Needs*. Washington, DC: Migration Policy Institute.

Printed in the United States of America.

TABLE OF CONTENTS

INTRODUCTION: Immigrants in a Changing Labor Market: An Overview 1
   Michael Fix, Demetrios G. Papademetriou, and Madeleine Sumption

PART ONE: WHAT KIND OF IMMIGRATION POLICY DOES THE US ECONOMY NEED?

CHAPTER 1: Immigration Policy and Less-Skilled Workers in the United States: Reflections on Future Directions for Reform 19
   Harry J. Holzer

CHAPTER 2: The Economics of Illegal Immigration in the United States: Policy Implications 53
   Gordon H. Hanson

CHAPTER 3: The Impact of Immigrants in Recession and Economic Expansion 69
   Giovanni Peri

CHAPTER 4: The Elusive Idea of Labor-Market 'Shortages' and the US Approach to Employment-Based Immigration Policy 93
   Madeleine Sumption

PART TWO: NEW BARRIERS TO IMMIGRANT INTEGRATION IN A WEAK ECONOMY

CHAPTER 5: How Immigrants and US Natives Fare during Recessions and Recoveries 123
   Pia M. Orrenius and Madeline Zavodny

CHAPTER 6: Eroding Gains: The Recession's Impact on Immigrants in Middle-Skilled Jobs 167
   Jeanne Batalova and Michael Fix

ACKNOWLEDGMENTS 199
ABOUT THE EDITORS AND AUTHORS 201
ABOUT THE LABOR MARKETS INITIATIVE 207

INTRODUCTION

IMMIGRANTS IN A CHANGING LABOR MARKET: AN OVERVIEW

Demetrios G. Papademetriou, Michael Fix, and Madeleine Sumption

Migration Policy Institute

I. A New Economic Landscape

The economic landscape facing immigration policymakers in the United States is undergoing a profound transformation. After two decades of almost uninterrupted growth, the US economy plunged from the prosperity of the mid-2000s into an unexpectedly deep and protracted recession, with a legacy of high unemployment projected to last for several more years even under favorable growth scenarios.

Five years after the economic crisis began, the share of men who held a job was at its lowest level since 1948 when the US Department of Labor started collecting the data.[1] In mid-2012 more than 40 percent of the unemployed had been jobless for more than six months.[2] Even when the recovery starts apace, available workers may not have the skills and qualifications that employers demand. The sheer scale, depth, and duration of the crisis deepen the risk that workers' skills will atrophy, and that jobs will go begging even as large numbers remain unemployed. At the same time, the unrelenting pace of technological change, coupled with long-term educational failures and a frayed workforce-development infrastructure, exacerbate the risk of mismatch between workers' skills and employers' expectations. In this context, the Great Recession and its impacts may continue to define the social and economic challenges facing the nation for the foreseeable future, with little prospect of a timely return to the 4 percent to 5 percent unemployment rates of the pre-2008 era.

---

1   Labor-force participation trends for women have changed enormously since the middle of the century, making male employment rates a more reliable indicator of economic conditions than the total employment rate.
2   US Labor Department, Bureau of Labor Statistics (BLS), "The Employment Situation, June 2012," www.bls.gov/news.release/archives/empsit_07062012.pdf.

At the same time, uncertainty about the nation's role in the global economy is greater than ever. The economic crisis and its aftermath have brought into sharp relief the narrowing gap between the United States and emerging economies such as China, whose economy grew by more than 40 percent between 2007 and 2011 while its American counterpart stagnated.[3] The desire to recover a slipping global market share in knowledge-intensive industries, such as high-tech manufacturing, has become a mainstay of the US political debate.[4] On the domestic front, concerns have grown over falling rates of entrepreneurship and the need to create an environment that better supports high-growth enterprises.[5] At the same time, the aging population is set to put unrelenting pressure on public finances, as the entitlements to which US society is now accustomed become less affordable.

In all fields of public policy, these trends have not only raised short-term questions about how best to respond to a rapidly changing economic environment, but have also prompted broader reflection on whether old policy models are sustainable and what changes will be needed to navigate the new economic landscape.

As the United States emerges from the crisis, questions abound about the appropriate role of immigration policy. Can the US labor market still accommodate steady flows of new immigrants without undermining the work and advancement opportunities of existing members of the labor force? Can it provide immigrants and their families with the opportunities they need to support their families and integrate economically? Should the crisis change our underlying assumptions about the impacts of immigration and its role in building a robust economy? In sum: what kind of immigration policy does the new US economy need?

---

[3] Calculated using historical data and 2011 projections from the International Monetary Fund (IMF), "World Economic Outlook Database," www.imf.org/external/pubs/ft/weo/2011/02/weodata/index.aspx.

[4] US high-tech manufacturing industries have a higher share of global output than any other country; but the US global share fell from 34 percent in 1998 to 28 percent in 2010, according to the National Science Foundation. By contrast, China's high-tech manufacturing share rose from 3 percent to 19 percent between 1995 and 2010, reaching nearly 50 percent in the computer industry. National Science Foundation (NSF), *Science and Engineering Indicators 2012* (Arlington, VA: National Science Foundation, January 2012), chapter 6, www.nsf.gov/statistics/seind12/c6/c6h.htm.

[5] While self-employment has risen alongside high unemployment in recent years, the creation of firms that have at least one employee has experienced a gradual longer-term decline, according to data from the Kauffman Foundation. Robert Fairlie, *Kauffman Index of Entrepreneurial Activity, 1996-2011* (Kansas City, MO: Kauffman Foundation, 2012), www.kauffman.org/uploadedFiles/KIEA_2012_report.pdf.

A. Changing Immigration Flows in the Postrecession Economy

Seismic shifts in the economic environment have been clearly reflected in immigration flows, even if their impact has been highly uneven. For more than 30 years, the United States has experienced historically high immigration levels. Fueled by an economy that generated seemingly unending demand for low-wage workers, many came to see illegal immigration as an inevitable feature of the US labor market. In the higher-skill labor market, tens of thousands of engineers and hundreds of thousands of computer scientists received visas to work for US employers.[6] The expanding economy appeared to absorb the additional labor with ease and many embraced its economic contribution with relatively few questions asked.

The crisis abruptly altered this picture, particularly at the low-wage end of the labor market. The growth in the unauthorized population ground to a halt between 2007 and 2011,[7] and net migration from Mexico fell to near zero. At the same time, fewer employers sought visas for immigrants in low-wage jobs. An exception to this trend was in agriculture, an immigrant-reliant industry where employment held steady,[8] while demand for H-2A agricultural worker visas fell only modestly.[9] Economic recovery may not reverse the decline in less-skilled immigration entirely — not least because the construction industry, whose collapse was a key driver of both legal and illegal flows at this skill level, may not rebound sufficiently for many years.[10] Meanwhile, other factors further militate against a return to pre-2007 levels of immigration into low-wage jobs, including massive investments in US border controls, aggressive interior enforcement measures, an improving Mexican economy, and — most importantly — demographic developments in Mexico, most notably a

---

6   United States Citizenship and Immigration Services (USCIS), "Characteristics of Specialty Occupation Workers (H-1B)," various years, www.uscis.gov/portal/site/uscis/menuitem.eb1d4c2a3e5b9ac89243c6a7543f6d1a/?vgnextoid=9a1d9ddf801b3210VgnVCM100000b92ca60aRCRD&vgnextchannel=9a1d9ddf801b3210VgnVCM100000b92ca60aRCRD.
7   According to US Department of Homeland Security (DHS) estimates. See Michael Hoefer, Nancy Rytina, and Bryan Baker, *Estimates of the Unauthorized Immigrant Population Residing in the United States: January 2011* (Washington, DC: DHS, 2012), www.dhs.gov/xlibrary/assets/statistics/publications/ois_ill_pe_2011.pdf.
8   The value of agricultural production in the United States grew 9 percent from 2007 to 2010, and despite a decrease in exports in 2009, net agricultural exports remained well above the levels of the early- and mid-2000s. Tom Hertz, "Hired Farm Labor Held Steady in Great Recession," *Amber Waves*, December 2011, www.ers.usda.gov/AmberWaves/December11/PDF/HiredFarmLabor.pdf; and US Census Bureau, "Table 849, Agricultural Exports and Imports — Value: 1990-2010," www.census.gov/compendia/statab/2012/tables/12s0849.pdf.
9   The number of H-2A visas issued fell by 15 percent between 2008 and 2010, but remained well above 2007 levels. US Department of State, "Nonimmigrant Visa Statistics," http://travel.state.gov/visa/statistics/nivstats/nivstats_4582.html.
10 BLS, "Occupational Outlook Handbook: Projections Overview," 2012, www.bls.gov/ooh/About/Projections-Overview.htm.

steady decline in the country's birth rate, which is reducing the total number of young people likely to migrate.

In the low and middle echelons of the skill spectrum, several areas of the labor market escaped the worst of the crisis. Unemployment among the college educated increased but remained below 5 percent throughout the late 2000s, and by 2011 the rate among doctoral and professional degree holders was as low as 2.5 percent despite the crisis.[11] Tech employers continued to cite access to talent as a top priority.[12] Meanwhile, health-sector employment not only grew over the course of the crisis, adding 1,360,000 jobs between January 2008 and June 2012,[13] but was projected to chalk up higher workforce growth than any other industry in the coming decade.[14] And although the labor-market effects of population aging cannot be predicted simplistically, a growing demand for health-care workers is widely expected across the skill spectrum, including in several large occupations with strong immigrant representation.

In the longer term, the demands on the immigration system will depend on a host of factors that are difficult to predict with confidence. For example, what if older workers work longer because they have lost their retirement savings, mistrust the old-age safety net, or simply find that their skills and experience command a high premium and who employers are willing to offer more flexible working conditions? How will continuing labor-market distress affect behavior among marginalized workers whose labor-force participation cannot be taken for granted, including the long-term unemployed, discouraged workers, the urban poor, or women who have left the labor force but may decide to return? How significantly will investments in productivity-enhancing technologies continue to widen the gap between workers with and without postsecondary education and training? As mechanization reduces demand for some categories of middle-skilled workers, will the transition from low- to middle-wage jobs become more unattainable? How will domestic workers react to the changing rewards the labor market offers: will they seek out higher education and quality technical training, or will the growth in educational attainment continue to stall?

---

11   Data on the college educated retrieved from BLS, "Labor Force Statistics Data Retrieval Tool: Current Population Survey," www.bls.gov/webapps/legacy/cpsatab4.htm; data on professional and doctoral degree holders from BLS, "Employment Projections: Education Pays," www.bls.gov/emp/ep_chart_001.htm.
12   Testimony of Brad Smith, General Counsel and Senior Vice President, Legal Corporate Affairs, Microsoft, before the US Senate Committee on the Judiciary, Subcommittee on Immigration, Refugees, and Border Security, *The Economic Imperative for Immigration Reform: High-Skilled Immigration as a Driver of Economic Growth,* 112th Cong., 1st sess., July 26, 2011, www.judiciary.senate.gov/pdf/11-7-26%20Smith%20Testimony.pdf.
13   BLS, "Employment, Hours, and Earnings from the Current Employment Statistics Survey: Series CES6562000001," http://data.bls.gov/timeseries/CES6562000001?data_tool=XGtable.
14   The largest growth is expected in the middle and lower end of the skill spectrum, with large projected employment increases for registered nurses and home health aides respectively. BLS, "Occupational Outlook Handbook 2012-13 Edition: Projections Overview."

As policymakers negotiate prospective immigration policy reforms in this uncertain economic landscape, a reassessment of immigration's economic role is warranted. This book examines the evidence on the impact of immigration and the policies that shape it, summarizing the state of the available knowledge and raising a series of questions: What has changed since the economic crisis? Does received wisdom on immigration's impact still hold in the postcrisis economy? How responsive has the immigration system been to shifting economic needs? And how can policymakers create systems that will cope with both expected and unexpected challenges in the postcrisis economy? The chapters comprise an updated selection of the papers produced for the Migration Policy Institute's Labor Markets Initiative, a three-year project that began in 2008.[15]

B. Principal Findings

From the early 1980s to the eve of the economic crisis in 2007, the immigrant population increased dramatically. Permanent visa issuances increased from between 500,000 and 600,000 per year in the early 1980s to more than 1 million in the mid-2000s, with family unification accounting for the largest share of inflows.[16] But very large shares also arrived illegally, particularly during the economic booms of the 1980s, 1990s, and 2000s. Others came as workers on temporary visas, whose number increased substantially after the *Immigration Act of 1990*; as refugees and asylum seekers; and as students, many of whom stayed on after graduation to join the US labor market. These flows brought into the labor market new arrivals with widely varying levels of formal education, occupational experience, and language proficiency.

The impact of this wave of immigration on the incomes and job prospects of existing members of the labor force is arguably the single most studied and debated question in the economics of immigration in the United States. The parameters of the current debate were firmly established in 1997 with the release of the National Research Council's survey of the evidence, *The New Americans*.[17] This report found that while immigration increases prosperity on average, some lower-income groups may lose out. This assessment remains the consensus view today, although a much richer research base now exists, allowing a more detailed assessment of immigrants' impact and its variation across different parts of the labor force.

---

15   The full range of publications produced for the project can be found at http://migrationpolicy.org/lmi/.
16   Immigration and Naturalization Service (INS), *Statistical Yearbook of the Immigration and Naturalization Service: 1985* (Washington, DC: INS, 1986); and DHS, *Yearbook of Immigration Statistics 2005* (Washington, DC: DHS, 2006), www.dhs.gov/xlibrary/assets/statistics/yearbook/2005/OIS_2005_Yearbook.pdf.
17   James P. Smith and Barry Edmonston, eds., *The New Americans: Economic, Demographic, and Fiscal Effects of Immigration* (Washington, DC: National Academy Press, 1997), www.nap.edu/catalog/5779.html.

In Chapter 1, Harry Holzer sets the stage by assessing recent evidence on the impact of immigration on earnings and employment prospects, focusing on the impact of less-skilled immigration. While most economists agree that highly skilled immigration brings broad economic benefits, the role of less-skilled newcomers and the policies that govern their admission and stay provoke much more disagreement. Research on the labor-market impact of less-skilled immigrants is sensitive to the methodology it employs; nonetheless, empirical studies have yielded some relatively consistent findings. First, even the more negative estimates of the impact on US workers competing for similar jobs suggest that in the long run, immigration accounts for only a small share of the deterioration in less-skilled Americans' earnings and employment rates. In the absence of immigration, Holzer argues, some workers' wages might rise somewhat in the short term, but the impact would be short-lived and probably not large enough to substantially improve the welfare of less-skilled Americans.

Second, less-skilled immigration has some benefits that have not yet been fully explored in empirical research, including benefits that accrue to consumers who purchase the goods and services less-skilled immigrants produce. Holzer argues that these benefits flow not just to high-income consumers in the form of cheaper restaurant tabs, landscaping, and child care (which has allowed many highly skilled women in particular to return to the labor market after having children), but also to low-income consumers in the form of lower prices for or greater availability of food, health care, and housing.

Third, there is no "optimal" level of immigration from an economic perspective. Even if the impacts of immigration could be measured with certainty, their range and complexity would prevent economists from making simple determinations about whether or not less-skilled immigration should be higher or lower. Moreover, the impact of a given level of immigration depends on the way policies are designed, including how easily employment-based immigrants are able to move from temporary status to permanent residence and whether they can switch between employers to seek out higher wages or move to areas or industries where demand is highest. Concrete evidence on the impacts of these and similar policy decisions remains relatively limited, in part because the necessary data are either not collected or not systematically analyzed.

The fact that a large share of less-skilled immigrants is illegally resident makes it particularly challenging to design effective policies to manage the flows. **In Chapter 2,** Gordon Hanson examines the ways in which illegal entry and status shape the economic impact of immigration on the low-wage echelons of the labor market.

Despite the extremely contentious debate on illegal immigration, Hanson finds that its overall *economic* impact is in fact quite small. Unauthorized immigrants make up a substantial share of the less-skilled labor force in the United States, providing a ready source of workers in a range of low-wage jobs from agriculture and food processing to construction and cleaning services. But while unauthorized immigrants provide significant benefits to employers in certain industries, they nonetheless make up a small share of the *total* labor force. At the same time, the economic benefits they bring are offset by some short-term costs on members of the workforce competing for similar jobs. Once these costs and benefits are taken into account, the net or average impact across the economy as a whole is essentially negligible. Even using more negative assumptions about immigrants' fiscal costs and the extent to which they compete with US workers for jobs, Hanson describes the overall impact of illegal immigration as essentially "a wash."

Illegal immigration also has proved more responsive to market conditions than legal immigration, making it a particularly appealing source of labor for some employers. As the economic crisis of the late 2000s has amply demonstrated, illegal entries can be highly sensitive to economic conditions. Legal, employment-based immigration policies at the less-skilled level have limited flexibility to respond to employer demand in this way. Green cards are almost entirely unavailable to low- and middle-skilled workers, while the two main low-skilled temporary visa programs (H-2A and H-2B) vary little over the economic cycle. Moreover, these employment-based flows are currently so small relative to the unauthorized population that their labor-market impact is not particularly significant.

One of the dilemmas these findings pose for policymakers is how to make legal immigration a more attractive option for employers who would otherwise turn to unauthorized labor, without deregulating the system entirely. Expanding legal, employment-based immigration and allowing inflows to fluctuate with the economy would enable the system to become more responsive to demand. But a more market-driven legal immigration system would also have the consequence of expanding the low-wage labor force by admitting new immigrants who would *not* otherwise have come illegally. This possibility is generally not welcomed, especially at a time when many individuals working in the same occupations as unauthorized immigrants face difficult economic circumstances.

Legal, employment-based visas will not replace illegal immigration for all employers. For some employers in fields, such as hospitality and construction, last-minute hiring or short-duration contract work is commonplace and legal visas cannot easily accommodate these practices. For many employers, however, legal routes could be made more flexible. In his chapter Hanson argues that policymakers could create incentives for employers to hire legally — and for immigrants to immigrate legally — if the rules rewarded compliance with a chance to seek lawful permanent residence; this option is essentially unavailable to less-skilled, work-based immigrants and their employers under the current system.

The idea of creating a system that responds more closely to shifting economic needs is taken up further **in Chapter 3**, in which Giovanni Peri analyzes the impact of immigration over the course of the economic cycle. Despite a broad consensus among economists that the average impact of immigration in the long run is small but positive, the impact in the short run raises much more uncertainty — uncertainty that has intensified with rising unemployment and concerns about competition for a shrinking number of jobs.

Immigration's effects in the short run (that is, for periods of up to about five years) depend on the speed with which the economy adjusts to accommodate new arrivals by creating more jobs. In this chapter Peri presents the first detailed empirical analysis examining this adjustment process in the United States, both in good times and during periods of economic weakness. When the economy is growing, Peri finds, it creates enough jobs to accommodate new immigrants while leaving US-born workers' employment prospects unharmed — even in the relatively short run and also for less-educated individuals. When economic growth is weak, however, new immigrants have a small negative impact on US-born employment rates for the first few years after their arrival. Regardless of the state of the economy at arrival, Peri finds that the long-run impact of immigration remains small and positive.

These findings suggest that the US economy could retain some of the long-term benefit of immigration at a lower short-term cost if new immigration responded more strongly to the state of the economy. Net immigration already responds to labor-market conditions to some extent, rising in booms and falling during recessions, but this flexibility is limited and comes primarily from unregulated flows, such as illegal immigration. The legal immigration system, by contrast, is not designed to respond quickly to employer demand, because only a small share of overall immigration is employment based and because numerical limits reduce any natural fluctuations in inflows that might otherwise occur.[18]

---

18 For some flows, this unresponsiveness is inevitable. Immigration motivated by family unification, for example, remained essentially unchanged over the course of the crisis. New immigration of immediate relatives of US citizens, whose visas are not governed by numerical limits and hence have the potential to respond more quickly to economic conditions, rose from 2008 to 2009 and then fell by 15 percent from 2009 to 2011; however, this drop is no more dramatic than other fluctuations in the flows of immediate relatives that have occurred over the past decade. The backlogs of family-sponsored immigrants waiting for visas fell during the recession, suggesting that some may have decided against immigration or delayed their plans. However, these backlogs are sufficiently large that lower demand in the family preference class does not translate into fewer arrivals; total family visa issuances remained roughly constant between 2007 and 2011. Sources: Communication with DHS officials (family-immigration backlogs); and DHS, *Yearbook of Immigration Statistics: 2011* (Washington, DC: DHS, 2012), www.dhs.gov/files/statistics/publications/LPR11.shtm (numbers of new arrivals).

Demand for labor varies not just over the business cycle, but also across sectors, industries, and occupations within the US economy. Large differences in wage growth and unemployment between workers with different occupational skills suggest that some parts of the economy have greater need for new workers than others. As Madeleine Sumption discusses **in Chapter 4**, this observation has often led to calls for a more targeted immigration policy that would channel employment-based workers to the areas of the economy in which they are most needed, and away from areas in which they are not.

There is no single way to define what the labor market "needs," however. Some countries have conducted statistical analyses of occupations thought to face a shortage of workers, in which immigration is thought to be most beneficial. These exercises respond to a desire for transparent, objective, and evidence-based criteria for admitting immigrant workers, but can be problematic in practice. First, statistical measures of shortages are unreliable and provide only a rough guide to actual conditions facing employers as they seek to recruit workers with the right skills. Second, analysis based on past data arrives after several months' delay and provides only limited information on the extent to which increased training or other responses may be addressing a suspected shortage. Third, governments have limited options for translating a list of shortage occupations into immigration policy in a useful way. And fourth, increasing or reducing immigration in specific occupations in the short run provides no guarantee of successful immigrant integration in the long term. As a result, the chapter argues that while policies should respond to broad changes in economic conditions, attempts to fine-tune immigration flows too closely may not be worth the resources they consume. In fact, immigration systems that rely too heavily on occupation-specific rules might do more harm than good, if they overcorrect for perceived shortages while preventing beneficial flows on the basis of imperfect statistical measures.

The volume concludes with two chapters assessing immigrant integration in the United States in the light of the economic crisis. **In Chapter 5**, Pia Orrenius and Madeline Zavodny show that immigrants were on a steady trajectory toward better economic outcomes during the economic booms of the 1990s and 2000s. But recessions — and particularly the Great Recession — have put this favorable development in jeopardy, particularly for Latinos. Immigrant poverty rates, which fell steadily in the 1990s and during the 2004-06 housing boom, have risen sharply since 2007.

Several factors drive these trends, including the fact that immigrants are more likely to have low levels of formal education and are more concentrated in hard-hit occupations and industries such as construction (particularly Latino men). Immigrants also have a shorter tenure in their jobs since many of them have arrived only recently, drawn to the country by the booming labor market of the mid-2000s.

As Michael Fix and Jeanne Batalova show **in Chapter 6**, pre-recession job growth for the immigrant population was more evenly distributed across skill levels than analysts typically assumed. Growth was distributed not just across high- and low-skill jobs but was also very significant in middle-skill jobs.[19] The great majority of these jobs pay good wages, making them an important vehicle for escaping poverty and achieving financial stability. Interestingly, most immigrants in these jobs have entered — and prospered — outside of the employment-based visa systems.

Following the recession, however, growth became far more uneven, with middle-skilled job growth sustained in the health sector but collapsing in construction. As a result, the widest pathway to the middle class for those immigrants without strong academic or English language skills has been substantially narrowed. These developments put even greater pressure on the nation's work preparation systems to open the way to well-paying jobs at a time of rising immigrant poverty rates, and underscore the risks that severe financial pressure on community colleges pose for immigrant integration.

II. Conclusion

Paradoxically, the economic collapse provided a brief respite from some of the most dysfunctional aspects of the employment-based immigration system. Pressure for illegal immigration into lower-wage jobs decreased. Visa quotas for skilled workers had been exhausted in a matter of days immediately before the crisis, leaving many employers unable to hire skilled workers for most of the year, but took several months to fill from 2009 to 2011 before returning to pre-recession time frames in 2012.[20] Employer demand for low-skilled H-2B visas remained comfortably below the cap from 2009 to the time of writing in 2012. As a result, private-sector pressure for more reliable access to work visas ebbed in many industries.

Economic recovery is not likely to replicate all of the same migration pull forces that characterized the pre-2008 era. Nonetheless, as the economy recovers and unemployment falls, some of the old pressures on the immigration system will return across the skill spectrum and it will become more difficult — and more irresponsible — to ignore them. For employers hiring at the bachelor's level and above, creating an immigration system that delivers predictable outcomes for applicants and employers remains a priority even in the short run. In other words, the need for fundamental reform has not diminished.

---

19 Middle-skilled jobs are defined in this context as those that typically require more than a high school degree but less than a four-year college degree.

20 H-1B visa limits for skilled professionals were exhausted in months, rather than days, in the 2009, 2010, and 2011 calendar years. In 2012 (fiscal year 2013), the cap was exhausted in 71 days, compared to 131 days in 2005 and 55 days in 2006.

For more than ten years, successive administrations, key congressional leaders, and a wide range of stakeholders have sought comprehensive immigration reform (CIR) legislation, but their efforts have fallen victim to a deeply polarized political system. The economic downturn has made certain aspects of reform more difficult — most notably new temporary work programs at the low-skilled level. Nonetheless, the recent reduction in new illegal immigration may also have created the space for Congress to take action. These developments have fueled an ongoing debate between those who believe that CIR can be enacted, and those who believe that more can be achieved with an incremental approach. Regardless of the form immigration legislation will eventually take, the first steps toward reform in the near term seem most likely to focus on certain highly educated immigrants whose economic value is most widely accepted. In particular, several recent legislative proposals have focused on immigrants with backgrounds in science, technology, engineering, and math — especially those who gained their education in the United States.

As policymakers evaluate immigration reform proposals in a difficult political and economic environment, what should they take away from the research and analysis that have accumulated to date? One conclusion that emerges clearly from the chapters prepared for this volume is that immigration would be more consistent with the interests of employers, existing members of the labor force, taxpayers, and consumers, if policies were more flexible and more responsive to economic needs.

Flexibility can come in a number of forms. These include more frequent adjustments to numerical limits and eligibility criteria, to curb the extraordinary pressure that oversubscribed visas have put on the immigration system during years of high demand. Numerical limits themselves could also be made less rigid by allowing employers to hire outside of caps under certain circumstances.[21] While no single, "optimal" level of immigration can be set a priori from an economic perspective, and while numbers almost certainly matter less than the ways in which immigrants are selected and admitted, a more thoughtful approach to determining the numbers is warranted. Elsewhere, the Migration Policy Institute has recommended that a Standing Commission on Labor Markets, Economic Competitiveness, and Immigration could help to overcome the inertia that has plagued the setting of

---

21 For example, cap exemptions could be made in return for a fee. For more details on this proposal, see Demetrios G. Papademetriou and Madeleine Sumption, *Eight Policies to Boost the Economic Contribution of Employment-based Immigration* (Washington, DC: Migration Policy Institute, 2011), www.migrationpolicy.org/pubs/competitivenessstrategies-2011.pdf.

numerical limits for employment-based immigrants.[22] This body could advise Congress on sensible adjustments to visa policies and numerical limits, while building analytical capacity to support future reforms.

Among the most important of these analytical tasks would be to generate and systematically evaluate much more detailed information on the link between admission policies and the successful incorporation of immigrants. Without the capacity to examine basic indicators such as the earnings and employment prospects of immigrants who enter under different routes, the successes and challenges of integration cannot inform immigration policy — and the United States foregoes what is arguably the most important feedback mechanism in any well-functioning immigration system. Indeed, the United States remains far behind other countries in its ability to generate the data and analysis that would bring a more nuanced understanding of the effects of different immigration policy decisions.

The immigration system could also better accommodate the natural dynamics of the labor market by creating a more predictable transition to permanent status. At the highly skilled level, a path to permanent residence exists, but long delays before eligible applicants receive their green cards tether immigrants to their employers and sharply curtail their ability to move to the jobs in which their skills are most needed.[23] At the less-skilled level, a path to permanent status is essentially unavailable, despite the fact that demand for immigrants at this level is ongoing and that on-the-job experience is a crucial determinant of productivity.[24]

Another overarching lesson that arises from the chapters is the need to strike a good balance between long- and short-term concerns. As Holzer points out in Chapter 1, policies with short-term costs may have longer-term benefits, and vice versa. For example, admitting less-skilled immigrants willing to work for low wages can have some benefits for employers and consumers in the short run, but may increase the cost of integrating immigrants and their families in the long run. Similarly, workers who are admitted (or arrive illegally) to meet short-term "shortages" may not be guaranteed employment several years later, especially if they work in naturally cyclical industries. These dynamics

---

22　Demetrios G. Papademetriou, Doris Meissner, Marc R. Rosenblum, and Madeleine Sumption, *Harnessing the Advantages of Immigration for a 21st Century Economy: A Standing Commission on Labor Markets, Economic Competitiveness, and Immigration* (Washington, DC: Migration Policy Institute, 2009), www.migrationpolicy.org/pubs/StandingCommission_May09.pdf.

23　Immigrants on temporary work visas who have applied for a green card are not legally prohibited from switching employers, but doing so may jeopardize their green-card applications and is thus considered inadvisable.

24　Demetrios G. Papademetriou, Doris Meissner, Marc R. Rosenblum, and Madeleine Sumption, *Aligning Temporary Immigration Visas with US Labor Market Needs: The Case for a New System of Provisional Visas* (Washington, DC: Migration Policy Institute, 2009), www.migrationpolicy.org/pubs/Provisional_visas.pdf.

make good policy particularly difficult at the less-skilled level, where the visa system arguably diverges furthest from market demand but where any move to increase immigration flows creates understandable unease.

In the booming labor market of the mid-2000s, historically high immigrant inflows were absorbed with relative ease. Unemployment was low, immigrant poverty rates were in steady decline, and in many quarters the notion took hold that large-scale immigration was essential to economic prosperity. Years of economic weakness, however, brought this assumption into question. Of course, high unemployment does not eliminate the need for new immigration. As the chapters in this book have explained, the benefits to be reaped from immigration remain substantial, but in the new economic landscape more care — and more caution — will be needed to ensure that immigration policies are sufficiently selective and that the country is *making the most of the human capital it already possesses.*

Some of the economic changes that lie ahead can be anticipated; others cannot. The demand for a growing health-care workforce, for example, can be forecast years or even decades in advance, while contractions of the kind the US construction industry experienced in the late 2000s are highly unpredictable; no immigration system can perfectly navigate these changes. But with some much-needed reforms in the short term and efforts to build an evidence base that would support rational improvements in the long term, the system could do much more to bring in immigrants who make the country more prosperous and who have the capacity to integrate successfully over the years to come.

Works Cited

Fairlie, Robert. 2012. *Kauffman Index of Entrepreneurial Activity, 1996-2011*. Kansas City, MO: Kauffman Foundation. www.kauffman.org/uploadedFiles/KIEA_2012_report.pdf.

Hertz, Tom. 2011. Hired Farm Labor Held Steady in Great Recession. *Amber Waves*, December 2011. www.ers.usda.gov/AmberWaves/December11/PDF/HiredFarmLabor.pdf.

Hoefer, Michael, Nancy Rytina, and Bryan Baker. 2012. *Estimates of the Unauthorized Immigrant Population Residing in the United States: January 2011*. Washington, DC: Department of Homeland Security. www.dhs.gov/xlibrary/assets/statistics/publications/ois_ill_pe_2011.pdf.

Immigration and Naturalization Service (INS).1986. *Statistical Yearbook of the Immigration and Naturalization Service: 1985*. Washington, DC: INS.

International Monetary Fund (IMF). 2011. World Economic Outlook Database. www.imf.org/external/pubs/ft/weo/2011/02/weodata/index.aspx.

National Science Foundation (NSF). 2012. *Science and Engineering Indicators 2012*, Chapter 6. Arlington, VA: NSF. www.nsf.gov/statistics/seind12/c6/c6h.htm.

Papademetriou, Demetrios G. and Madeleine Sumption. 2011. *Eight Policies to Boost the Economic Contribution of Employment-based Immigration*. Washington, DC: Migration Policy Institute. www.migrationpolicy.org/pubs/competitivenessstrategies-2011.pdf.

Papademetriou, Demetrios G., Doris Meissner, Marc R. Rosenblum, and Madeleine Sumption. 2009. *Harnessing the Advantages of Immigration for a 21st Century Economy: A Standing Commission on Labor Markets, Economic Competitiveness, and Immigration*. Washington, DC: Migration Policy Institute. www.migrationpolicy.org/pubs/StandingCommission_May09.pdf.

———. 2009. *Aligning Temporary Immigration Visas with US Labor Market Needs: The Case for a New System of Provisional Visas*. Washington, DC: Migration Policy Institute. www.migrationpolicy.org/pubs/Provisional_visas.pdf.

Smith, Brad. 2011. Testimony of General Counsel and Senior Vice President, Legal Corporate Affairs, Microsoft, before the US Senate Committee on the Judiciary, Subcommittee on Immigration, Refugees, and Border Security. *The Economic Imperative for Immigration Reform: High-Skilled Immigration as a Driver of Economic Growth*, 112th Cong., 1st sess., July 26, 2011. www.judiciary.senate.gov/pdf/11-7-26%20Smith%20Testimony.pdf.

Smith, James P. and Barry Edmonston, eds. 1997. *The New Americans: Economic, Demographic, and Fiscal Effects of Immigration*. Washington, DC: National Academy Press. www.nap.edu/catalog/5779.html.

US Census Bureau. Table 849, Agricultural Exports and Imports — Value: 1990-2010. www.census.gov/compendia/statab/2012/tables/12s0849.pdf.

US Citizenship and Immigration Services (USCIS). Various years. Characteristics of Specialty Occupation Workers (H-1B). www.uscis.gov/portal/site/uscis/menuitem.eb1d4c2a3e5b9ac89243c6a7543f6d1a/?vgnextoid=9a1d9ddf801b3210VgnVCM100000b92ca60aRCRD&vgnextchannel=9a1d9ddf801b-3210VgnVCM100000b92ca60aRCRD.

US Department of Homeland Security (DHS). Various years. *Yearbook of Immigration Statistics*. Washington, DC: DHS. www.dhs.gov/files/statistics/publications/LPR11.shtm.

US Department of Labor, Bureau of Labor Statistics (BLS). 2012. The Employment Situation, June 2012. www.bls.gov/news.release/archives/empsit_07062012.pdf.

———. 2012. Occupational Outlook Handbook 2012-13 Edition: Projections Overview. www.bls.gov/ooh/About/Projections-Overview.htm.

———. 2012. Employment Projections: Education Pays. www.bls.gov/emp/ep_chart_001.htm.

———. 2012. Employment, Hours, and Earnings from the Current Employment Statistics Survey: Series CES6562000001. http://data.bls.gov/timeseries/CES6562000001?data_tool=XGtable.

———. Labor Force Statistics Data Retrieval Tool: Current Population Survey. www.bls.gov/webapps/legacy/cpsatab4.htm.

US Department of State. Various years. Nonimmigrant Visa Statistics. http://travel.state.gov/visa/statistics/nivstats/nivstats_4582.html.

PART ONE

WHAT KIND OF IMMIGRATION POLICY DOES THE US ECONOMY NEED?

CHAPTER 1

IMMIGRATION POLICY AND LESS-SKILLED WORKERS IN THE UNITED STATES: REFLECTIONS ON FUTURE DIRECTIONS FOR REFORM

By Harry J. Holzer

Georgetown University

Introduction

The economic role of less-skilled immigrants is one of the most controversial questions in the immigration debate. Economists have reached a consensus on the benefits of highly skilled immigration, but less-skilled newcomers and the policies that govern their admission and stay continue to provoke disagreement. When the United States takes up reform of the still-dysfunctional US immigration system, the usual claims and counterclaims will be made about how legislation would affect the labor market, with advocates on all sides claiming to know its effects with virtual certainty.

In light of this, it is worth reviewing what is known from the research literature on immigration and the labor market and what has yet to be learned. I do so in this chapter from the personal perspective of a labor economist who has spent time in both the academic and policy worlds.[1] As such, I have some understanding of how good policy can and should be informed by rigorous research, but also know that policymaking in the real world often requires us to make our best judgments without all the information we would ideally like to have.

This chapter focuses primarily on immigration in the labor market for

---

1   I served as chief economist of the US Department of Labor in the Clinton administration, between my academic stints at Michigan State University and Georgetown University. I also now serve as a fellow at the Urban Institute and public policy professor at Georgetown University in Washington, DC, and am a member of the Migration Policy Institute's Labor Markets Advisory Group.

less-skilled or less-educated workers in the United States — i.e., those with a high school diploma or less. There seems to be little disagreement among economists and immigration analysts more broadly that attracting and retaining more highly educated foreign "talent" would be beneficial to the US economy,[2] even if these individuals compete somewhat with US-born highly educated workers and graduate students. Highly skilled immigrants clearly add to the potential for economic innovation and national competitiveness, and there seems to be little dispute among respected scholars and analysts about the potential benefits of encouraging more of them to reside here.

In contrast, stronger disagreements characterize the research on the economic costs and benefits of less-educated immigrants, both legal and unauthorized. The most divisive policy proposals in the immigration reform debate also focus on this population.

Accordingly, this chapter begins with a review of what I consider to be the general goals of US immigration policy, as well as the most important questions that should drive reform. It then turns to the research literature to review the extent to which these questions have or have not been convincingly answered, and also considers a range of policy proposals whose impacts we may or may not be able to predict with some precision. The chapter closes with some discussion of how we should proceed on immigration reform in light of what we do and do not know on this topic.

I. Immigration Reform: General Goals and Primary Questions

Before proceeding to the research literature and to potential areas of agreement and disagreement among analysts, the chapter begins by considering what ought to be the general goals of immigration policy regarding low-skilled workers. From a purely economic perspective, and one that prioritizes the interests of American citizens (whether they are US born or naturalized immigrants), the primary goals of immigration policy should be to:

- maximize the benefits of less-skilled immigration to the productivity of the US economy and the well-being of US consumers;

---

2   See George Borjas, "Assimilation, Changes in Cohort Quality, and the Earnings of Immigrants," *Journal of Labor Economics* 3, no. 4 (1985): 463-89; Richard B. Freeman, *America Works* (New York: Russell Sage Foundation, 2007a); Jennifer Hunt, "How Much Does Immigration Boost Innovation?" (Montreal, Canada: McGill University, unpublished, 2008); Bertelsmann Stiftung and Migration Policy Institute, eds., *Talent, Competitiveness and Migration* (Gütersloh: Bertelsmann Stiftung and Migration Policy Institute, 2009).

- minimize the potential costs of such immigration to native-born Americans, especially the least-educated workers; and, whenever possible,

- help less-educated immigrants who stay in the country gain opportunities for effective integration and upward mobility without hurting US-born Americans.

Of course, there may well be conflicts and tradeoffs involved in the pursuit of such goals. For instance, US consumers might well benefit from immigration policies that allow nearly unlimited inflows of less-educated immigrants (legally or illegally), while less-educated US-born workers might well be hurt by such policies. And allowing for policies that enhance upward mobility prospects for immigrants might impose costs on some Americans and drain public resources that might otherwise be available to them. At least theoretically, we might therefore seek to identify some optimal levels of less-skilled immigration in light of these tradeoffs.

Furthermore, important distributional concerns must be taken into account: for example, a heavy influx of less-skilled immigrants might enhance the net real earnings (due to higher earnings and lower consumer prices) of higher-income native-born consumers while reducing them for lower-income US workers. It is impossible to identify an optimal level of immigration in the presence of these distributional factors without having some sense of what weights to put on the well-being of groups of Americans who are differently affected by immigration. My own preference is to put relatively more weight on the well-being of those who are now relatively more disadvantaged, among both consumers and workers, at least among the native-born.

Furthermore, the well-being of legal immigrants who have become naturalized citizens should arguably receive at least some consideration here, and perhaps just as much as that of the US-born. But doing so creates some conceptual difficulties; for instance, it generates inconsistencies over time in how we view immigrants from the same source countries who arrive only a few years apart, since the newer arrivals likely compete heavily with and therefore impose costs on their own fellow nationals who came earlier but are now naturalized. Thinking of unskilled legal immigrants as a group that will ultimately settle in the country permanently might also change how we view the costs and benefits associated with them before their arrival, as noted below.

Of course, immigration policy always will (and should), to some extent, reflect political, social, and humanitarian concerns as well as national economic interests. But the focus of this analysis is on the economic aspect.

Subject to these caveats, national immigration policy should be designed to serve broad economic goals. But, in attempting to do so, a number of empirical questions arise which have been partially although not completely addressed in the research literature. Among these questions:

- What are the costs and benefits to native-born Americans associated with the immigration of unskilled workers, and to whom do they accrue? Can it be argued that the country presently has too many such immigrants, too few, or an optimal rate of inflow?

- To what extent do these benefits and costs change with the legal versus illegal status of unskilled immigrants? Among those here legally, does it matter whether they are temporary or permanent, and whether their status is based on employment, family reunification, or humanitarian status?

- To what extent does the United States overall — and not just the immigrants themselves — benefit from upgrading the skills of less-educated immigrants who are permanent residents?

The next section considers the extent to which we can answer these questions, based on the extant empirical research literature by economists and other social scientists. The section that follows will take up questions on the cost-effectiveness of specific policies to address these issues.

II. Empirical Research on Unskilled Immigrants: A Few Answers, Lots of Questions

When less-educated immigrants — i.e., those with high school diplomas or less — come to the United States, what costs and benefits do they generate for native-born Americans at different income or skill levels?

A. Costs: Lower Earnings among Native-Born Workers

There is no question that immigrants have greatly expanded the number of high school dropouts in the US labor market — perhaps by one-third or more since 1980.[3] But it is less clear what their impacts have been on native-born dropouts and other less-educated groups, including African Americans.

---

3   George Borjas, "Immigration Policy and Human Capital" in *Reshaping the American Workforce in a Changing Economy*, eds. Harry J. Holzer and Demetra Nightingale (Washington, DC: Urban Institute Press, 2007).

The extent to which immigrant workers compete in the labor market with native-born Americans has been the subject of extensive research and debate among labor economists. Most immigration analysts are familiar with the differing findings of David Card of the University of California at Berkeley and George Borjas of Harvard, in which the former finds very little impact of less-educated immigrants on less-educated US-born workers while the latter finds a more substantial negative impact. What is perhaps less well understood is why their results differ, what problems are associated with each researcher's methods, and whether any consensus might emerge from these findings.

Card's work[4] focuses primarily on differences between US metropolitan statistical areas (MSAs), some of which have had much higher immigration levels than others. Borjas and others have argued that these "cross-sectional" estimates understate the likely negative impact of migration for two reasons: 1) immigrants are attracted to strong labor markets, especially those where they might be more easily absorbed; and 2) native-born workers emigrate out of these labor markets in response to immigration, and thus any negative impacts on wages are not observed where the immigrants actually reside.[5] While Card claims to address these issues through a variety of statistical techniques, questions persist about the ability of these methods to resolve the statistical biases in the cross-MSA work. Card also disputes the notion of substantial native outmigration in response to immigrant entry into MSAs, though the issue is not yet resolved empirically.[6]

In contrast, Borjas studies differences in immigrant penetration and native labor market outcomes across nationwide groupings of workers according to their educational attainment and work experience, for the five decennial years over the period 1960-2000. With four education and eight experience groupings in each year, he generates 160 national groups (each with the same level of education and experience) from which to compare immigrant presence and employment outcomes.[7] But questions remain over the extent to which these findings are robust to other controls, and to whether he is really capturing the effects of a greater supply of less-skilled labor (induced by immigration) as

---

[4] David Card, "Is the New Immigration Really So Bad?" *Economic Journal* 115 no. 506 (2005): 300-323; David Card, "Immigration and Inequality," *American Economic Review* 99 no. 2 (2009): 1-21.

[5] George Borjas, Richard Freeman, and Lawrence Katz, "Searching for the Effect of Immigration in the Labor Market," *American Economic Review* 86 no. 2 (1996): 246-51.

[6] For different views on how to interpret the data on cross-MSA migration of natives in response to immigration, see George Borjas, "Native Internal Migration and the Labor Market Impact of Immigration," *Journal of Human Resources* 41 no. 2 (2006): 221-58; and David Card, "Immigration Inflows, Native Outflows, and the Local Labor Market Impacts of Higher Immigration," *Journal of Labor Economics* 19 no. 1 (2001): 22-64. http://davidcard.berkeley.edu/papers/immig-inflows.pdf.

[7] George Borjas, "The Labor Demand Curve IS Downward Sloping: Reexaming the Impacts of Immigration on the Labor Market," *Quarterly Journal of Economics* 118 no. 4 (2003): 1335-74.

opposed to reductions in the demand for such labor (because of technological change, rising international trade, or other forces).[8] Borjas also acknowledges that the long-run impacts of immigration are likely to be smaller than the short-run impacts, given that inflows of capital in the long run might partially or fully offset those impacts.[9]

In my view, Card's estimates are likely lower bounds to the true, negative impacts of immigration on less-educated natives while Borjas' estimates are likely upper bounds. Some other authors[10] using Card's methods have recently generated modest negative effects of unskilled immigration on native employment outcomes among less-educated Americans, while others find much more modest negative effects using a national-level analysis similar to that of Borjas.[11] Also, since Borjas' own long-run estimates do not differ too greatly from some of these other cross-sectional estimates, it seems likely that immigration to the United States has generated quite modest negative impacts on the employment and earnings of native-born high school dropouts, and perhaps the most

---

8   By estimating negative effects of immigration on wages over a 40-year period, but with the largest amounts of immigration occurring in the last 20 years, it is possible that the observed negative effects of immigration supply might really be capturing the decline in the relative demand for less-educated labor that occurred during this same period due to technological change and other global forces, as noted by Claudia Goldin and Lawrence Katz and many others; Claudia Goldin and Lawrence Katz, *The Race Between Education and Technology* (Cambridge, MA: Harvard University Press, 2008). Borjas' attempts to control for these other demand shifts through the inclusion of year-by-education dummy variables in his estimated equations may or may not be sufficient to fully capture these effects.

9   Borjas notes that if capital is fully mobile, then the long-run effects of immigration on US labor markets in the aggregate must be zero, since capital inflows will fully offset labor inflows. But he still believes that immigration will negatively affect less-educated workers and positively affect more-educated labor over longer periods of time, though much more modestly than in the short run; he estimates that immigration between 1980 and 2000 decreased the earnings of less-educated native-born workers by 4 percent in the long run rather than 9 percent in the short run. Stephen Raphael notes that when black male incarceration rates are added to Borjas' empirical specification, his effects largely disappear; Stephen Raphael and Lucas Ronconi, "The Effects of Labor Market Competition with Immigrants on the Wages and Employment of Natives: What Does Existing Research Tell Us?" *DuBois Review: Social Science Research on Race* 4 no. 2 (2007): 413-32. www.irle.berkeley.edu/cwed/ronconi/immigration_existing_research.pdf. Since these incarceration rates likely proxy for a wide range of demand-side (and perhaps supply-side) factors affecting employment outcomes of young black men, it is likely that Borjas' estimates are capturing at least some of these demand shifts over time and across groups. Ibid. George Borjas, "Wage Trends among Disadvantaged Minorities," in *Working and Poor: How Economic and Policy Changes are Affecting Low-Wage Workers*, eds. Rebecca M. Blank, Sheldon H. Danziger, and Robert F. Schoeni (New York: Russell Sage Foundation, 2006b).

10 Deborah Reed, and Sheldon H. Danziger, "The Effects of Recent Immigration on Racial/Ethnic Labor Market Differentials," *American Economic Review* 97 no. 2 (2007): 373-7; Christopher Smith, "Essays on the Youth and Entry Level Labor Markets" (PhD dissertation, MIT, 2008); Patricia Cortes, "The Effect of Low-Skilled Immigration on US Prices: Evidence from CPI Data," *Journal of Political Economy* 116 no. 3 (2008): 381-422.

11 See Gianmarco Ottaviano and Giovanni Peri, "Rethinking the Effects of Immigration on Wages" (NBER Working Paper 12497, 2006), www.nber.org/papers/w12497.pdf?new_window=1.

disadvantaged and least skilled of high school graduates. In this view, immigration would only account for a small percentage of the decline in relative wages experienced by the least educated workers.

But, if true, another question emerges: why are the impacts of so large an influx of less-educated workers so small on the labor market outcomes of native-born workers? Both theory and evidence suggest three possible answers. First, immigrants generate additional product demand and therefore labor demand as well as supply, since they are consumers in the United States as well as producers. While it is unlikely that they consume enough to fully offset their impacts on low-skill labor markets, a partial offset is likely.[12]

Second, immigrants are imperfect substitutes for native-born workers of the same educational level.[13] In fact, the least-educated immigrants concentrate in jobs that require virtually no verbal interaction with customers and no reading/writing work of any kind. Accordingly, they directly compete mostly with earlier cohorts of immigrants from the same countries in the same industries, while natives move to other jobs in those industries. Indeed, estimates of negative impacts of immigrants are always much larger on other immigrants than on native-born workers in the same educational categories.[14] Immigrants might then complement these other native-born workers instead of substituting for them, even if the latter have educational levels that are similar.

Third, production techniques shift in response to less-educated immigrant labor, with employers less likely to substitute capital and/or technology for less-educated labor when more immigrants are available. While this might reduce productivity growth within industries, it also means that many low-skilled jobs that are now available to immigrants would likely not exist in their absence, as they would be replaced by capital and technology.[15]

It is noteworthy that the limited negative impact of unskilled immigrants on the labor market prospects of the native born might be a

---

12   Since immigrants have lower average incomes than the US born, they presumably consume less per person. Since their labor force impact is much more concentrated on the bottom end of the labor market, their modest consumption is unlikely to fully offset their negative impacts on wages for less-skilled groups, while their consumption likely contributes to positive impacts on more-educated groups. Immigrants' consumption is also reduced when they send remittances home.
13   Ottaviano and Peri, "Rethinking the Effects of Immigration on Wages."
14   Cortes, "The Effect of Low-Skilled Immigration on US Prices: Evidence from CPI Data."
15   Ethan Lewis finds that such effects are largely *within-industry* — meaning that it is not the proliferation of industries that use low-wage immigrants when they enter an area, but rather a shift from capital to labor inputs within existing industries. If true, then production is more capital-intensive in the absence of these immigrants, and at least some of the jobs they hold would no longer be available to natives at higher wages. Ethan Lewis, "Immigration, Skill Mix and the Choice of Technique" (Working Paper, Federal Reserve Bank of Philadelphia, 2005), www.philadelphiafed.org/research-and-data/publications/working-papers//2005/wp05-8.pdf.

relatively unique American phenomenon, reflecting the flexibility of US labor markets in adjusting to external supply shocks. Indeed, evidence by economists Joshua Angrist and Adriana Kugler suggests more negative effects of immigration on the employment of native-born European workers, because employment regulations in Europe raise the costs and limit the extent of the new job creation that is needed to absorb the flows of new immigrant workers.[16]

Of course, other questions remain. Would native-born workers even be interested in the kinds of jobs that immigrants often fill? What wages would be high enough to draw US-born workers into these jobs, and could these jobs still exist at such wages? Perhaps the wages that would be needed to attract US-born workers vary by industrial sector, depending on work conditions and the social status of jobs across sectors. It seems unlikely that many native-born workers would find low-wage, low-status work in agriculture, restaurants, or landscaping very appealing, absent large wage increases which themselves might cause many of the jobs to disappear.[17]

The answers might also vary across US-born groups. In particular, the stunning declines in recent decades in employment among less-educated young black men immediately raise questions about whether African Americans have been hurt more by less-skilled immigrants than other groups of less-educated US-born workers, as Borjas and his colleagues contend.[18] Indeed, there is some evidence that, where both groups are available for low-wage and low-skill work, employers actually prefer the immigrants, and believe that they have a stronger work ethic and lower rates of turnover out of low-wage jobs.[19] So perhaps native-born African Americans have borne a disproportionately large share of the burden associated with unskilled immigration.

Of course, young black men tend to "disconnect" from school and

---

16 Joshua Angrist and Adriana Kugler, "Protective or Counter-Productive? Labour Market Institutions and the Effect of Immigration on EU Natives," *The Economic Journal* 113 no. 2 (2003): 302-31, www.nber.org/papers/w8660.pdf?new_window=1.

17 The extent to which these jobs would be available to native-born workers in the absence of immigrants, and at wages that would be sufficiently high to appeal to them, rests on the relative magnitudes of "elasticities" of labor demand among employers in the relevant sectors and labor supply among the workers to those sectors. (Elasticities are measures of employers' or workers' sensitivity to prices). High wages are more likely to reduce employers' hiring in the long run than the short run, as capital and technology that might substitute for low-skilled workers are more variable over longer periods of time. Meanwhile, supply elasticities by workers to sectors that are seen as having very low status or unappealing working conditions are likely quite low, implying that very substantial wage increases would be necessary for the workers to take such jobs — often likely higher than employers would pay over the longer term.

18 Borjas, "Wage Trends among Disadvantaged Minorities."

19 Joleen Kirschenman and Kathryn Neckerman, "We'd Love to Hire Them But..." in *The Urban Underclass*, eds. Christopher Jencks and Paul E. Peterson (Washington, DC: Brookings Institution, 1991), http://digitalcommons.uconn.edu/cgi/viewcontent.cgi?article=1004&context=cpilj.

the workforce at early ages, often in response to a perceived lack of better-paying jobs.[20] Absent immigrants, would some employers raise wages enough to encourage some of these young men to remain attached to the labor force? In some sectors — notably construction and manufacturing — wages might be high enough even today to entice young black men into the markets, even in the presence of immigrants, if they could be hired; but whether employers would hire young black men into these jobs if immigrants were not available remains questionable because of other factors such as discrimination and weak informal job networks among young blacks.[21]

No doubt, many local labor markets that now rely heavily on low-wage immigrants would adjust to a new "equilibrium" in their absence with modestly higher wages for native-born unskilled workers in certain industries. But part of the adjustment process would also likely involve short-term disruptions, with some employers leaving their current industries altogether in response to rising labor costs. While we should perhaps not worry too much about the costs of short-run disruptions and the reallocation of employers and their capital across industries and local markets, this additional dimension of costs to lower immigration should at least be noted. And it is likely that some capital might be moved to offshore rather than domestic uses, thus generating long-term reductions in US output and employment rather than just short-term reallocations.

Finally, the fiscal impacts of less-educated immigrants should be noted. On net, these immigrants often draw on local public services, especially emergency rooms and public schools. Many noncitizens are ineligible for public benefits.[22] Less-skilled immigrants typically pay taxes, including for Social Security, even when they are unauthorized. Most analysts suggest that the fiscal impacts of unskilled immigrants are mixed, perhaps generating a net drain on local public resources (at least in the short run) and somewhat less negative (or even positive) impacts at the federal level. The fiscal impacts also improve across generations as the incomes of immigrant children and grandchildren grow in absolute and relative terms.

Thus, a variety of costs to US-born workers as a result of less-educated immigration are uncertain in magnitude. The likely extent and speed of the US labor market's adjustment to any curtailing of less-skilled

---

20 See Peter Edelman, Harry J. Holzer, and Paul Offner, *Reconnecting Disadvantaged Young Men* (Washington, DC: Urban Institute Press, 2006) for more recent evidence on the growing extent over time to which young black men disconnect from both school and the labor market and for policy recommendations to deal with this phenomenon.

21 For a discussion of relative "reservation" (or lowest acceptable) wages among black and white youth, see Harry J. Holzer, "Black Youth Nonemployment: Duration and Job Search," in *The Black Youth Employment Crisis*, eds. Richard B. Freeman and Harry J. Holzer, (Chicago: University of Chicago Press, 1986).

22 Michael Fix, "Comment on 'Welfare Reform and Immigration'" in *The New World of Welfare*, eds. Rebecca M. Blank and Ron Haskins (Washington, DC: Brookings Institution, 2001).

immigration is also unclear, especially when considering the great deal of uncertainty that surrounds future labor market trends and outcomes. If, for instance, baby boomer retirements in the next decade or two dramatically reduce the supply of less- as well as more-educated US-born labor, then immigrant competition to less-educated US-born workers who remain in the labor force will generate less severe costs and greater relative benefits to the US economy.[23] If, on the other hand, baby boomer retirements are more modest than expected, given the inadequacy of their savings and recent declines in the values of their assets; if the United States experiences a period of persistent low growth; or if, as Richard Freeman argues,[24] globalization and offshoring imply much greater effective supplies of less-educated labor to US employers, then the costs of low-skilled immigration to US-born workers will be more substantial. Exactly which scenario is more accurate is hard to ascertain at present, but will have important consequences for the ratio of costs and benefits to the US economy generated by low-skilled immigrants.

B. Benefits: For Employers, Consumers, and the Economy

If low-skilled immigration imposes modest costs on native-born less-educated workers, what benefits does it generate for native-born Americans, and who exactly enjoys these benefits?

Clearly, the current employers of these immigrants are the most direct beneficiaries of the lower wages that they are paid. George Borjas, Gordon Hanson, and others have calculated the value of the "surplus" (or profit) accruing to employers, at least in the short term, because of lower-wage immigrant labor, net of the costs borne by workers.[25] These aggregate surplus estimates are invariably small, when computed as percentages of Gross Domestic Product (GDP), because immigrants remain fairly small parts of the workforce and their impacts on wages are small as well.[26] However, for particular economic sectors and local areas, these contributions might be more important; and in the long run, if the higher profits attract more capital to industries or areas that rely on low-skilled immigrants or to the economy as a whole, these patterns will likely raise the economic benefit of immigration and allow it to be spread to others, such as newly hired US workers in these sectors and locations.

---

23 See Carol D'Amico and Richard Judy, *Workforce 2020* (New York: Hudson Institute, 1997).
24 Richard B. Freeman, "Is a Great Labor Shortage Coming? Replacement Demand in the Age of Globalization" in *Reshaping the American Workforce in a Changing Economy*, eds. Harry J. Holzer and Demetra Nightingale, (Washington, DC: Urban Institute Press, 2007).
25 George Borjas, "The Economic Benefits from Immigration," *Journal of Economic Perspectives* 9 no. 2 (1995): 3-22; see Chapter 2 of this volume, Gordon Hanson, *The Economics of Illegal Immigration in the United States: Policy Implications*.
26 For instance, Hanson, in *The Economics of Illegal Immigration in the United States*, estimates that unauthorized immigrants add just 0.03 percent to the nation's GDP in the aggregate, though their impact on specific regions and industries could be much larger than that.

Another kind of benefit to the economy flows to consumers and derives from the lower prices of goods and services produced as a result of lower wages. The best-known calculation of these benefits to date is by Patricia Cortes, who estimated the benefits to consumers of immigrant contributions to the production of "nontraded" goods, since the prices of "traded" goods[27] are set in broader markets.[28] To do so, she estimated price differences across metropolitan areas with different levels of immigrant intensity in the production in each.

Cortes estimates that immigrants lower the prices of products consumed by highly educated consumers by 0.4 percent of GDP and for less-educated consumers by 0.3 percent.[29] She argues that highly educated or high-income consumers benefit more because they use more "immigrant-intensive" products (like child care, restaurant food, landscaping, and the like) than do lower-income consumers. Furthermore, Cortes calculates that since immigrants also lower the wages of less-educated US workers (with much bigger negative effects on earlier immigrants than on the native born), the net effects of immigration overall are positive for the highly educated and negative for the less-educated, though both magnitudes are modest.[30]

While compelling, it seems likely that Cortes' methods result in some underestimation of the magnitudes of consumer benefits, particularly for less-educated Americans. For one thing, her list of industries is limited by the availability of local consumer price data by industry and it omits some key immigrant-intensive industries like construction and housing, which are particularly important to lower-income consumers. More importantly, what is "traded" at the metropolitan level (because it is produced[31] in other locations in the United States) is often "nontraded" at the national level, and these impacts are left out of her calculations. Local food and clothing costs from domestic agriculture and garment production might well be included in this category.

---

27 Nontraded goods must be produced and consumed in the same location; they include personally delivered services such as health care or gardening or freshly prepared food that cannot be shipped. Traded goods can be produced in one location and sold in another; they include many manufactured goods, but also some services such as IT.
28 Cortes, "The Effect of Low-Skilled Immigration on US Prices: Evidence from CPI Data," 381-422.
29 Ibid.
30 Cortes estimates that the flow of low-skilled immigrants into the United States in the period 1980-2000 increased the purchasing power of highly educated native-born workers by 0.32 percent and decreased that of dropouts overall by 1 percent or less, and of Hispanic high school dropouts by up to 4 percent. Native-born high school graduates, on net, benefit from immigration in her estimates.
31 Cortes does estimate impacts of immigration on prices of "traded" products from relatively immigrant-intensive industries that include garments and some food sectors that she can identify, and she finds no significant effects. Whether this would be true for all such sectors that heavily use immigrants in domestic production is unclear.

In critical industries such as health and elder care, the contribution of immigrant labor may be underestimated even more. As Americans age and live longer and the strong demand for these services continues to grow, these labor markets might fail to "equilibrate" — wages and prices may not be able to rise sufficiently if they are limited by the reimbursement policies of third-party insurers.[32] The results would be persistent shortages of workers, even in low-wage and low-skill positions such as nurses' aides. In such situations, immigration's contribution might be to allow a greater *quantity* of these services to be provided, rather than to reduce consumer prices.

Finally, since food, clothing, housing, and medical care account for much of the consumer budgets of the low-income relative to higher-income Americans, the immigrant contributions to the former group are likely understated in Cortes' calculations.

Of course, the estimates of immigration surpluses for employers and consumers are static in nature, and do not include the possible contributions of less-educated immigrants to the efficiency or growth of the US economy over time. Will Somerville and Madeleine Sumption argue that immigrants likely contribute to both, at least partly because they relocate more quickly than native-born workers in response to product or labor demand shifts.[33] It is, of course, hard to directly test these hypotheses and to estimate the magnitudes of their effects.

Somerville and Sumption also argue that immigrant concentrations in lower-wage industries might induce native-born workers to relocate to higher-paying jobs that use language and computational skills more intensively, since natives have greater communication skills compared to immigrants with the same education level.[34] In a 2009 paper, Patricia Cortes and Jose Tessada argue that low-skilled immigrants complement and thereby augment the labor supply of highly educated native-born women with children by providing cheaper household services.[35] In both cases, less-educated immigrants raise the earnings and labor supply of American workers at different levels, which no doubt benefits those groups directly and the US economy more broadly.

In sum, the estimates to date of the economic benefits of unskilled

---

32 Robin Stone and Joshua Wiener, *Who Will Care for Us? Addressing the Long-Term Care Workforce Crisis* (Washington, DC: Institute for the Future of Aging Services, 2001), www.urban.org/UploadedPDF/Who_will_Care_for_Us.pdf.
33 Will Somerville and Madeleine Sumption, *Immigration and the Labor Market: Theory, Evidence, and Policy* (Washington, DC: Migration Policy Institute, 2009), www.migrationpolicy.org/pubs/Immigration-and-the-Labour-Market.pdf.
34 Giovanni Peri and Chad Sparber, "Task Specialization, Comparative Advantages, and the Effects of Immigration on Wages" (NBER Working Paper 13389, 2007), www.nber.org/papers/w13389.
35 Patricia Cortes and Jose Tessada, "How Low-Skilled Immigration Is Changing the Labor Supply of Highly Educated American Women" (Working paper, 2009), www.inesad.edu.bo/bcde2009/A2%20Cortes%20Tessada.pdf.

immigrant labor appear quite modest in the aggregate. But these estimates likely understate the true magnitudes of these benefits, and especially those that accrue to specific local areas and economic sectors as well as particular demographic groups. The notion that these benefits accrue much more to higher-income than lower-income Americans also seems overstated.

Accordingly, given the mix of benefits and costs associated with less-skilled immigration, and uncertainties over their relative magnitudes both today and in the future, we cannot really argue that we will have too many or too few low-skilled immigrants over the next few decades. Of course, we would generally prefer that less-educated US-born Americans obtain higher rates of educational achievement and attainment, which would improve their own labor market outcomes and reduce overall inequality.[36] Large flows of low-skilled immigrants who remain in the country for many years also raise integration issues in the long term, making the case for continuing unskilled flows more tenuous. Still, with the mix of benefits and costs associated with such immigration noted above, it is difficult to make a strong case for many fewer such immigrants in the near future, or for many more.

C. Do the Costs and Benefits Vary by Immigrant Category?

The above discussion highlights the fact that the impacts of less-skilled immigrants on the native born will vary, according to the skills, sectors employed, and demographics of the latter. But they might also vary according to certain categories of immigrants themselves.

For instance, we know very little about the extent to which legal and unauthorized immigrants have different impacts on the labor market outcomes of the native born, since most of the data used to study labor market impacts cannot distinguish between them. Of course, the characteristics of the two groups of immigrants likely differ, with unauthorized immigrants having lower levels of cognitive or verbal skills and less formal education.[37] The local areas and sectors in which the two groups are hired also differ. Unauthorized immigrants are heavily Mexican in origin and are most likely hired in small establishments with very informal human resource policies that operate under the radar of law enforcement authorities.

Because unauthorized immigrants have fewer options in the formal

---

36 See Claudia Goldin and Lawrence Katz, *The Race Between Education and Technology* (Cambridge, MA: Harvard University Press, 2008) for a historical review of how rising levels of education in the United States have helped to alleviate rising inequality associated with technological change and rising demand for skills, and how these increases in the past three decades have failed to keep pace with technological change.

37 Gordon Hanson, "Illegal Migration from Mexico to the United States," *Journal of Economic Literature* 44 no. 4 (2007): 869-924.

labor market, it appears that many have lower pay and benefits than similar legal immigrants.[38] All else being equal, this implies that they pose a greater competitive threat than legal immigrant workers to the jobs of the native born who might otherwise work in these sectors. Of course, their lower wages might also imply greater benefits from these immigrants in terms of employer surplus or consumer prices, though Gordon Hanson argues that these benefits remain quite modest.[39]

Some evidence also suggests that unauthorized immigrants' employment in the United States is more responsive to the business cycle, and that they are the first ones let go during a serious downturn such as the present one. At the same time, their illegal status might well impede their ability to find employment in other sectors, thus limiting their adaptability to changes in the economic environment. The fact that the influx of unauthorized immigrants has clearly declined in response to the Great Recession, more than the flow of legal immigrants, reflects their greater inability to find employment or public benefits during this downturn. Thus, while their responsiveness to employment fluctuations might be a buffer for native-born workers, it exacts a very high human cost on the unauthorized immigrants themselves.

What about the relative impacts of various other categories of immigrants — such as those who are here on temporary visas rather than permanent ones, or those whose legal entry is employment-based rather than driven by family unification? In reality, very few unskilled immigrants enter the United States through temporary and/or employment-based visas: the H-2A program for seasonal agricultural workers and the H-2B program for nonagricultural workers account for very small percentages of the total.[40] Family reunification accounts for the vast majority of low-skilled immigrants admitted legally.[41]

The evidence to date suggests that temporary workers are among the lowest paid of all unskilled immigrants, and only partly because they are now so heavily concentrated in agriculture.[42] The upward

---

38 Sherrie Kossoudji and Deborah Cobb-Clark estimate wage penalties of 14 percent to 24 percent for those here illegally, while Francisco Rivera-Batiz and others find even larger effects. Sherrie Kossoudji and Deborah Cobb-Clark, "Coming Out of the Shadows: Learning About Legal Status and Wages from the Legalized Population," *Journal of Labor Economics* 20 no. 3 (2002): 598-628; Francisco Rivera-Batiz, "Undocumented Workers in the Labor Market: An Analysis of Earnings of Legal and Illegal Mexican Immigrants in the United States," *Journal of Population Economics* 12 no. 1 (1999): 91-116. See Gordon Hanson, "Illegal Migration from Mexico to the United States," *Journal of Economic Literature* 44 no. 4 (2007): 869-924 for a discussion of these estimates.
39 Hanson, *The Economics of Illegal Immigration in the United States*.
40 In recent years, 100,000 to 150,000 workers have been authorized to work in the United States on H-2A or H-2B visas in any given year. US Department of State, "Nonimmigrant Visa Statistics," http://travel.state.gov/visa/statistics/nivstats/nivstats_4582.html.
41 Ibid.
42 Madeleine Sumption, *Low-Skilled Immigration to the United States* (Washington, DC: Migration Policy Institute, 2010, unpublished).

mobility of these immigrants is impeded by the fact that they cannot usually stay legally for more than one year at a time, and that their visa and therefore their legal employment is heavily tied to their current employers; thus the market external to their current jobs offer little in the way of alternative opportunities to those experiencing unusually low wages and poor working conditions.

Because employment-based immigration is more responsive than other forms of legal immigration to cyclical or sectoral employment conditions, these immigrants provide potentially less competition to native-born workers in times of slack labor markets. On the other hand, those here on low-skilled H-2 visas might overstay and become unauthorized immigrants, who may ultimately be more competitive with less-educated US-born workers (although most overstayers, in fact, enter on tourist visas).

All of this perhaps suggests that employment-based immigration can mitigate some of the harmful competition to native-born unskilled workers, but only if the immigrants can be convinced to not ultimately become illegal and their employers are convinced not to hire them illegally as well. This, in turn, might imply the need for a path to permanent immigration status for those here on temporary employment-based visas, to provide an incentive for the workers to accept the legal path, as well as strong sanctions for both employers and workers who continue to engage in illegal employment.

D. Immigrant Integration: What Are the Stakes for Native-Born Workers?

There has been some dispute in recent years about whether newer cohorts of immigrants to the United States integrate and advance economically more slowly, both within and across generations, than previous cohorts did. In particular, Borjas has argued that the most recent waves of immigrants arrive further behind native-born Americans, in educational attainment and earnings, than did previous cohorts, and thus take longer to assimilate.[43] Borjas and Lawrence Katz note that this is particularly true of recent cohorts of Mexicans, who remain significantly behind their native-born counterparts even after two generations in the United States.[44]

On the other hand, Card questions whether this is true of immigrants overall. Much depends not only on labor market conditions when the immigrants arrive — in terms of earnings gaps between those with more or less education — but also the selection mechanisms that determine which immigrants come to the United States from which source

---

43 Borjas, "Assimilation, Changes in Cohort Quality, and the Earnings of Immigrants."
44 George Borjas and Lawrence Katz, "Evolution of the Mexican-Born Workforce in the United States" (NBER Working Paper 11281, 2006), www.nber.org/chapters/c0098.pdf.

countries, who remains in the United States, and who returns home.⁴⁵ All else being equal, the more egalitarian the labor market of the source country, the more likely that highly educated workers there will emigrate to the United States, where income inequality between more- and less-educated workers is relatively great and thus the highly skilled receive a high return on educational investments. Darren Lubotsky, in particular, argues that labor market conditions in Mexico, whose labor market is not considered egalitarian, generate unskilled immigration to the United States, though he also argues that the least successful immigrants in the United States are the ones most likely to return home.⁴⁶

No doubt, immigrants who stay in the United States have a strong interest in economic advancement and integration. And, to the extent that many become citizens, perhaps we have some obligation to help them succeed, just as we would any other Americans. But do native-born Americans, and our economy more broadly, have much interest in the extent to which less-skilled immigrants progress while here? If not, how supportive should we be of their advancement? If so, what policies should we support to encourage immigrant integration? And does all of this change how we might view the costs and benefits of such immigration in the first place, implying perhaps an even greater preference for more skilled immigrants at the outset?

On the plus side, the evidence reviewed above suggests that more highly skilled immigrants contribute more to the American economy over time and compete less with the most disadvantaged workers. Thus, to the extent that skill levels can be raised for the least-educated immigrants who are here, we might reduce the competition they present to native-born workers with low levels of education. More educated immigrants might generate even better-educated offspring of immigrants in future generations, which would benefit the economy overall.

Furthermore, increasing immigrant economic success over time would bring fiscal benefits, as immigrants and their children draw fewer public benefits while generating more tax revenues on their higher incomes. To the extent that poverty in the United States among children generates long-term economic costs — by reducing productivity,

---

45   Card, "Immigration Inflows, Native Outflows, and the Local Labor Market Impacts of Higher Immigration."
46   Lubotsky uses the fact of selective return migration to Mexico to argue that those immigrants have been somewhat less successful over time in integrating into the United States than had previously been thought. Pablo Ibarraran and Darren Lubotsky, "Mexican Immigration and Self-Selection: New Evidence from the 2000 Mexican Census" (NBER Working Paper 11456, 2005), www.nber.org/papers/w11456, Darren Lubotsky, "Chutes or Ladders? A Longitudinal Analysis of Immigrant Earnings," *Journal of Political Economy* 115 no. 5 (2007): 820-67.

raising crime rates, and weakening health — reducing poverty among immigrants and their children might well reduce these costs (though it is unclear whether immigrant poverty generates the same aggregate costs as it does among natives).[47]

But improved integration could also have some costs, in the form of workforce development programs. Immigrants are currently underrepresented in workforce training programs, especially if they lack English language skills.[48] However, the public resources available for employment and training services for both immigrants and the US born are extremely limited at the federal level, and there is little sign that greater resources will be made substantially more available anytime soon, particularly in an era of fiscal belt-tightening. The low attention and resources that workforce training programs have historically received suggests that policymakers may be reluctant to increase spending sufficiently to increase participation among both native-born workers and less-skilled immigrants, creating at least some possibility of competition for available resources between them.

In the labor market, questions also arise about the benefits and costs of greater immigrant integration to the native born. If less-educated immigrants' limited English literacy and communication skills reduce the extent to which employers can substitute them for most native-born workers in many low-skilled jobs, as argued above, then just modestly improving those skills might raise their substitutability and thus the degree of competition they provide to somewhat more-educated native-born workers. Immigrants might then be able more effectively to compete for a wider range of jobs now held more by native-born workers and less by other immigrants like themselves. Of course, doing so would also lessen the competition that they provide to less-educated native-born workers as well as immigrants who have arrived earlier. In other words, immigrant integration would likely increase competition with some groups of US-born workers while reducing it for others, leading to a "dilution" of competition across a broader section of the workforce.

---

47 For instance, immigrant poverty is likely less associated with crime and incarceration or very low labor force participation than poverty among natives (and especially African Americans), and these outcomes are large parts of what drive the aggregate cost of child poverty in the United States. Harry J. Holzer, Diane Schanzenbach, Greg Duncan, and Jens Ludwig, *The Economic Costs of Poverty: Subsequent Effects of Children Growing Up Poor* (Washington, DC: Center for American Progress, 2007).

48 In addition, immigrants experience high rates of noncompletion in training programs, and only one-third of students with English as a second language progressed more than one level in a six level system, according to a 2006 evaluation. US Department of Education, Office of Vocational and Adult Education, *Adult Education and Family Literacy Act Program Year 2003-2004. Report to Congress* (Washington, DC: US Department of Education: 2006) www2.ed.gov/about/reports/annual/ovae/2004aefla.pdf.

In the end, the net impacts of such educational upgrading among immigrants would depend heavily on the particular occupational and industrial patterns of immigrant versus native penetration, which themselves might vary across local labor markets. In some industries, like construction, where immigrants already compete very effectively with the native born for low-skilled jobs but less so in the higher-skilled crafts (e.g., plumbing, electrical work, and advanced carpentry), immigrant upgrading might reduce already scarce opportunities for good jobs for the less-educated native born, at least in the short term. In others, such as health care, where worker shortages in positions requiring some certification are a persistent problem, the greater availability of moderately skilled immigrant labor should not hurt native-born employment prospects.

This discussion raises a number of issues. For one thing, how strong is the labor market for "middle-skilled" jobs in the United States — i.e., those that require some certification beyond high school but less than a bachelor's degree? If the supply of workers with such credentials were to substantially increase, would demand be sufficient in the longer run to absorb them without wage losses for those in those jobs right now? Are there some industries where a limited number of "good jobs" offering potential advancement for less-educated workers are rationed, at least in the short term? Certainly such rationing occurs during a recession as severe as the recent one — but will this last for many years to come?

Some research suggests that the market for middle-skilled jobs remains fairly robust in the longer run, though there is some variation across specific sectors.[49] Construction will likely remain depressed for some time, given the recession and the bursting of the housing bubble. In other industries, where higher earnings accrue more to those with externally obtained credentials rather than just on-the-job experience, competition for job slots and key on-the-job training should matter somewhat less, and especially over time. And Randy Capps et al. have recently shown that immigrant penetration into the middle-skilled market has been somewhat greater than was previously realized, though the on-the-job skills obtained by many less-educated immigrants in construction contribute quite heavily to this finding.[50]

---

49 Harry J. Holzer and Robert Lerman, *America's Forgotten Middle-Skill Jobs: Education and Training Requirements in the Next Decade and Beyond* (Washington, DC: The Workforce Alliance, 2007); Anthony Carnevale, Nicole Smith, and Jeff Strohl, *Help Wanted: Projections of Jobs and Education Requirements Through 2018* (Center on Education and the Workforce, Georgetown University, 2010), www.urban.org/UploadedPDF/411633_forgottenjobs.pdf.

50 In construction, jobs held by high school dropouts in the crafts where training is gained informally, in what the Bureau of Labor Statistics calls "moderate on-the-job training" or "long-term on-the-job training" can be considered "middle-skilled" jobs. Randy Capps, Michael Fix, and Serena Yi-Ying Lin, *Still An Hourglass? Immigrant Workers in Middle-Skilled Jobs* (Washington, DC: Migration Policy Institute, 2010), www.migrationpolicy.org/pubs/sectoralbrief-Sept2010.pdf. See also Holzer and Lerman, *America's Forgotten Middle-Skill Jobs*, for more discussion.

Overall, US labor markets will almost certainly be able to absorb more middle-skilled workers over time. It appears to be in the national interest to generate more such workers out of the current pool of the unskilled, and to reduce their poverty rates and raise their average incomes over time, even if the exact pattern of immigrant-native competition in the short- and medium-terms that would be generated under these circumstances remains a bit more uncertain at present.

On the other hand, does this imply that that we should simply limit unskilled immigration at the outset in favor of the more-skilled? Not necessarily. While this study has acknowledged the benefits of skilled immigration and the need to encourage more of it, unskilled immigration also appears to have some net benefits. Perhaps the most sensible and justifiable strategy is to continue allowing an amount of unskilled immigration that generates such benefits, while ultimately helping only those who stay legally and eventually become citizens here (as well as their offspring) to integrate and advance economically. If and when they do so, they would then be replaced by other cohorts of the unskilled, some of whom would ultimately stay and advance as well.

III. Immigration Policy

What do the analyses above imply for immigration reform policy? What legislative proposals have been forwarded in recent years, and which seem most likely to further the goals set out above for immigration policy? Where does considerable uncertainty about the likely effects of immigration reform remain, and how should we proceed, in light of such uncertainty?

Between 2005 and 2007, several pieces of immigration reform legislation were proposed in both the US House of Representatives and the Senate, with each chamber passing one of two very different bills.[51] The Senate-passed bill, the *Comprehensive Immigration Reform Act of 2006* (S.2611), was sponsored by Senator Arlen Specter (R-PA) and cosponsored by a bipartisan group of senators, with support from the Bush White House.[52] It included a number of provisions that had also been included in various forms in previous Senate bills, including:

- tougher border enforcement at the US-Mexico border along with stricter sanctions against employers hiring unauthorized workers;

---

51 For a comparison of the provisions in the comprehensive immigration reform proposals, see Migration Policy Institute (MPI), "Side-By-Side Comparison of 2006 and 2007 Senate Legislation and 2009 CIR ASAP Bill" (Washington, DC: MPI, 2009) www.migrationpolicy.org/pubs/CIRASAPsidebyside.pdf.

52 The cosponsors included Republican Senators Sam Brownback (KS), Lindsey Graham (SC), Chuck Hagel (NE), Mel Martinez (FL), and John McCain (AZ), along with Democratic Senator Edward Kennedy (MA).

- a path to citizenship for most current unauthorized residents, after the payment of back taxes and fines and some delay; and,

- a temporary "guest worker" program for unskilled immigrants.[53]

After this bill failed to be enacted (because of differences with the House), another somewhat similar Senate bill was proposed as the *Comprehensive Immigration Reform Act of 2007* (S.1639); this bill was sponsored by Senator Harry Reid (D-NV) and strongly supported by a coalition of Democratic senators joined by some Republicans and with the strong support of the Bush White House. In addition to somewhat different versions of the three features above,[54] S.1639 would have also reduced family reunification as the basis for admitting immigrants and replaced it with a "merit system" in which points would be allocated for a range of skills plus family connections. This bill (and an earlier version) also included provisions of the *DREAM Act*, which would tender eventual legal permanent residence and ultimately citizenship to many unauthorized immigrants brought to the country as minors, provided they meet higher educational or military service requirements.

In contrast, the House's major actions on immigration focused entirely on border control and cracking down on illegal immigration, with passage of the *Border Protection, Anti-Terrorism, and Illegal Immigration Control Act of 2005*, or H.R. 4437.[55] The bill, which never became law, would have mandated the construction of up to 700 miles of fences along the Mexican border, required all employers to eventually use electronic verification of employees, stiffened fines for hiring illegal workers, and made it a felony for any US citizen to knowingly aid or assist unauthorized immigrants.

Which of the legislative proposals — House or Senate — would further the goals outlined earlier of maximizing net benefits to the US economy and to immigrants who are here while minimizing hardship for less-educated US-born Americans? And what additional changes might be considered to make the achievement of these goals more likely?

---

53 *Comprehensive Immigration Reform Act of 2006*, S.2611, 109th Cong. 2nd sess. (April 7, 2006).

54 For instance, S. 1639 would have allowed 200,000 guest workers (reduced from 400,000 by amendment) for up to two years, after which they would have been required to return home. The bill would have added 370 miles of fencing on the Mexican border, along with the hiring of 20,000 more Border Patrol agents and the mandatory use of an electronic verification system for hiring eligibility. Current unauthorized residents could apply for a green card after waiting eight years, and paying a $2,000 fine on top of all back taxes. *A Bill to Provide For Comprehensive Immigration Reform And For Other Purposes*, S. 1639, 110th Cong, 2007.

55 *The Border Protection, Anti-Terrorism, and Illegal Immigration Control Act of 2005*, H.R. 4437, 109th Cong, 1st sess., (December 6, 2005).

A. The Senate Bill: Closer to the Mark

Offering a personal assessment, I find the measures of H.R. 4437 not only harsh and punitive but also potentially economically costly. The bill would have required the expenditures of many additional billions of dollars annually on enforcement measures, above those that are already occurring, that may or may not be cost-effective ways of limiting immigration; and it would cause major disruptions and impose higher costs on many domestic industries and employers, at least in the short term, while raising prices for consumers. Any benefits to native-born workers or to fiscal balance at various levels of government would be likely to be modest.

On the other hand, at least some version of the three broad provisions contained in the various Senate bills make sense from a policy perspective to further the goals outlined above. Converting today's unauthorized immigrants into legal ones would no doubt limit their ability to undercut the wages of native-born workers, as they would now earn market-level wages while also greatly improving their own chances for integration and upward mobility as well as those of their descendants. Providing for a temporary worker program, under the right conditions, would be another means of converting unauthorized to legal immigrants by channeling future flows of the former into the latter. This conversion could potentially be done by keeping the supply of unskilled immigrants at roughly current levels — thus preventing huge disruptions and costs that would be imposed on the relevant industries and their consumers from a sudden curtailment of these immigrants, while enhanced worksite and border enforcement would help prevent local areas (especially those on or near the Mexican border or in major urban centers) from being flooded with large increases in their numbers. The visa levels for temporary immigrants could also be based on economic necessity, thus generating a better fit with fluctuating US economic needs. Overall, the country would thus be able to maintain much of the net benefit currently associated with unskilled immigration while limiting some of its costs, both economic and human.

Still, there are a number of areas in which the Senate bills seen to date can be improved, as addressed below. I address each of these issues below.

B. Helpful Adjustments

Some modifications to the provisions included in those bills would raise the net benefits they provide to both native-born Americans and immigrants themselves. Among them:

1. Guest Workers: Prospects for Better Jobs and Citizenship

Guest worker provisions are quite sensible at one level, since they provide a potential legal avenue for those immigrants who would otherwise enter illegally in the future. Yet these provisions also have at least two major downsides. First, since guest worker provisions usually tie workers to the employers who sponsor them, the workers can be exploited and abused without having recourse to other jobs in the external labor market. Second, without any prospect of future permanent residence or citizenship, many legal guest workers would ultimately become unauthorized residents when their guest term expires — or they might simply opt to come illegally at the outset.

Both of these potential downsides to guest worker programs can be remedied rather easily. After some period of time — say six months to a year — guest workers should be entitled to switch jobs as they please, with all of the protections that other workers have when so doing. And they should have the option of obtaining permanent residence and ultimately citizenship after some period of time, as long as they comply with the terms of their visas. These protections and options would provide an incentive for temporary workers to choose the legal path over the illegal one and also improve their abilities to enjoy earnings growth and integration over time. As legal workers, enforcement of wage and hour regulations could be accomplished more directly.

Indeed, these visas might be considered explicitly "provisional" rather than "temporary," which would clarify the ultimate option of permanent residence and citizenship for these workers.[56] Whether temporary visas should remain available to some if provisional visas go to others would remain an open question under these circumstances.[57]

2. Fees for Guest Workers (or Provisional Visa Holders)

Given the strain that unskilled and especially illegal immigration can place on public finances at the local level at least in the short term and given that those workers generate important benefits to some Americans (especially employers) but some costs to others (native-born unskilled workers), it makes sense that employers should pay fees in order to generate revenue and to provide some potential compensation to those hurt by the arrival of these immigrants.[58] This notion, in addition to being fair, makes basic economic sense — in that those whose economic activities impose costs (or "negative externalities") on others

---

[56] Demetrios G. Papademetriou, Doris Meissner, Marc R. Rosenblum, and Madeleine Sumption, *Aligning Temporary Immigration Visas with US Labor Market Needs: The Case for a New System of Provisional Visas* (Washington, DC: MPI, 2009), www.migrationpolicy.org/pubs/Provisional_visas.pdf.

[57] For instance, it might make sense to allow temporary visas for certain categories of work, like seasonal agricultural work, without granting provisional visas to those workers.

[58] See Hanson, *The Economics of Illegal Immigration in the United States*; and Richard B. Freeman and Harry J. Holzer, "Guest Worker Proposals Memorandum," (Judiciary Committee, US Senate: Mimeo, 2006).

in society should have to pay for any damage they cause.⁵⁹

Of course, care would be needed when setting the appropriate fee levels. Given that the goal is to provide an incentive for both workers and their employers to choose the legal rather than the illegal route, these fees must not be so steep as to dissuade them from doing so. Given the very low incomes and assets of recent Mexican and other immigrant workers, the payment should be directly levied on employers.⁶⁰

3. Macroeconomic Adjustments to the Numbers Admitted

One related reform, already been touched upon in some measure in the earlier Senate bills, would be to adjust the flows of legal guest (or provisional) workers over time to match shifts in employer demand. These adjustments could occur within the industries and regions that tend to depend heavily today on unskilled immigrants, or in response to aggregate shifts in the labor market (such as the recent recession). This mechanism for recalibrating flows could recreate some of the economic responsiveness to conditions that exists today among unauthorized immigrants, while allowing more flexibility in terms of where these workers flow to meet the demand.

Of course, exactly how decisions about such adjustments should be made, and by whom, remain open questions. Arguments for a professional commission to make such recommendations, based on data analysis over the short and long runs, certainly have some merit.⁶¹

4. State-Level Variation and Research/Evaluation

Immigration is primarily a federal concern, and should be primarily regulated through federal policy. But given the extent to which local economic conditions as well as immigrant flows vary, it makes sense that federal reforms should allow for some state-level variability in the how these policies are designed and implemented. For instance, guest worker flows might be based on state-level rather than federal unemployment rates, while policies to aid with immigrant integration will vary across states as well. Alternatively, any fees collected for

---

59 Economists generally believe that prices of goods and services paid by consumers should reflect not only the costs of producing the good or service but also the costs imposed on the rest of society through negative externalities. The most efficient mechanism for assigning these costs is a "Pigouvian" tax (named for early 20th century British economist A.C. Pigou) that captures the per-unit costs imposed on society. The revenues from such a tax are then presumably used to remediate the social costs.
60 Economists believe that the ultimate "incidence" of such a tax may not fall on the employer, but would be shared between employers and employees, with the latter perhaps paying some of it through lower wages. The exact distribution of the tax would depend on elasticities of labor supply and demand, as noted above.
61 Demetrios G. Papademetriou, Doris Meissner, Marc R. Rosenblum, and Madeleine Sumption, *Harnessing the Advantages of Immigration for a 21st Century Economy: A Standing Commission on Labor Markets, Economic Competitiveness, and Immigration* (Washington, DC: MPI, 2009), www.migrationpolicy.org/pubs/StandingCommission_May09.pdf.

immigrant entry might be distributed across states according to how many immigrants have recently arrived.

Such variation would allow for research and evaluation of the impacts of different policies for and flows of immigrants on their own outcomes and those of natives. This research would importantly inform policymakers and economists about the costs and benefits of different approaches and therefore enable potential adjustments as time goes on.

C. The Many Remaining Uncertainties

Having laid out some specific suggestions for legislative reforms, we need to honestly acknowledge just how much remains unknown.

Very simply, it is hard to know how the labor market behavior of unauthorized immigrants and employers would respond to any set of legislative changes, and so it is hard to know the likely impact of any such reform. More specifically:

- How effective would new enforcement strategies be in deterring unauthorized immigrants from entering the country and potential employers from hiring them?

- Would the guest worker provisions outlined above be sufficiently attractive, in combination with enforcement efforts, to create an incentive for these workers to become legal and for employers to hire them legally?

- If successful, would the new legal status of many such immigrants and their receipt of market-clearing wages generate a more level playing field in which native-born workers would compete more effectively for at least some of the jobs now held by unauthorized immigrants?

- Would native workers become more interested in some of these jobs, especially if wages rise? How many such jobs would remain available as wages in these sectors rise as well?

- To what extent would granting legal status generate upward earnings mobility and more effective integration for workers who become legal, if they stay permanently in the United States?

- Would a more robust set of workforce development policies be cost-effective at improving the skills and earnings of less-educated immigrants or their native-born counterparts?

What we can observe to date on each of these issues is either not terribly informative or not terribly encouraging. For instance, a 2010 evaluation of the E-Verify electronic verification program among employers suggests high rates of false positives — about 50 percent or more — because of extensive identity fraud (with large numbers of stolen or borrowed Social Security numbers) among unauthorized immigrants.[62] The program is also costly while covering a fairly small number of employers and jobs.[63] Whether some type of biometric identification can be devised and implemented on a broad scale without a high error rate remains to be seen. Further increasing border enforcement is even costlier and less reliable.

Given the enormous imbalances in earnings levels between the United States and Mexico, it is possible that the flow of unauthorized immigrants will remain large, even in the presence of a competing legal program. Hanson has argued that the creation of a new, legal path to citizenship for those currently here illegally might encourage more people to come illegally in hopes of a future legalization.[64]

With regards to how employers and native-born workers would respond to changes in the legal status of immigrant workers, we do not really know exactly how the various stocks and flows of legal and unauthorized workers would change, and thus the extent to which earnings of currently unauthorized workers would rise. And for any such earnings increase, it is hard to know exactly how native-born workers would respond — whether jobs would continue to be available, and whether US-born workers would continue to compete for these jobs. These issues involve questions of labor demand and supply elasticities — or how employers and workers respond to changes in wage levels — in specific occupational or industry contexts. Our existing empirical evidence tells us relatively little about the relevant behaviors in these contexts and thus provides little to easily inform decisions on immigration policy changes.

Finally, we have too little evidence on the extent of earnings progress and upward mobility among less-educated immigrants in different employment categories who remain in the country, or on how various workforce development or education programs affect their mobility.

Having said all this, it is important to note that the likely benefits of implementing comprehensive immigration reform still exceed the costs, in my opinion. Not knowing the exact impacts of such measures on outcomes does not become an argument for inaction, given the costs and inefficiencies created by the current system. It merely implies that there remains much to learn, and that any reforms should leave clear opportunities to learn about impacts in order to inform any future reform efforts.

---

62 Department of Homeland Security (DHS), *Westat Evaluation of the E-Verify Program: USCIS Synopsis of Findings and Policy Implications* (Washington, DC: DHS, 2010). www.uscis.gov/ USCIS/Native%20Docs/Westat%20Evaluation%20of%20the%20E-Verify%20Program.pdf
63 Ibid.
64 Hanson, "Illegal Migration from Mexico to the United States."

D. A Few Broader Issues

Besides the specific changes discussed above, some other broader issues will continue to be debated. The biggest is whether the United States should continue to have an immigration system that generates a mix of immigrants that is so heavily tilted towards the unskilled — especially given the arguments that the greatest economic benefits for the country derive from those with the highest levels of education.

Since the current mix of immigrants is heavily driven by a system that places its primary emphasis on family reunification, any policy that would significantly change this mix would have to challenge this pillar of current immigration law. Indeed, the points system proposed in the 2007 Senate legislation would have done just that. Other ways of doing so would be to dramatically expand the numbers of H-1B visas or employment-based green cards for highly educated immigrants, perhaps in ways described above that would create clearer pathways to permanent citizenship for these workers.

Of course, economic considerations are not the only relevant ones for immigration policy; social, political, and humanitarian concerns matter as well, and for these reasons a strong emphasis on family reunification will likely survive. But given the enormous effects this system has on the mix of immigrants and therefore on the economic effects of immigration, the issue should remain one that is openly discussed and debated.

The other big issue — one that is less directly addressed through immigration reform and more through our education, workforce development, and income-transfer policies — involves how can prospects for upward mobility and integration be improved for less-educated immigrants who stay legally in the United States. A fuller treatment of this issue clearly goes beyond the scope of this chapter. But I believe that more concerted efforts to improve the prospects of both immigrant and US workers through education and workforce development services will be required.

Simply put, a range of policies that create pathways for advancement for disadvantaged youth and adults — through high-quality career and technical education, community college efforts, and related workforce supports and services — should be implemented to maximize the chances that these populations can advance when opportunities arise in higher-wage sectors with middle-skilled jobs.[65] Of course, such policies would potentially benefit immigrants as well as the native-born. Policies that specifically address the needs of immigrants — such as adult basic education or remedial language efforts in the schools — deserve some support as well.

---

65   Harry J. Holzer, Julia Lane, and David Rosenblum, *Where Are All the Good Jobs Going? What National and Local Job Quality and Dynamics Mean for US Workers* (New York: Russell Sage Foundation, 2011).

Other efforts to directly raise the quality of jobs in the labor market — including higher minimum wages, more collective bargaining, and other public efforts to help and provide an incentive for employers to create "good jobs" — would benefit both native and immigrant workers and should be considered as well. Expanded public supports for low-wage workers should be on the nation's agenda too, even in a fiscal climate that requires major deficit reduction over time.[66]

IV. Conclusion

The treatment of less-educated immigrants, and especially the unauthorized, continues to be the most controversial aspect of any potential reform legislation. What principles should guide policies on this topic? What do we know from research on this issue, and what important questions remain largely unanswered? And, in light of what we know and don't know, how should we move ahead on policy?

Immigration reform legislation will no doubt be driven by a range of social and political as well as economic concerns, as it should be. But certainly the economic issues deserve to be among our top concerns. It is reasonable to ask what kinds of reforms would best serve the interests of native-born American workers, consumers, and employers as well as the overall economy going forward. There is a widespread consensus that highly educated immigrants have much to offer the US economy, but much less agreement on what is gained from those who are less educated.

Still, my review of the literature indicates that we know some things with fairly reasonable certainty. Though the extent to which less-educated immigrants compete with and harm their native-born US counterparts has been very heavily debated in the economics profession, the overall findings of this literature suggest quite modest negative impacts. Fiscal costs also appear to be modest. The benefits of low-skilled immigration accrue not only to employers (who benefit from paying lower wages) and high-income consumers (who benefit from cheaper child care, landscaping, and restaurant meals) but also to low-income consumers (in the form of cheaper and more available food, housing, and medical care), workers who can specialize in jobs that require somewhat greater communication and arithmetic skills, and the economy overall.

---

[66] Higher minimum wages can raise the earnings of less-educated workers, but perhaps with some loss of employment to those groups. See David Neumark and William Wascher, *Minimum Wages* (Cambridge, MA: MIT Press, 2009). Collective bargaining can also improve worker outcomes, but there are also potential employment losses if their higher wages are not offset by higher productivity, especially in more competitive product markets. See Freeman and Holzer, "Memorandum." The use of tax credits or technical assistance to create incentives for more employers to offer higher wages and benefits and better advancement opportunities to its workers is discussed in Holzer et al., *Where Are All the Good Jobs Going?*

While the effects of different categories of immigration are often unclear, it seems reasonable that those who are unauthorized pose greater threats to native-born workers in the form of the below-market wages they are often paid. Greater efforts to improve the upward mobility of these immigrants might make them more competitive with Americans in certain sectors and areas, but less so in others; and economic projections suggest that there will be strong enough demand in the "middle-skill" job categories that the labor market can likely absorb larger numbers of both native-born and immigrant workers in this category without great difficulty. Greater skills and earnings among immigrants will likely mean even more improvements in the education and skills of future generations of their offspring, implying greater economic benefits and fewer costs associated with poverty.

In all, it is hard to make the case that the current volume of unskilled immigration to the United States is too high and needs to be sharply curtailed. Any such efforts would certainly lead to disruptions in the labor supply of many industries in various regions of the country in the short term, and might raise costs in the long term as well. It is also hard to make the case that unskilled immigration should be expanded dramatically, on the basis of the benefits and costs it creates. Accounting for future demographic changes, including the imminent retirements of baby boomers, does not greatly change this picture. On the other hand, transforming the current stock of unauthorized immigrants into legal ones and providing for future legal flows is certainly better for them and mostly better for native-born Americans as well.

Accordingly, immigration reform that creates pathways to legal status and citizenship for those already here, and that provides an incentive for employers and immigrants to use newly legal routes, seems very sensible. A range of efforts would improve the incentives of both groups to choose the legal over the illegal route — such as stronger enforcement, allowing legal immigrants to move freely in the US labor market once they are here, and providing them a path to permanent status. Charging employers some modest fees to offset short-term fiscal costs and modifying the flows in response to changing macroeconomic conditions would further improve the ratio of benefits to costs that accrue to the United States from such a policy change.

Still, the potential effects of reform efforts are sufficiently uncertain that policy changes should be undertaken with some caution. Exactly how employers and immigrants would respond to any legislative changes cannot be predicted with any certainty, just as the responses of less-educated US-born workers to any changes in job market circumstances are unclear too. How future shifts in the domestic labor supply of unskilled workers associated with baby boomer retirements compare with any shifts in demand caused by ongoing technological change, other forms of globalization, and the like, and what these forces mean for the future evolution of earnings and employment for unskilled workers remains unclear.

It makes sense to pursue immigration reform in ways that allow us to experiment with different approaches and to evaluate the labor market impacts of such policy changes as time goes on. Giving states some flexibility in implementing these reforms would provide greater scope to observe variations in market outcomes and policies and to learn from them. Allowing for policies to adapt to future changes — such as having a commission that would direct the loosening or tightening of restrictions according to macroeconomic changes — would be sensible as well.

Having said all this, it is also clear that changes in immigration policy would leave many other issues and concerns unaddressed. While unskilled immigration has clearly not been the major source of economic difficulty experienced by less-educated native-born Americans in recent years, the loss of earnings and employment they have experienced in the past few decades remains profound, and needs greater policy attention. A range of education and workforce development policies that would benefit all low-skilled workers — both native-born and immigrant — deserves greater funding and support. These would include high-quality career and technical education for youth, greater supports for disadvantaged youth and adults at community colleges, and better integration of education and training providers with a workforce system that is more closely linked to employer demand. Direct efforts to improve job quality and expand public supports for the working poor have merit as well.

More serious efforts in this regard could more than offset the modest costs to native-born workers associated with unskilled immigration, and would thus enable us to more fully enjoy the benefits that it provides.

Works Cited

Angrist, Joshua and Adriana Kugler. 2003. Protective or Counter-Productive? Labour Market Institutions and the Effect of Immigration on EU Natives. *The Economic Journal* 113 (2): 302–31, www.nber.org/papers/w8660.pdf?new_window=1.

Bertelsmann Stiftung and Migration Policy Institute (MPI). 2009. *Talent, Competitiveness and Migration,* eds. Bertelsmann Stiftung and MPI. Gütersloh: Bertelsmann Stiftung.

Borjas, George. 1985. Assimilation, Changes in Cohort Quality, and the Earnings of Immigrants. *Journal of Labor Economics* 3 (4): 463-89.

_____. 1995. The Economic Benefits from Immigration. *Journal of Economic Perspectives* 9 (2): 3-22.

_____. 2003. The Labor Demand Curve IS Downward Sloping: Reexamining the Impacts of Immigration on the Labor Market. *Quarterly Journal of Economics* 118 (4): 1335–74.

_____. 2006a. Native Internal Migration and the Labor Market Impact of Immigration. *Journal of Human Resources* 41 (2): 221-58.

_____. 2006b. Wage Trends among Disadvantaged Minorities. In *Working and Poor: How Economic and Policy Changes are Affecting Low-Wage Workers*, eds. Rebecca M. Blank, Sheldon H. Danziger, and Robert F. Schoeni. New York: Russell Sage Foundation.

_____. 2007. Immigration Policy and Human Capital. In *Reshaping the American Workforce in a Changing Economy*, eds. Harry J. Holzer and Demetra Nightingale. Washington, DC: Urban Institute Press.

Borjas, George and Lawrence Katz. 2006. Evolution of the Mexican-Born Workforce in the United States. NBER Working Paper 11281. www.nber.org/papers/w11281.

Borjas, George, Richard B. Freeman, and Lawrence Katz. 1996. Searching for the Effect of Immigration in the Labor Market. *American Economic Review* 86 (2): 246-51.

Capps, Randy, Michael Fix, and Serena Yi-Ying Lin. 2010. *Still An Hourglass? Immigrant Workers in Middle-Skilled Jobs*. Washington, DC: Migration Policy Institute. www.migrationpolicy.org/pubs/sectoralbrief-Sept2010.pdf.

Card, David. 2001. Immigration Inflows, Native Outflows, and the Local Labor Market Impacts of Higher Immigration. *Journal of Labor Economics* 19 (1): 22-64. http://davidcard.berkeley.edu/papers/immig-inflows.pdf.

_____. 2005. Is the New Immigration Really So Bad? *Economic Journal* 115 (506): 30023.

_____. 2009. Immigration and Inequality. *American Economic Review* 99 (2): 1-21.

Carnevale, Anthony, Nicole Smith, and Jeff Strohl. 2010. *Help Wanted: Projections of Jobs and Education Requirements Through 2018*. Washington, DC: Center on Education and the Workforce, Georgetown University.

Cortes, Patricia. 2008. The Effect of Low-Skilled Immigration on US Prices: Evidence from CPI Data. *Journal of Political Economy* 116 (3): 381-422.

Cortes, Patricia and Jose Tessada. 2009. How Low-Skilled Immigration is Changing the Labor Supply of Highly Educated American Women. Working Paper. www.inesad.edu.bo/bcde2009/A2%20Cortes%20Tessada.pdf.

Department of Homeland Security (DHS). 2010. *Westat Evaluation of the E-Verify Program: USCIS Synopsis of Findings and Policy Implications*. Washington, DC: DHS. www.uscis.gov/USCIS/Native%20Docs/Westat%20Evaluation%20 of%20the%20E-Verify%20Program.pdf.

D'Amico, Carol and Richard Judy. 1997. *Workforce 2020*. New York: Hudson Institute.

Edelman, Peter, Harry J. Holzer, and Paul Offner. 2006. *Reconnecting Disadvantaged Young Men*. Washington, DC: Urban Institute Press.

Fix, Michael. 2001. Comment on 'Welfare Reform and Immigration.' In *The New World of Welfare*, eds. Rebecca M. Blank and Ron Haskins. Washington, DC: Brookings Institution.

Freeman, Richard B. 2007. *America Works*. New York: Russell Sage Foundation.

_____. 2007. Is a Great Labor Shortage Coming? Replacement Demand in the Age of Globalization. In *Reshaping the American Workforce in a Changing Economy*, eds. Harry J. Holzer and Demetra Nightingale. Washington, DC: Urban Institute Press.

Freeman, Richard B. and Harry J. Holzer. 2006. Guest Worker Proposals Memorandum. Judiciary Committee, US Senate: Mimeo.

Goldin, Claudia and Lawrence Katz. 2008. *The Race Between Education and Technology*. Cambridge, MA: Harvard University Press.

Hanson, Gordon. 2007. Illegal Migration from Mexico to the United States. *Journal of Economic Literature* 44 (4): 869–924.

_____. 2013. The Economics and Policy of Illegal Immigration in the United States. In *Immigrants in a Changing Labor Market: Responding to Economic Need*, eds. Michael Fix, Demetrios G. Papademetriou, and Madeleine Sumption. Washington, DC: Migration Policy Institute.

Holzer, Harry J. 1986. Black Youth Nonemployment: Duration and Job Search. In *The Black Youth Employment Crisis*, eds. Richard B. Freeman and Harry J. Holzer. Chicago: University of Chicago Press.

_____. 2009. Workforce Development as an Antipoverty Strategy: What Do We Know? What Should We Do? In *Changing Poverty, Changing Policies*, eds. Maria Cancian and Sheldon H. Danziger. New York: Russell Sage Foundation.

Holzer, Harry J. and Robert Lerman. 2007. *America's Forgotten Middle-Skill Jobs: Education and Training Requirements in the Next Decade and Beyond*. Washington, DC: The Workforce Alliance.

Holzer, Harry J., Julia Lane, David Rosenblum, and Fredrik Andersson. 2011. *Where Are All the Good Jobs Going? What National and Local Job Quality and Dynamics Mean for US Workers*. New York: Russell Sage Foundation.

Holzer, Harry J., Diane Schanzenbach, Greg Duncan, and Jens Ludwig. 2007. *The Economic Costs of Poverty: Subsequent Effects of Children Growing Up Poor.* Washington, DC: Center for American Progress.

House Resolution 4437. 2005. *The Border Protection, Anti-Terrorism, and Illegal Immigration Control Act of 2005*, 109th Cong., 1st sess. http://thomas.loc.gov/cgi-bin/bdquery/z?d109:h.r.04437:.

Hunt, Jennifer. 2008. How Much Does Immigration Boost Innovation? Unpublished paper, McGill University.

Ibarraran, Pablo and Darren Lubotsky. 2005. Mexican Immigration and Self-Selection: New Evidence from the 2000 Mexican Census. NBER Working Paper 11456. www.nber.org/papers/w11456.

Kirschenman, Joleen and Kathryn Neckerman. 1991. We'd Love to Hire Them But... In *The Urban Underclass*, eds. Christopher Jencks and Paul E. Peterson. Washington, DC: Brookings Institution. http://digitalcommons.uconn.edu/cgi/viewcontent.cgi?article=1004&context=cpilj.

Kossoudji, Sherrie and Deborah Cobb-Clark. 2002. Coming Out of the Shadows: Learning About Legal Status and Wages from the Legalized Population. *Journal of Labor Economics* 20 (3): 598-628.

Lewis, Ethan. 2005. Immigration, Skill Mix and the Choice of Technique. Working Paper, Federal Reserve Bank of Philadelphia. www.philadelphiafed.org/research-and-data/publications/working-papers//2005/wp05-8.pdf.

Lubotsky, Darren. 2007. Chutes or Ladders? A Longitudinal Analysis of Immigrant Earnings. *Journal of Political Economy* 115 (5): 820-867.

Migration Policy Institute (MPI). 2009. Side-By-Side Comparison of 2006 and 2007 Senate Legislation and 2009 CIR ASAP Bill. Washington, DC: MPI. www.migrationpolicy.org/pubs/CIRASAPsidebyside.pdf.

Neumark, David and William Wascher. 2009. *Minimum Wages.* Cambridge, MA: MIT Press.

Ottaviano, Gianmarco and Giovanni Peri. 2006. Rethinking the Effects of Immigration on Wages. NBER Working Paper 12497. www.nber.org/papers/w12497.pdf?new_window=1.

Papademetriou, Demetrios G., Doris Meissner, Marc R. Rosenblum, and Madeleine Sumption. 2009a. *Aligning Temporary Immigration Visas with US Labor Market Needs: The Case for a New System of Provisional Visas.* Washington, DC: Migration Policy Institute.

_____. 2009b. *Harnessing the Advantages of Immigration for a 21st Century Economy: A Standing Commission on Labor Markets, Economic Competitiveness, and Immigration.* Washington, DC: Migration Policy Institute. www.migrationpolicy.org/pubs/standingcommission_may09.pdf.

Peri, Giovanni and Chad Sparber. 2007. Task Specialization, Comparative Advantages, and the Effects of Immigration on Wages. NBER Working Paper 13389. www.nber.org/papers/w13389.

Raphael, Steven and Lucas Ronconi. 2007. The Effects of Labor Market Competition with Immigrants on the Wages and Employment of Natives: What Does Existing Research Tell Us? *DuBois Review: Social Science Research on Race*, 4 (2): 413-32. www.irle.berkeley.edu/cwed/ronconi/immigration_existing_research.pdf.

Reed, Deborah and Sheldon H. Danziger. 2007. The Effects of Recent Immigration on Racial/Ethnic Labor Market Differentials. *American Economic Review* 97 (2): 373-7.

Rivera-Batiz, Francisco. 1999. Undocumented Workers in the Labor Market: An Analysis of Earnings of Legal and Illegal Mexican Immigrants in the United States. *Journal of Population Economics* 12 (1): 91-116.

Senate Bill 2611. 2006. *Comprehensive Immigration Reform Act of 2006*. 109th Cong., 2nd sess. http://thomas.loc.gov/cgi-bin/bdquery/z?d109:SN02611:@@@L&summ2=m.

Senate Bill 1639. 2007. *A Bill to Provide For Comprehensive Immigration Reform And For Other Purposes.* 110th Cong., 1st sess. http://thomas.loc.gov/cgi-bin/bdquery/z?d110:SN1639:.

Smith, Christopher. 2008. Essays on the Youth and Entry Level Labor Markets. PhD Dissertation, Department of Economics, MIT.

Somerville, Will and Madeleine Sumption. 2009. *Immigration and the Labor Market: Theory, Evidence and Policy*. Washington, DC: Migration Policy Institute. www.migrationpolicy.org/pubs/Immigration-and-the-Labour-Market.pdf.

Stone, Robin and Joshua Wiener. 2001. *Who Will Care for Us? Addressing the Long-Term Care Workforce Crisis*. Washington, DC: Institute for the Future of Aging Services. www.urban.org/UploadedPDF/Who_will_Care_for_Us.pdf.

Sumption, Madeleine. 2010. *Low-Skilled Immigration to the United States* (Unpublished). Washington, DC: Migration Policy Institute.

CHAPTER 2

THE ECONOMICS AND POLICY OF ILLEGAL IMMIGRATION IN THE UNITED STATES

Gordon H. Hanson

University of California-San Diego
and National Bureau of Economic Research

Introduction

"America's immigration system is outdated, unsuited to the needs of our economy and to the values of our country. We should not be content with laws that punish hard-working people and deny businesses willing workers and invite chaos at our border."

George W. Bush, February 2, 2005

"We need immigration reform that will secure our borders, and... that finally brings the 12 million people who are here illegally out of the shadows... We must assert our values and reconcile our principles as a nation of immigrants and a nation of laws."

Barack Obama, June 28, 2008

"My biggest failure so far is we haven't gotten comprehensive immigration reform done ... But it's not because for lack of trying or desire, and I'm confident we are going to accomplish that."

Barack Obama, September 19, 2012

President Barack Obama, like President George W. Bush and countless others before him, has declared that our immigration system is broken and in need of an overhaul. While the two presidents would not agree on all the details of a reform plan — with Bush focusing, in his second term, on enforcement initiatives and a temporary worker program; and Obama in favor of giving the unauthorized population a path to legal residence — they share a belief that high levels of illegal immigration are an indictment of the current policy regime and that immigrants by and large make positive contributions to America.

There are currently an estimated 11.1 million unauthorized immigrants living in the United States, with an average of 500,000 new entrants arriving annually over the course of the 2000s.[1] As many as two-thirds of unauthorized immigrants have been estimated to enter the country by crossing the US-Mexico border, with the remaining 30 percent to 40 percent arriving on temporary entry visas and then staying on after their visas expire.[2] Though the economic crisis and persistently high levels of unemployment in the United States appear to have staunched the growth of the unauthorized population, higher levels of illegal entry are likely to resume, if past experience is any guide, once the US economy recovers.

If leaders from different parties and with quite different political orientations can agree on a broad mandate for immigration reform, why has Congress not passed such legislation? A conventional, but incomplete, answer for why immigration reform has not occurred is that it is another casualty of the partisan divide gripping Washington. Democrats and Republicans often disagree on immigration; and there also is conflict within the parties themselves, which has complicated the formation of coalitions to support reform. Another reason is that the illegal immigration, despite its faults, has been sufficiently beneficial to US employers that they are doubtful about the capacity of Congress to improve the situation and therefore unwilling to take the political risk of supporting reform. Unauthorized entry is the primary means through which the US economy gains access to low-skilled foreign labor. As long as unauthorized immigrants are able to enter the United States and interior enforcement does not prevent employers from hiring them, inflows of unauthorized labor are essentially regulated by the market and can respond to the demands of US business, helping raise US productivity in the process. This was essentially the case in the early 2000s, when hundreds of thousands of unauthorized immigrants were able to find work in the United States.

In recent years, enormous investments in border control and growing interior enforcement may have begun to change this dynamic, although their impact is far from clear and cannot be easily separated from the

---

1 Jeffrey S. Passel and D'Vera Cohn, *Unauthorized Immigrants: 11.1 Million in 2011* (Washington, DC: Pew Hispanic Center, 2012), www.pewhispanic.org/2012/12/06/unauthorized-immigrants-11-1-million-in-2011; Jeffrey S. Passel and D'Vera Cohn, *A Portrait of Unauthorized Immigrants in the United States* (Washington, DC: Pew Hispanic Center, 2009), http://pewresearch.org/pubs/1190/portrait-unauthorized-immigrants-states.

2 Office of the Inspector General, US Department of Justice, *Follow-Up Report on INS Efforts To Improve The Control Of Nonimmigrant Overstays*, Report No. I-2002-006 (Washington, DC: Office of the Inspector General, US Department of Justice, 2002), www.justice.gov/oig/reports/INS/e0206/intro.htm#bac; Rey Koslowski, *Real Challenges for Virtual Borders: The Implementation of US-VISIT* (Washington, DC: Migration Policy Institute, 2005), 5, www.migrationpolicy.org/pubs/Koslowski_Report.pdf; and US Government Accountability Office, *Overstay Tracking: A Key Component of Homeland Security and a Layered Defense*, GAO-04-82 (Washington, DC: US Government Accountability Office, 2004), www.gao.gov/new.items/d0482.pdf.

effects of the economic downturn. Nonetheless, many employers continue to recruit unauthorized workers, suggesting that their appeal as a flexible labor force remains robust. The obvious downsides of such a system include the overt flouting of US immigration laws and the insecurity and abuse to which unauthorized migrants are often exposed.

I. The Economics and Policy of Illegal Immigration

Legal mechanisms for low-skilled immigration, at least in their current form, are not designed to meet the changing demands of US employers. To enter legally, foreign workers either have to obtain a green card (given US immigration law, this effectively requires them to have close family members in the United States), or secure a temporary work visa. The H-2A and H-2B visa programs are the main temporary avenues through which low-skilled workers enter the country. The total supply of H-2A and H-2B visas is scarcely 1 percent of the current unauthorized population, making foreign guest workers a negligible part of the low-skilled US labor force.

Given the vast scale of illegal immigration and few existing channels for legal entry, there is pressure on Washington to resolve America's immigration problem and President Obama has repeatedly promised that he will tackle the issue — a pledge he has reiterated as a major priority for the early part of his second term. Policies to tackle unauthorized immigrant and employment tend to embrace one or both of two major competing theories currently en vogue:

- An enforcement strategy, which would likely rely on security at the border and in the US interior (including additional legal status verification obligations for employers) to prevent future illegal immigration and employment of unauthorized workers, and convince those here unlawfully to leave the country; and

- A starkly different accommodation strategy, under which the United States would legalize unauthorized immigrants in the country and offer expanded legal options to absorb future prospective migrants.

Any new reform effort will have to take a stand on preventing versus facilitating inflows of low-skilled foreign labor. The immigration legislation Congress contemplated but did not pass in 2007, for example, was a blend of enforcement and accommodation approaches — pairing a path to legal status for unauthorized immigrants and a new temporary worker program with stepped-up border and interior enforcement. While the debate on immigration reform in mid- to late-2000s focused primarily on the need for a "comprehensive" package of this kind, the failure to pass any reform bills has increased the likelihood that different parts of the package may be considered separately.

To weigh the relative merits of enforcement and accommodation strategies, this chapter lays out a set of stylized facts about illegal immigration in the United States and concludes with a set of recommendations for policymakers. Are unauthorized immigrants important to the US economy? Would reducing low-skilled immigration be good for the United States? Is the type of immigration reform Congress would pass liable to make the country better or worse off?

A. Unauthorized Immigrants Are a Large Part of the Low-Skilled US Labor Force

Over the last 50 years, the United States has raised the education level of its adult population dramatically. Whereas in 1960 half of US-born working-age adults had not completed high school, today the figure is just 8 percent. Though the share of low-skilled native-born individuals in the US labor force has fallen, employers continue to require less-educated workers in US agriculture, construction, food processing, building cleaning and maintenance, and other low-end jobs. Immigrants, unauthorized immigrants in particular, have stepped in to provide a ready source of manpower. Unauthorized immigrant workers have been an important source of low-skilled labor supply to the US economy for many decades.

The Pew Hispanic Center estimates that the number of unauthorized immigrants in the US labor force was 8 million in 2008, up from 6.3 million in 2003 but down slightly from the 2007 peak of 8.4 million.[3] Just as the 2002 to 2007 economic expansion increased employment of unauthorized immigrants, the illegally resident labor force has stalled during the economic crisis and slow recovery. The vast majority of unauthorized immigrants work in low-skilled occupations, owing both to their immigration status and their low levels of schooling. Forty-seven percent of unauthorized immigrants between 25 and 64 years of age have not completed the equivalent of a US high school education; they account for 20 percent of working-age adults in the United States with less than a high school degree. Unsurprisingly, unauthorized immigrants have a significant presence in industries intensive in the use of low-skilled labor. In 2008, they represented 25 percent of farm workers, 19 percent of building and maintenance staff, 17 percent of construction labor, 12 percent of employees in food preparation and serving, 10 percent of production labor, and 5 percent of the total civil-

---

3   Passel and Cohn, *Unauthorized Immigrant Population: National and State Trends*, 2010 (Washington, DC: Pew Hispanic Center, 2011), www.pewhispanic.org/files/reports/133.pdf.

ian labor force.[4] The US economy could no doubt survive the departure of these workers, but it would cause disruptions in labor-intensive industries and the regions in which they are concentrated.

The majority of unauthorized immigrants come from countries near the United States, with 59 percent being from Mexico, 15 percent from Central America and the Caribbean, and 7 percent from South America.[5] The vast majority of these individuals from nearby countries enter the United States by crossing the US-Mexico border. The remaining 19 percent of unauthorized immigrants are divided among Asia (11 percent), Canada and Europe (4 percent), and other countries (4 percent), most of whom enter on and then overstay temporary visas. With over four-fifths of unauthorized immigrants coming from the Western Hemisphere, managing US borders is clearly a central function of US immigration policy.

While unauthorized migrants are in the country illegally, many are, in some respects, well integrated into US society. They work in formal businesses, own their own homes, shop in neighborhood stores, attend local churches, and send their children to public schools. More than half have payroll taxes deducted from their paychecks[6] and a smaller but still significant number pays federal income taxes.[7] Until the Department of Homeland Security enacted stricter interior enforcement policies in 2006, their presence in the country was unofficially tolerated, at least once they had succeeded in getting past the US Border Patrol. Unauthorized migrants who eschewed criminal activity were largely left alone. In his second term, President Bush shifted away from a policy of unofficial tolerance by stepping up efforts to prosecute unauthorized immigrants using unauthorized Social Security numbers (in order to hide their unlawful status from employers) and enlisting the help of local law enforcement in tracking down unauthorized immigrants in the US interior. Recently, President Obama has scaled back worksite enforcement raids on the one hand, but has also expanded programs for auditing employers to ensure compliance with employment verification laws on the other.

Low-skilled foreign workers seeking to enter the United States legally have two options. One is to obtain a green card. The *Immigration Act of 1990* set an overall annual cap on the number of green cards at 675,000, with specific quotas assigned to immigrants who are family-sponsored

---

4   Jeffrey S. Passel and D'Vera Cohn, *A Portrait of Unauthorized Immigrants in the United States* (Washington, DC: Pew Hispanic Center, 2009), http://pewresearch.org/pubs/1190/portrait-unauthorized-immigrants-states.
5   Ibid.
6   Council of Economic Advisers, *Economic Report of the President* (Washington, DC: Council of Economic Advisers, 2005), www.gpo.gov/fdsys/pkg/ERP-2005/pdf/ERP-2005.pdf.
7   Steven A. Camarota, *The High Cost of Cheap Labor: Illegal Immigration and the Federal Budget* (Washington, DC: Center for Immigration Studies, 2004), www.cis.org/articles/2004/fiscal.html.

(480,000), skilled employees (140,000), or entering by lottery (55,000).[8] Immediate relatives of US citizens enter without restriction; refugees and asylees have their own visa category. To qualify for a green card, a low-skilled foreign worker would have to have a close relative who is a US citizen or legal resident, obtain one of 5,000 employment-based visas available each year to low-skilled workers, be a refugee, or win one of the scarce lottery visas. The second option is to obtain a temporary work visa under the H-2A (seasonal agricultural worker) or H-2B (seasonal nonagricultural worker) visa programs, which permit visa holders to work for a US employer for up to one year. H-2B visas are capped at 66,000 per year; H-2A visas have no cap but are subject to onerous requirements and strict work rules which limit their use. On average, H-2A and H-2B visa issuances have been roughly comparable, although the number of H-2A visas issued has grown steadily, while H-2B inflows have fluctuated.[9] In light of the 8 million unauthorized immigrants working in the United States, the roughly 150,000 temporary low-skilled legal immigrants who are in the country at any one moment are an inconsequential component of domestic low-skilled employment.

Were the United States to restrict or eliminate illegal immigration through greater enforcement, the clear losers would be business owners in labor-intensive industries, including agriculture, construction, lodging, restaurants, food processing, and building maintenance and cleaning services. Not surprisingly, these are the industries that fight hardest against restrictions on low-skilled immigration.

B. Illegal Immigration Responds to Market Conditions in Ways that Legal Immigration Presently Cannot

Illegal immigration occurs because foreign workers can earn much more in the United States than they can at home and US immigration restrictions prevent them from entering the country through legal means. Consider the gain to emigration for a young urban male in Mexico who has completed nine years of education (which in Mexico is equivalent to finishing secondary school). Simply by moving to the United States, the worker's annual income would rise by 2.5 times, even after controlling for cost-of-living differences between the two countries.[10] The income gain from migration is a result of international differences in labor productivity, with labor in the United States being far more productive than in Mexico.

---

8 US Department of Homeland Security (DHS), *2008 Yearbook of Immigration Statistics* (Washington, DC: DHS, 2009), www.dhs.gov/xlibrary/assets/statistics/yearbook/2008/ois_yb_2008.pdf.

9 US Department of State, "Classes of Nonimmigrants Issued Visas (Detailed Breakdown) Fiscal Years 2004-2008," www.travel.state.gov/pdf/NIVClassIssued-DetailedFY2004-2008.pdf.

10 Michael Clemons, Claudio Montenegro, and Lant Pritchett, "The Place Premium: Wage Differences for Identical Workers across the US Border," (working paper No. 148, Center on Global Development, Washington, DC, December 2008), www.cgdev.org/content/publications/detail/16352.

Illegal immigration is not entirely unregulated. To a certain extent, the US government affects the inflow of unauthorized immigrants by choosing how intensively to enforce the border and deter the employment of unauthorized workers. The Border Patrol has more than doubled since 2001, with 20,000 agents who police US borders, ports, and airports, seeking to apprehend individuals attempting to enter the country illegally. Beyond the increased agent deployment, other measures have strengthened the enforcement presence, including the construction of fencing at key crossing points at the US-Mexico border, use of technology such as unmanned aerial vehicles to patrol remote border locations, and increased detention and prosecution of would-be crossers. As a result, illegal migrants are forced to pay higher prices to smugglers to get into the country — a development that weakens the incentive to migrate to the United States. In 2008, the price for smuggler services at the US-Mexico border averaged $2,750, up from $1,250 in the late 1990s (adjusted for inflation).[11]

While enforcement clearly plays a role in illegal migration patterns, the variation in illegal immigration over time is largely a response to changes in the US macroeconomy, as well as the economies of migrants' home countries. In the United States, wages for low-skilled labor rise and fall over the business cycle.[12] Individuals' earnings peak during expansions, as rising demand for goods and services push prices up, allowing each worker to generate more revenue per hour worked and hence to earn more. Correspondingly, wages drop during downturns, as falling demand lets prices drop, bringing wages down, too. The value to business of having access to low-skilled labor is greatest when economic growth is high and least when it is low.

Over the last two decades the inflow of unauthorized immigrants has broadly tracked economic performance. During the US economic expansion of 2002 to 2007, unauthorized migrants came in large numbers, particularly at the peak of the US housing boom. In 2008, 21 percent of unauthorized migrants in the United States were employed in construction. In the mid-1990s, when the United States enjoyed rapid growth and Mexico suffered a financial crisis, illegal entry was also at high levels.[13] With the collapse of the US housing market and rapid rises in unemployment in 2008, by contrast, illegal inflows slowed dramatically to one third of the level that prevailed in the first half of the 2000s.[14]

---

11 For example, see The Mexican Migration Project, "Border Crossing Costs" 1980-2008, http://mmp.opr.princeton.edu/results/001costs-en.aspx.
12 Katherine Abraham and John Haltiwanger, "Real Wages over the Business Cycle," *Journal of Economic Literature*, 33 (1995): 1216-64.
13 Gordon Hanson and Antonio Spilimbergo, "Illegal Immigration, Border Enforcement and Relative Wages: Evidence from Apprehensions at the U.S.-Mexico Border," *American Economic Review*, 89 (1999): 1337-57.
14 D'Vera Cohn and Jeffrey Passel, "U.S. Unauthorized Flows Are Sharply Down Since Mid-Decade" (Washington, DC: Pew Hispanic Center, 2010), www.pewhispanic.org/2010/09/01/us-unauthorized-immigration-flows-are-down-sharply-since-mid-decade/.

Once in the country, unauthorized migrants are mobile geographically, moving between and within states in response to regional business cycles. Today, unauthorized immigrants have a presence in most parts of the United States, having spread out beyond the handful of traditional gateway states where they once were nearly totally concentrated.

Because of policy constraints on the number of visas, some types of legal immigration are largely unresponsive to market forces, however. The number of green cards available each year is fixed by law and does not adjust in response to changes in the US economy. Congress could in principle vary the number of temporary work visas according to US macroeconomic conditions, but in practice adjusts the supply only modestly and on an *ad hoc* basis. And although Congress temporarily expanded low-skilled seasonal work visas from 2004 to 2008 through the H-2R program for "returning workers,"[15] the total supply of temporary legal low-skilled workers remained tiny relative to the number of unauthorized immigrants employed in US industry. Meanwhile, employer take-up of the uncapped but highly regulated H-2A (agricultural) visas grew by only 20,000 during the 2002 to 2007 economic expansion; and the annual inflow of nonagricultural low-skilled workers rose by less than 70,000 over the same period,[16] even as US employers hired hundreds of thousands of illegally resident workers in booming industries such as construction. In other words, US visa programs are simply not designed to accommodate the changing demands of US industry. Under current policies, if businesses want to hire additional low-skilled foreign workers in a time of economic expansion, their primary option is to employ unauthorized immigrants.

High unemployment in the past five years may have made the creation of a new temporary visa route for legal, less-skilled workers difficult as the demand for both unauthorized immigrants and temporary visaholders has fallen. But in the long run, if Congress chooses to use increased legal immigration as a means to reduce illegal inflows, it will have to revamp entirely the manner in which employment visas are allocated. Visas would need to be supplied flexibly, made responsive to market conditions, and provided to the workers in demand by US business. Not since the "bracero" guest worker program, which lasted from the 1940s to the early 1960s, has the United States run such a system.

---

15 The H-2R program allowed individuals who had previously worked in the United States with an H-2B (nonagricultural) visa to receive a cap-exempt H-2R visa.

16 Note that without the one-off measure exempting returning H-2B workers from the 66,000 cap from 2005-2007, this increase would have been almost negligible. US Department of State, "Classes of Nonimmigrants Issued Visas (Detailed Breakdown) Fiscal Years 2004-2008," www.travel.state.gov/pdf/NIVClassIssued-DetailedFY2006-2010.pdf; and US Department of State, "Classes of Nonimmigrants Issued Visas (Detailed Breakdown) Fiscal Years 2002-2006," http://travel.state.gov/pdf/FY06AnnualReportTableXVIA.pdf.

C. The Overall Impact of Illegal Immigration on the US Economy Is Small

Economic theory suggests that illegal immigration has both positive and negative impacts on the US economy and its workers. The arrival of foreign workers increases the domestic supply of low-skilled labor, putting downward pressure on US wages. Low-skilled workers, native and foreign born, see their wages fall,[17] while employers enjoy higher income, both because their labor costs are lower and because their businesses are more productive. As a result, immigration has two effects: it redistributes income from low-skilled native workers to employers and it creates a net gain in national income by allowing employers to use their land, capital, and technology more productively. Economists refer to this net gain to the US economy as the immigration surplus. The size of the surplus depends on the productive potential of the arriving labor. In 2010, unauthorized immigrants accounted for 5.2 percent of the US civilian labor force.[18] Applying standard economic methods, the surplus from illegal immigration, or the net gain to US workers and employers exclusive of any labor income paid to the unauthorized immigrants themselves, is approximately 0.03 percent of US GDP.[19] The arriving labor does contribute to a significantly larger expansion in overall US GDP, as unauthorized workers increase the total amount of output the US economy generates. But the vast majority of this additional wealth goes to unauthorized immigrants themselves, leaving only a small gain in US native income. This small income gain to US employers (net of the wages losses to US workers) results primarily from the modest scale of illegal immigration in the overall workforce.[20]

The 0.03 percent of GDP figure for the immigration surplus is based on many restrictive assumptions. It is meant more as an indicator of the order of magnitude of illegal immigration's impact on the US economy than as a precise estimate. Reasonable changes in the underlying economic model could easily make the impact larger or smaller. But note that even if the impact is too small by a factor of ten — which is unlike-

---

17   George J. Borjas, "The Labor Demand Curve Is Downward Sloping: Reexamining the Impact of Immigration on the Labor Market," *Quarterly Journal of Economics* 118 (2003): 1335-74.
18   Passel and Cohn, *Unauthorized Immigrant Population: National and State Trends, 2010.*
19   From George J. Borjas, *Heaven's Door: Immigration Policy and the American Economy* (Princeton, NJ: Princeton University Press, 1999), the formula for the immigration surplus is: 0.5 X labor's share of national income X wage elasticity X (immigrant share of the labor force).² Labor's share of national income is approximately 0.7. The wage elasticity is the percent change in wages from a 1 percent increase in labor supply due to immigration, which I take to be 0.3, as reported in Borjas *The Labor Demand Curve Is Downward Sloping*. This formulation of the immigration surplus is based on a simple static model of the US economy, in which there are two factors of production, capital and labor, with immigration having no dynamic effects on economic outcomes. As such, it is useful for gauging the short-run consequences of immigration only.
20   In other words, the increase in US GDP from illegal immigration equals the immigration surplus plus the total labor income paid to unauthorized immigrants, meaning that US GDP rises by much more than US native income, with foreign workers pocketing the difference.

ly, unless illegal immigration somehow has large unmeasured effects on innovation and technological progress — it would still be less than *one-third of 1 percent* of GDP.

The fact that illegal immigration has a small net impact on US native income is not inconsistent with unauthorized workers being an important source of low-skilled labor. The two findings are reconciled by the fact that low-skilled labor accounts for a small share of the US labor force, and that most of the economic output that illegal immigration generates accrues to the immigrants themselves. In 2007, workers with less than a high school education, whether native or foreign born, accounted for just 8 percent of total hours worked, down from 21 percent in 1980. While unauthorized immigrants have grown substantially as a share of the US low-skilled labor force (at least until 2007), the share of the low-skilled in total US employment is on the wane.

It is worth noting that there is a population for which illegal immigration is a big deal: the migrants themselves (and their family members). Unauthorized immigrants gain substantially more by living and working in the United States than any US group (such as low-skilled native workers) loses. For unauthorized immigrants from Mexico, who account for 59 percent of the total unauthorized population, the total gain in labor income from moving to the United States was equivalent to approximately $170 billion in 2008, or 1.2 percent of US GDP.[21] Considering how immigration affects global welfare, the gain in income to immigrants far outweighs the net loss to US natives, which has been estimated as high as 9 percent for high school dropouts over a 20-year period,[22] meaning that on net illegal migration from Mexico to the United States raises global economic well-being.[23] Yet, US policymakers, by virtue of their mandate as public servants, naturally spend much more time worrying about the welfare of US residents than that of would-be immigrants. Consequently, the relatively large income gain that immigrants enjoy receives little weight in US policy decisions.

A second important effect of immigration on national income occurs through changes in the net tax burden on US households. Many unauthorized immigrants contribute to government coffers at the local, state, and federal levels by paying income, payroll, property, and sales taxes. They also increase government expenditure by using public services, including fire and police protection, public roads and bridges,

---

21 Gordon H. Hanson, "The Economic Consequences of the International Migration of Labor," *Annual Review of Economics*, 2009: 179-208, www.nber.org/papers/w14490.

22 Estimates of the impact on low-skilled native workers are highly disputed. See Borjas, *The Labor Demand Curve Is Downward Sloping: Reexamining the Impact of Immigration on the Labor Market*.

23 The astute reader will observe that the impact of migration on global income depends on the net impact on the receiving country, the net impact on the migrants, and the net impact on the sending country. The third component is not considered here, but appears to be too small to change the conclusion that migration from Mexico to the United States raises global welfare (Hanson, *The Economic Consequences of the International Migration of Labor*).

publically funded emergency health care, and, most importantly, public education — though not all at the same levels as the native born. Whether illegal immigration causes the tax burden on natives to rise or fall depends on how much income immigrants earn, the size and structure of their families, and whether they receive public benefits. Based on the profile of immigrant households in the US Current Population Survey, households headed by an unauthorized immigrant appear to generate a short-run net fiscal cost of approximately 0.1 percent of US GDP.[24] Adding the small positive immigration surplus to the small negative net fiscal impact, the total short-run change in US national income from illegal immigration is -0.07 percent of GDP. While the value is negative, indicating illegal immigration on net lowers US national income, it is close enough to zero to be essentially a wash.

A provocative addendum to the discussion of the fiscal impacts of illegal immigration is that for the US taxpayer an attractive feature of keeping low-skilled immigration illegal is that it mitigates the fiscal cost of admitting foreign workers. Noncitizens in the United States are ineligible to receive most federally funded entitlement programs. Even though most households headed by unauthorized immigrants are poor, they make minimal use of Temporary Assistance for Needy Families, Supplemental Security Income, energy assistance, housing subsidies, or other welfare programs.[25] Whereas individuals receiving a green card are eligible to receive these benefits after five years of residence in the United States, unauthorized immigrants have no such option. Unauthorized immigrants do draw on public expenditure in other ways, especially through their children, who may attend public schools and, if they are born in the United States, receive Medicaid and participate in school breakfast and lunch programs. Access to public education and publicly funded emergency health care appear to be largely responsible for the negative impact of illegal immigration on US public finances.[26]

The magnitudes of the costs and benefits of illegal immigration hold several important lessons for policymakers. One is that notwithstanding all of the focus and controversy surrounding illegal immigration, the fate of the US economy is not riding on the country's policy toward unauthorized workers. Allowing a few more or a few less unauthorized immigrants into the country would not have dire consequences. At the same time, Congress can increase the net benefit that the United

---

24 See Camarota, *The High Cost of Cheap Labor: Illegal Immigration and the Federal Budget*; Hanson 2007. Short-run means that future taxes and spending associated with immigration are ignored. Obviously, there are many caveats in estimating the fiscal impacts of immigration. For illuminating discussions on this point, see James P. Smith and Barry Edmonston, eds., *The New Americans: Economic, Demographic, and Fiscal Effects of Immigration* (Washington, DC: National Academy Press, 1997) and Borjas, *Heaven's Door: Immigration Policy and the American Economy*.

25 Camarota, *The High Cost of Cheap Labor: Illegal Immigration and the Federal Budget*. Unauthorized immigrants are not eligible for most welfare programs, although households including a US-citizen spouse or dependent children have greater access to these benefits.

26 Ibid.

States derives from each low-skilled immigrant by reducing his or her fiscal impact, either by charging immigrants an entry fee or taxing the employers that hire them (which, obviously, would require them to be legal). Reducing government benefits to the unauthorized population is not a meaningful option, given that the primary benefits they receive are in the form of public education, to which their access is constitutionally guaranteed, and Medicaid for their US-born children.

D. Enforcement against Illegal Immigration Is Expensive (Relative to the Potential Gains from Eliminating Illegal Entry)

The US government devotes considerable resources to enforcement against illegal immigration. Most activity occurs at the borders, particularly the US-Mexico border, where Border Patrol agents monitor points of entry. Nationwide, the Border Patrol made 340,000 apprehensions in 2011, down from 723,000 in 2008 and more than 1 million in 2006.[27] The vast majority of these individuals were caught along the US-Mexico border. Between 1992 and 2008, total annual officer hours worked by the US Border Patrol increased by a factor of four. The 21,000 Border Patrol agents currently in the field are an increase from 11,000 in 2004. Additional resources have been devoted to building and maintaining physical barriers along the border and upgrading the technology and equipment agents have at their disposal. Interior enforcement efforts include monitoring and auditing employee roles at US worksites, working with local law enforcement to find and deport unauthorized immigrants who have committed crimes (under the Secure Communities and 287(g) programs), and expanding E-Verify (an electronic system run by the Department of Homeland Security that allows US employers to verify the eligibility of their workers, now mandatory for federal contractors).[28] The cost of enforcement against illegal entry is large. In 2012, the budgets for US Customs and Border Protection (which oversees border enforcement) and US Immigration and Customs Enforcement (which oversees interior enforcement) were $11.7 billion and $5.9 billion, respectively.[29]

Illegal immigration is not, of course, the only reason for increased

---

27 See US Department of Homeland Security, *Immigration Enforcement Actions, 2008: Annual Report, Office of Immigration Statistics*, July 2009, www.dhs.gov/xlibrary/assets/statistics/publications/enforcement_ar_08.pdf; John Simanski and Lesley M. Sapp, *Immigration Enforcement Actions: 2011* (Washington, DC: Department of Homeland Security, September 2012), www.dhs.gov/sites/default/files/publications/immigration-statistics/enforcement_ar_2011.pdf.

28 See Randal C. Archibold, "US Alters Disputed Immigration Rules for Police," *The New York Times*, October 16, 2009; Julia Preston, "US Identifies 111,000 Immigrants with Criminal Records," *The New York Times*, November 11, 2009; and Neil A. Lewis, "Immigration Officials to Audit 1,000 More Companies," *The New York Times*, November 19, 2009.

29 DHS, *FY 2013 Budget in Brief* (Washington, DC: DHS, 2012), www.dhs.gov/xlibrary/assets/mgmt/dhs-budget-in-brief-fy2013.pdf.

border enforcement; since the Sept. 11, 2001 terrorist attacks, national security and terrorism concerns have also driven spending. As a thought experiment, however, it is interesting to consider whether border enforcement is worth the expense. In economic terms, the justification for border enforcement is to keep unauthorized immigrants out of the country, thereby avoiding the negative net economic impact that their presence entails. This negative impact, as we have seen, appears to be small. Suppose the United States were to increase enforcement to the point where it eliminated illegal immigration entirely, by shutting down new inflows and convincing those in the country to return home. Suppose the annual gain to the United States was 0.07 percent of GDP, or $10 billion, as we calculated earlier. Eliminating illegal immigration would be justified only if the extra annual enforcement costs were less than $10 billion. Enforcement during the mid-2000s, which cost $10-$15 billion a year, allowed 500,000 new unauthorized immigrants to enter the country annually. Unless the next $10 billion in enforcement is much more effective than the first $15 billion, it is difficult to see how one could justify a pure enforcement strategy to address illegal immigration, at least in terms of standard cost-benefit analysis.

II. Conclusion

Whether any future congressional action on immigration will occur through comprehensive new legislation or piecemeal reforms is unknown. What is certain is that with large numbers of unauthorized immigrants residing in the United States the issue is not going to disappear any time soon.

The unauthorized population is a major source of low-skilled foreign labor in the United States. These workers account for about 5 percent of the US labor force, but are far more significant to the sectors that use low-skilled labor intensively, including farming, construction, low-end manufacturing, the hospitality industry, and building cleaning and maintenance. An enforcement-only strategy that did not facilitate legal labor inflows but which sought to cut low-skilled immigration drastically would hurt these industries. While business gains from having access to low-skilled foreign workers, the aggregate productivity bonus to the US economy is small. Also modest is the fiscal cost of illegal immigration. Because the net impact of illegal immigration on the US economy does not appear to be very large, one would be hard pressed to justify a substantial increase in spending on border and interior enforcement, at least in terms of its economic return. This does not mean enforcement should be lax, but rather that beginning from current levels of spending, sizeable increases in enforcement resources could easily cost far more than the tax savings they generated from reduced illegal presence in the United States.

A constructive immigration policy would allow low-skilled immigration to occur in a manner that generated maximum productivity gains to the US economy, while limiting the fiscal cost of immigration and keeping enforcement spending contained. Effectively, this means converting existing inflows of unauthorized immigrants into inflows of legal immigrants.

Which policies would help this to happen? First, to keep the expense of immigration enforcement in check, low-skilled foreign workers need legal channels of entry into the US labor market. They also need incentives to play by the rules set forth in legal work visas. Low-skilled labor would be more likely to avoid illegal entry if there were meaningful enforcement of immigration laws at US worksites and workers were rewarded for their compliance by having the chance to seek legal permanent residence.

Congress ultimately will have to decide on the overall level of low-skilled immigration that makes sense for the country as a whole. But taking the average inflow across time as given, low-skilled immigration would do more to benefit the US economy if it were allowed to fluctuate from year to year in response to macroeconomic conditions and be channeled through mechanisms that limited adverse fiscal effects. The productivity benefit from immigration is higher when businesses can choose which workers they want to hire and when they want to hire them, which requires making the supply of visas flexible and responsive to changing economic conditions.

Finally, the net fiscal cost of low-skilled immigration would be lower if foreign workers paid a fee for the right to work legally in the United States or employers were taxed for hiring them.

While it is not cost-effective to reduce illegal immigration to zero, by enacting policies such as these Congress should be capable of reducing it by a large measure, expanding legal immigration options and helping the US economy at the same time.

Works Cited

Abraham, Katherine and John Haltiwanger. 1995. Real Wages over the Business Cycle. *Journal of Economic Literature* 33: 1216-64.

Archibold, Randal C. 2009. US Alters Disputed Immigration Rules for Police. *The New York Times*, October 16, 2009. www.nytimes.com/2009/10/17/us/17immig.html.

Borjas, George J. 1999. *Heaven's Door: Immigration Policy and the American Economy*. Princeton, NJ: Princeton University Press.

_____. 2003. The Labor Demand Curve Is Downward Sloping: Reexamining the Impact of Immigration on the Labor Market. *Quarterly Journal of Economics* 118: 1335-74.

Camarota, Steven A. 2004. *The High Cost of Cheap Labor: Illegal Immigration and the Federal Budget*. Washington, DC: Center for Immigration Studies. www.cis.org/articles/2004/fiscal.html.

Clemons, Michael, Claudio Montenegro, and Lant Pritchett. 2008. The Place Premium: Wage Differences for Identical Workers across the US Border. Center on Global Development Working Paper No. 148.

Council of Economic Advisers. 2005. *Economic Report of the President*. Washington, DC: Council of Economic Advisers. www.gpo.gov/fdsys/pkg/ERP-2005/pdf/ERP-2005.pdf.

Gathmann, Christina. 2008. Effects of Enforcement on Illegal Markets: Evidence from Migrant Smuggling on the Southwestern Border. *Journal of Public Economics* 92(10-11): 1926-41.

Hanson, Gordon H. 2005. *Why Does Immigration Divide America? Public Finance and Political Opposition to Open Borders*. Washington, DC: Institute for International Economics.

_____. 2007. *The Economic Logic of Illegal Immigration*. Council Special Report No. 26, Council on Foreign Relations.

_____. 2009. The Economic Consequences of the International Migration of Labor. *Annual Review of Economics*. www.nber.org/papers/w14490.

Hanson, Gordon H., and Antonio Spilimbergo. 1999. Illegal Immigration, Border Enforcement and Relative Wages: Evidence from Apprehensions at the US-Mexico Border. *American Economic Review* 89: 1337-57.

Koslowski, Rey. 2005. *Real Challenges for Virtual Borders: The Implementation of US-VISIT*. Washington, DC: Migration Policy Institute. www.migrationpolicy.org/pubs/Koslowski_Report.pdf.

Lewis, Neil A. 2009. Immigration Officials to Audit 1,000 More Companies. *The New York Times,* November 19, 2009. www.nytimes.com/2009/11/20/us/20immig.html.

Passel, Jeffrey S. and D'Vera Cohn. 2009. *A Portrait of Unauthorized Immigrants in the United States*. Washington, DC: Pew Hispanic Center. http://pewresearch.org/pubs/1190/portrait-unauthorized-immigrants-states.

Passel, Jeffrey S. and D'Vera Cohn. 2011. *Unauthorized Immigrant Population: National and State Trends, 2010.* Washington, DC: Pew Hispanic Center. www.pewhispanic.org/files/reports/133.pdf.

Passel, Jeffrey S. and D'Vera Cohn. 2012. *Unauthorized Immigrants: 11.1 Million in 2011.* Washington, DC: Pew Hispanic Center. www.pewhispanic.org/2012/12/06/unauthorized-immigrants-11-1-million-in-2011.

Preston, Julia. 2009. US Identifies 111,000 Immigrants with Criminal Records. *The New York Times*, November 11, 2009. www.nytimes.com/2009/11/13/us/13ice.html.

Simanski, John and Lesley M. Sapp. 2012. *Immigration Enforcement Actions: 2011.* Washington, DC: Department of Homeland Security. www.dhs.gov/sites/default/files/publications/immigration-statistics/enforcement_ar_2011.pdf.

Smith, James P. and Barry Edmonston, eds. 1997. *The New Americans: Economic, Demographic, and Fiscal Effects of Immigration.* Washington, DC: National Academy Press.

US Department of Homeland Security. 2009. *Yearbook of Immigration Statistics.* www.dhs.gov/xlibrary/assets/statistics/yearbook/2008/ois_yb_2008.pdf.

_____. 2009. *Immigration Enforcement Actions, 2008: Annual Report.* Washington, DC: Office of Immigration Statistics. www.dhs.gov/xlibrary/assets/statistics/publications/enforcement_ar_08.pdf

_____. 2012. *FY 2013 Budget in Brief.* Washington, DC: DHS. www.dhs.gov/xlibrary/assets/mgmt/dhs-budget-in-brief-fy2013.pdf.

US Department of Justice, Office of the Inspector General. 2002. *Follow-Up Report on INS Efforts To Improve The Control Of Nonimmigrant Overstays*, Report No. I-2002-006. Washington, DC. www.justice.gov/oig/reports/INS/e0206/intro.htm#bac.

US Department of State. Classes of Nonimmigrants Issued Visas (Detailed Breakdown) Fiscal Years 2004-2008. www.travel.state.gov/pdf/NIVClassIssued-DetailedFY2004-2008.pdf.

_____. Classes of Nonimmigrants Issued Visas (Detailed Breakdown) Fiscal Years 2006-2010. www.travel.state.gov/pdf/NIVClassIssued-Detailed-FY2006-2010.pdf.

_____. Classes of Nonimmigrants Issued Visas (Detailed Breakdown) Fiscal Years 2002-2006. http://travel.state.gov/pdf/FY06AnnualReportTableXVIA.pdf.

US Government Accountability Office. 2004. *Overstay Tracking: A Key Component of Homeland Security and a Layered Defense*, GAO-04-82. Washington, DC. www.gao.gov/new.items/d0482.pdf.

CHAPTER 3

THE IMPACT OF IMMIGRANTS IN RECESSION AND ECONOMIC EXPANSION

By Giovanni Peri

University of California, Davis

Introduction

The recent recession may be over, but the US labor market remains far from full recovery. Unemployment rates in the United States peaked in 2010 at an annual average of 9.6 percent, a level not experienced for two decades. Between January 2009 and January 2010, about 3.9 million jobs were lost. Despite improvements in the economic outlook, unemployment still hovered around 8 percent in late 2012.[1] It is natural, therefore, to revisit questions about the impact of immigrants on the labor market and on the economy through the lens of this economic situation. Are the short-run effects of net immigration[2] on native workers' employment and income less beneficial (or more harmful) if immigrants enter the United States during a period of economic weakness? Does the economy have the same capacity to "absorb" new workers when immigrants join the US economy in a recession? Do the *long-run* gains or losses to the US economy from immigration depend on the phase of the cycle during which immigrants enter the country? These questions have become particularly relevant in recent years; the present analysis tries to address them.

Most (though not all) economic research over the past decade has emphasized the potential gains that result from immigration to the United States. Immigration can boost the supply of skills different

---

1   Bureau of Labor Statistics (BLS), "E-1 Employment Status of the Civilian Noninstitutional Population by Sex and Age, Seasonally Adjusted," www.bls.gov/web/empsit/cpsee_e01.pdf.
2   Net immigration is equal to the inflow of immigrants minus the outflow of returnees and remigrants.

from and complementary to those of natives,[3] increase the supply of low-cost services,[4] contribute to innovation,[5] and create incentives for investment and efficiency gains.[6] Quantifying these gains is not easy, but steady progress has been made in identifying and measuring them. There is broad consensus that the long-run impact of immigration on the average income of Americans is small but positive.[7] In particular, recent studies have identified measurable gains for the highly educated and small, often not significant, losses for less-educated workers. These empirical analyses, however, have focused on the long run.[8] But the recent economic recession and its persistent labor-market consequences make the long run seem rather distant, and more pressing concerns about the short run have taken center stage.[9]

Immigration's economic benefits mostly result from immigrant and native workers' occupational choices, accompanied by employers' investments and the reorganization of firms. For instance, immigrants are usually allocated to manual-intensive jobs, promoting competition and pushing natives to perform communication-intensive tasks more efficiently. This process, at the same time, reorganizes firms' structures, producing efficiency gains and pushing natives toward cognitive- and communication-intensive jobs that are better paid. These effects may take a few years to unfold fully. In the meantime and before the adjustments take place, do immigrants crowd out natives from the labor market? How long does it take for firms to adjust their investments and organization in order to benefit from the new supply of skills? Are these processes easier and less costly during an economic expansion than in an economic downturn?

---

3   See, for instance, Gianmarco Ottaviano and Giovanni Peri, "Immigration and National Wages: Clarifying the Theory and the Empirics" (working paper 14188, National Bureau of Economic Research, July 2008), www.nber.org/papers/w14188.
4   Patricia Cortes, "The Effect of Low-Skilled Immigration on U.S. Prices: Evidence from CPI Data," *Journal of Political Economy* 116, no. 3 (2008): 381–422.
5   William R. Kerr and William F. Lincoln, "The Supply Side of Innovation: H-1B Visa Reforms and U.S. Ethnic Invention," *Journal of Labor Economics* 28, no. 3 (2010): 473–508, www.people.hbs.edu/wkerr/Kerr_Lincoln_JOLE3_H1B_Paper.pdf; Marjolaine Gauthier-Loiselle and Jennifer Hunt, "How Much Does Immigration Boost Innovation?" *American Economic Journal: Macroeconomics* 2, no. 2 (2010): 31–56.
6   Giovanni Peri and Chad Sparber, "Task Specialization, Immigration and Wages," *American Economic Journal: Applied Economics* 1, no. 3 (2009): 135–69.
7   David Card, "Immigration and Inequality" (working paper 14683, National Bureau of Economic Research, Cambridge, MA, 2009), www.nber.org/papers/w14683.pdf.
8   Most of the economic analysis is based on periods at least ten years apart. This is because the analysis relied on decennial census data as the main source of labor-market information identifying individuals' nativity.
9   Throughout this chapter, the "short run" refers to periods of between one and four years unless otherwise specified. The "long run" refers to periods of seven to ten years and above.

Until very recently no comprehensive analysis of the short-run effects of immigration on the US labor market was possible.[10] The reason is that annual representative data from the Current Population Survey, typically used to analyze production and labor markets, have contained information on the place of birth of individuals only since 1994 (as opposed to the decennial census that has always included that information). Hence, it is only during the past few years that sufficient data have accumulated to analyze the short-run (yearly) impacts of net immigration on labor-market outcomes. Moreover, between 1994 and 2007, only the mild 2001 recession provided variation in the economic cycle. While several influential academic papers have emphasized how the short-run effects of immigration on wages and employment could be different from long-run effects, those differences were based on theoretical assumptions rather than on empirically estimated evidence.

Using empirical methods in line with the best practices used to analyze and quantify the long-run effects of immigration, this chapter provides some evidence to inform these questions. It begins by analyzing the short-run impact of immigration on employment, income, and other factors that affect income, such as investment, hours worked, and productive efficiency, examining the speed with which the economy adjusts to accommodate new immigrants. It then extends this analysis to investigate how these short-run effects, and possibly the medium-run effects (over four or five years), depend on the state of the economy when immigrants enter the labor market. Finally, it discusses the implications the results may have for immigration policy.

The results suggest that in the long run, immigrants do not reduce native employment rates, but they do increase productivity and hence average income. This finding is consistent with much existing literature on the impact of immigration on the United States. New analysis of the short-run impacts of immigration in this chapter, however, finds some mild negative effects: immigration may slightly reduce native employment at first, because the economic adjustment process is not immediate. Lower average income is also likely in the short run. The long-run gains to productivity and income become significant after seven to ten years. The results moreover suggest that the short-run impact of immigration depends on the state of the economy. When the economy is growing, new immigration creates jobs in sufficient numbers to leave native employment unharmed, even in the relatively short run. During downturns, however, new immigrants are found to have a small negative impact on native employment in the short run (but not the long run). During recessions the economy does not appear to respond as quickly to new immigrants in terms of new job creation and productivity boosts.

---

10 The only paper I know of that analyzes the effects of immigration on wage and native employment in the United States using annual panel data is by Silvia Barcellos, "The Dynamics of Immigration and Wages" (RAND working paper WR-755, March 2010), www.rand.org/pubs/working_papers/2010/RAND_WR755.pdf.

I. The Impact of Net Immigration on Employment and Gross Domestic Product

Methodological Approach

The goal of this study is to identify and measure the impact of immigration on employment and income or gross domestic product (GDP) in the United States. Income per worker depends on how productive workers are and it is the main determinant of the worker's wage: in a competitive market, more productive workers are paid higher salaries as they are more valuable to the firm.

The difficulty in identifying the effects of immigration on economic variables is that we do not observe what would have happened if immigration levels were different; therefore, to infer such effects we compare states with high immigration to states with low immigration. More precisely we account for most other productive differences (sector specialization, research spending, and others) and measure what differences arise in states that have experienced large immigrant inflows compared to states that receive small inflows. Such differences allow us to infer the impact of immigrants on the economy.

To be more confident that we are isolating the real impact of immigration and not a reflection of the fact that immigrants choose to go to areas with faster growth, we isolate only variations in net immigration not affected by state-specific economic conditions. In particular we isolate net immigration caused by geographical proximity to the border (because border states tend to get more immigration), and historical migration patterns (because immigrants are drawn to areas with previous immigrant communities). Those flows are driven mostly by geography and preference but still affect the economy, so the response to them is a measure of immigrants' impact on economic variables.[11]

We choose the state economies from 1960 to 2006 as units of our analysis to provide a measure of the aggregate impact of immigration. While effects on employment, income, and wages may vary by occupation (and possibly industry), here we present the aggregate effects that summarize the economic consequences for the average American worker.

---

11 A more technical explanation of the method of estimation is contained in Appendix A. For a more detailed description of the methodology, see Giovanni Peri, "The Effect of Immigration on Productivity: Evidence from U.S. States" (working paper 15507, November 2009, National Bureau of Economic Research, Cambridge, MA), www.nber.org/papers/w15507.

Before presenting the actual estimates, let us briefly discuss the channels through which net immigration affects the components of income. The empirical analysis will look at each of these components, and examine how immigration has affected them. First, and most naturally, net immigration can affect employment growth. If one more working immigrant produces no displacement of native workers, then for each new immigrant, total employment will increase by 1, and native employment will remain unchanged (in the Appendix tables that display the results, both are reported). An estimated response of total employment smaller than 1 implies that some native jobs are lost when immigrants enter employment (crowding out). An estimated response larger than 1 implies that some natives would gain jobs as a consequence of immigration (crowding in).

Second, immigration affects the amount of structure and equipment per worker. This is called physical capital per worker and it is an important determinant of firm productivity and workers' wages. Its adjustment depends on how quickly entrepreneurs invest. Eventually they can take advantage of the opportunity of a larger pool of potential employees and endow workers with productive capital by expanding their capacity, starting new businesses, or creating spinoffs. How fast investments respond to these opportunities and how long it takes to adjust physical capital in response to an inflow of immigrants are empirical questions, and our estimates will seek to provide an answer to them.

Third, the impact of immigration on hours per worker captures the effect on individual labor supply. This should depend in part on the average wage; hence, a positive average effect on worker's productivity and wages may result in higher individual labor supply.

Finally the analysis examines the impact of immigration on total factor productivity, which is a measure of the efficiency of production factors. Immigrants may affect this variable through several channels. By promoting efficient specialization of workers and better allocation of skills to tasks (as immigrants specialize in manual jobs) they may produce gains from specialization.[12] By encouraging the adoption of techniques that are more appropriate for less-educated workers they may increase their relative productivity.[13] Immigrants may also increase the range of services produced in the economy.[14] Finally the share of highly educated immigrants, as they are more specialized in technological and

---

12   Peri and Sparber, "Task Specialization, Immigration and Wages."
13   Ethan Lewis, "Immigration, Skill Mix, and the Choice of Technique" (working paper 05-08, Federal Reserve Bank of Philadelphia, Philadelphia, 2005), www.philadelphiafed.org/research-and-data/publications/working-papers//2005/wp05-8.pdf.
14   See, for instance, David Neumark and Francesca Mazzolari, "Beyond Wages: The Effect of Immigration on the Scale and Composition of Output" (working paper 14900, National Bureau of Economic Research, Cambridge, MA, 2009), www.nber.org/papers/w14900.pdf.

scientific occupations, may boost innovation.[15] All these effects may add to a measurable productivity effect. However, it seems plausible that they will materialize over a certain period of time and not in the very short run as immigrants enter the country.[16]

II. The Short- and Long-Run Effects of Net Immigration on Average (over the Whole Business Cycle)

Detailed empirical results are described in Appendix B, which shows estimates of the effects of net immigration on each of the components of GDP described above. Three patterns emerge clearly that are worth emphasizing.

First, ***there is only very limited evidence that immigrants crowd out natives from the workforce.*** In the short run (one to two years) the results imply a small negative effect on native employment, but the estimates are not significantly different from zero. In the long run, a small positive effect is estimated (also not significantly different from zero). Interestingly, the impact on hours per worker is similar, with small and nonsignificant effects in the short run and positive (this time significant) effects in the long run. These results are consistent with the idea that immigrant labor is somewhat differentiated and complementary to native labor, generating limited competition in the short run and in the long run even job opportunities for native workers.[17]

Second, ***immigration has a positive long-run effect on the average income of native workers. This effect accrues over some time.*** In the short run (one to two years) no effect is observed, while over the long run (ten years) a net inflow of immigrants equal to 1 percent of employment increases income per worker by 0.26 percent. This implies that total immigration to the United States over the period 1990-2006, representing an increase of employment by 11 percent, caused a 2.86 percent real wage increase for the average US worker. In another paper I focus on this effect and test its robustness to several controls and specifications.[18] This seems to be a strong and robust result.

---

15 See Kerr and Lincoln, "The Supply Side of Innovation;" and Gauthier-Loiselle and Hunt, "How Much Does Immigration Boost Innovation?" www.nber.org/papers/w14900.pdf.
16 Appendix B also reports the effect of immigration on workers' skill intensity. This is measured by the share of skilled workers (with college education) among all employees. Immigration has only a small negative impact on this share, as immigrants are somewhat overrepresented among workers with no college degree.
17 The results are also consistent with most of the literature. See, for example, David Card, "Immigrant Inflows, Native Outflows, and the Local Labor Market Impacts of Higher Immigration," *Journal of Labor Economics* 19, no. 1 (2001): 22–64.
18 See Peri, "The Effect of Immigration on Productivity."

The third result is that ***the long-run increase in income per native worker is mainly due to an increase in the economic efficiency of production (or "total-factor productivity").*** This effect takes four to seven years to become apparent. Moreover, while in the short run the intensity of physical capital per worker is decreased by net immigration, in the medium to long run firms expand their equipment and productive structures proportionally to their increase in workers. This long-run response of investments also means that the restructuring and specialization promoted by immigrants do not much change the machine-intensity of production. While some manual functions performed by immigrants may reduce the use of some type of machinery (e.g., tomato harvesters), the consequent increase in interactive-communication-managerial functions by natives may encourage the use of others (e.g., computers). Immigrants supplying labor and differentiated skills represent opportunities for firms to expand and increase their productive equipment and structures (capital). As this happens, the gains from specialization and efficiency produced by immigrants can be realized. This might be the reason for the slow response.

The patterns identified seem to support the following story. Immigration helps employment and productivity, but this process involves adjustments. Firms need to upgrade and expand their capital stock in order to take advantage of the new labor supply and create additional jobs. Immigrants, by specializing in manual tasks in which they have comparative advantages, push natives into more communication-intensive tasks. This generates gains from specialization and from comparative advantages but also takes some transitional time. For firms to adopt appropriate technologies and organizational structures to take advantage of the increased availability of manual labor also takes some time. Hence, while in the short run the inflow of immigrants may mildly reduce the amount of capital or equipment per worker and therefore income per native worker, in the long run it unambiguously increases efficiency and income.

Given the small short-run crowding effect of immigrants, it must be asked if there is an optimal way of absorbing immigrants in the short run that minimizes costs and still generates the benefits from their positive long-run effects? How does the short-run effect of immigrants depend on the economic cycle? To answer this question, the next section examines how the impact of immigration depends on the state of the economy.

III. Effects of Net Immigration during Economic Expansion and Downturn

This section examines the impact of net immigration during periods of relative economic weakness and strength.[19] While the estimated effects are not very precise, some patterns seem rather consistent.

On the one hand, immigration during *downturns* seems to have a small negative effect on both native employment and income per worker in the short run (one to two years); on the other, net immigration during economic *expansion* reduces native employment less in the short run and has no measureable negative effect on income per worker even within the first year.

Similarly, the responses of total factor productivity are estimated to be positive (or zero) in the short run when net immigration occurs during an expansion, while net immigration in a recession has a negative effect within the first year.

A third difference between expansion and downturn concerns the response of physical capital per worker. *During a downturn investments do not respond as quickly to immigration as in expansion.* This time the difference in response is close to being statistically significant within the two- and four-year intervals. Since the economy has unused capacity during downturns, this may make firms reluctant to expand their productive capacity and/or to adopt the technologies (and pay the fixed cost) that would best take advantage of immigrant labor. However, in the long run (seven- to ten-year intervals) no difference in adjustment is observed independent of the short-run effects.

It is worth emphasizing that the results imply that net immigration during expansionary periods may have positive short- and long-run effects on native jobs and hours worked. However, net immigration during a downturn may have a crowding-out effect on native jobs in the short run. This suggests a way in which immigration policy may help maximize the positive overall effects of immigration on natives by potentially allowing the labor demand from firms to affect foreign workers' time of entry. We will discuss this in the next section.

---

19   This chapter uses US states as the unit of analysis. To determine economic strength and weakness of a state economy, I use the state output gap, namely a measure of how far the economy is from its long-run trend, and I define downturns as periods in which the output gap for the state is smaller than zero and expansions as periods in which the output gap is larger than or equal to zero. I estimate separate responses depending on whether during the period the state economy exhibits on average a positive or zero output gap, which would imply strong demand or a negative output gap, which implies slow demand and some idle resources in the economy. I use the H-P filter, a standard procedure used to evaluate the long-run trend of output at the state level (gross state product, or GSP), and then take the difference between the actual GSP and the H-P filtered one to calculate the output gap.

The Impact of Less-Educated Immigrants

The analysis so far has focused on the aggregate and average effects of immigration. But distributional effects also exist. Some economists argue that the relatively large inflow of less- educated immigrants would hurt the employment and wages of less-educated natives. Appendix D shows the employment response to immigration of less-educated native workers only, in the short and long run, first averaging across periods (first row) and then separating the effects of inflows during economic upturns and downturns (second row). The results mirror the patterns for total native employment, but they are quantitatively larger and more statistically significant.

In the short run (one to two years) net immigration seems to crowd out less-educated native workers but only when it takes place in periods of economic weakness. Net immigration during economic upturns does not seem to affect employment of the less educated in the short run (one to two years). In the long run, there is some evidence that immigrants lead to positive job creation, even for less-educated natives.

IV. Implications and Discussion

Before talking about some implications, two clarifications are in order. First, the immigration data used in the study include authorized as well as unauthorized immigrants. The effect estimated, therefore, is the response to total net immigration. This is possible as I use data from the decennial census, the American Community Survey (ACS), and the Current Population Survey (CPS), which collect a representative sample of the population resident in the United States and record information about their place of birth — not their legal status.[20] The impact of authorized and unauthorized immigrants, estimated separately, might be quite different from each other.

Second, the estimated positive long-run effects of immigration on native income per worker are small but not negligible. In a state such as California, where the share of immigrants in employment increased from 25 percent in 1990 to 35 percent in 2007, the average income per worker would have increased by 2.6 percent in real terms over that period. Similar gains in income per worker would accrue in Texas (where the share of immigrant employment grew from 11 percent to 21 percent between 1990 and 2007) or in New York (where immigrant employment grew from 18 percent to 27 percent).

---

20 The difference between the count of foreign born from the Census/ACS and those registered with the Department of Homeland Security provide the estimates of unauthorized immigrants. Some adjustments are needed to account for a slight undercount of unauthorized immigrants as well as for immigrant mortality and remigration. See Michael Hoefer, Nancy Rytina, and Bryan Baker, *Estimates of the Unauthorized Immigrant Population Residing in the United States: January 2010* (Washington, DC: Office of Immigration Statistics, DHS, 2011), www.dhs.gov/xlibrary/assets/statistics/publications/ois_ill_pe_2010.pdf.

In order for immigration to boost productivity and income per worker, the state economy must make some adjustments, and this takes time. However, *most of these gains are realized within seven years.* The results suggest that if the gross inflow of new immigrants is allowed to vary with the strength of labor demand (downturns and expansions), it would minimize the short-run economic costs of adjustment. New immigrants could be allowed to flow into the United States in larger numbers during an expansion, when demand is stronger and firms are more willing to invest, than during a recession when they would temporarily crowd a depressed labor market. The details of such policy are not easy to implement and require consideration of the current US visa system. Moreover, the fact that the majority of new permanent residence permits are awarded based on family (and not employment) reasons make the current legal immigration system ill-suited to respond to economic incentives. Rather than spelling out the details of potential employment-based immigration policies, let me simply indicate some general ideas and facts to be kept in mind when designing such policies.

First, let me emphasize that the net inflow of immigrants into the United States already fluctuates to some extent with the economic cycle. Immigrants' tendency to arrive in larger numbers during periods of high labor demand has been identified in other countries as well. In general economists have estimated that for each 100 jobs lost in a country, 10 fewer immigrants enter (or 10 more leave). This is known as the 10 percent rule.[21] Figure 1 shows this pattern for the United States: each point on the graph represents the net US immigration rate and the percentage of the population that is employed, for a given year between 1994 and 2011. Again, there is a significant and positive correlation close to 10 percent. The natural fluctuation of net immigration, therefore, already provides a natural mechanism to decrease net inflows during downturns.

---

21 See, for instance, Timothy J. Hatton, and Jeffery G. Williamson, *Global Migration and the World Economy: Two Centuries of Policy and Performance* (Cambridge, MA: MIT Press, 2005).

Figure 1. US Net Immigration Rate and Employment Rate, 1994-2011

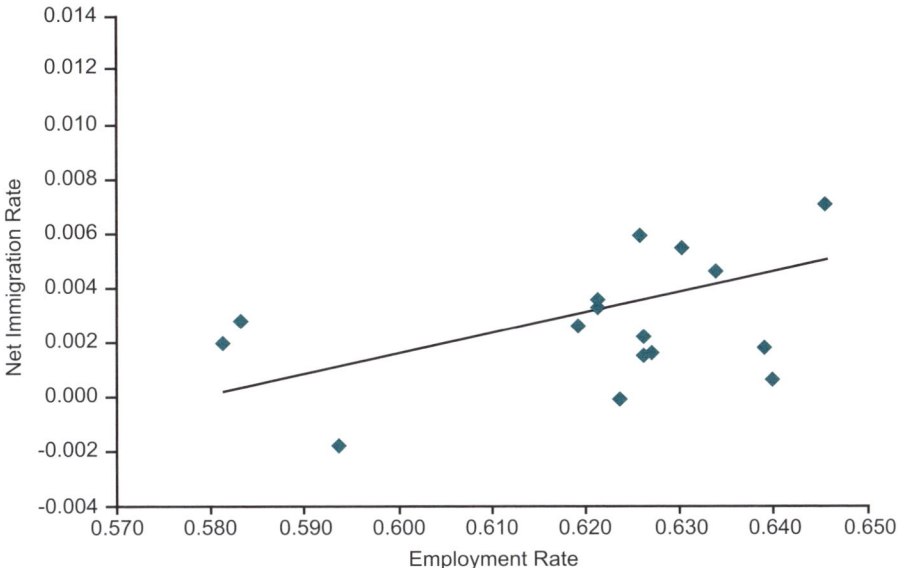

Note: The net immigration rate is calculated from CPS data and represents the increase in the number of foreign born as a proportion of the US population.
Source: Author's calculation using CPS data, 1994-2011.

What is also interesting, however, is that currently the adjustment of net total migration to the United States must take place only on the two "unregulated" margins: the return migration of authorized and unauthorized immigrants (who might leave in larger numbers during years of poor economic performance to go back to their country)[22] and the net flow of the unauthorized. In fact if we plot the new legal immigrants recorded in the Department of Homeland Security (DHS) data (as a proportion of the population) against the employment rate for the same 1994-2010 period (see Figure 2), there is no correlation at all between the two.

---

22 See, for instance, Dean Yang, "Why Do Migrants Return to Poor Countries? Evidence from Philippines' Migrants Response to Exchange Rate Shocks," *Review of Economics and Statistics* 88, no. 4 (2006): 715–35. In this study, Yang finds that a negative income shock to the migrant significantly increases the probability of return to the home country in that year.

Figure 2. US New Legal Immigrant Residents and Employment Rate, 1994-2010

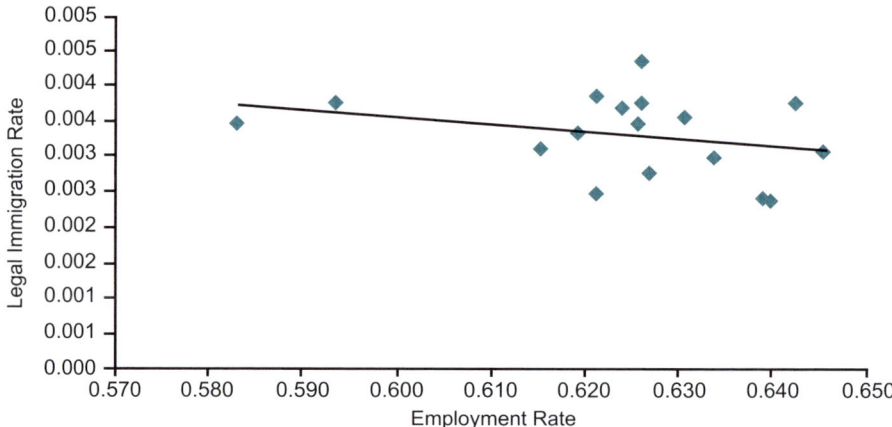

Note: The legal immigration rate is calculated as the number of green cards issued as a proportion of the US population. The correlation between new legal immigrant residents and the employment rate is not statistically significant.

Source: Author's calculations based on data from CPS and US Department of Homeland Security, Office of Immigration Statistics.

This is hardly a surprise, as around 70 percent of new green cards are awarded for family reasons (reunification and family sponsors).[23] The major temporary visas (H-1B and H-2B) have a fixed quota (inflows total around 200,000 together). The main 65,000 H-1B cap proved to be lower than the demand for these workers, even despite depressed labor demand from 2008 to 2011; and while the H-2B cap was not exhausted in 2010 or 2011, the majority of available visas were taken up. Meanwhile, the data available on the total inflow of unauthorized immigrants between 2000 and 2009 confirm that there was a net inflow of about 500,000 persons per year over the years 2001-06 (during the economic expansion) and a net outflow of about 500,000 annually in the years 2007-09 (during the recession).[24] The number of unauthorized migrants in 2010 was unchanged from 2009. One of the reasons that it is hard to reform the current immigration system, which is based in large part on the flow of unauthorized immigrants, is that for all the costs and inefficiencies this system entails, it has been more responsive than any legal program to economic incentives.

---

23 See Department of Homeland Security (DHS), *Yearbook of Immigration Statistics* (Washington, DC: DHS, 2008), www.dhs.gov/files/statistics/publications/yearbook.shtm.

24 Hoefer, Rytina, and Baker, *Estimates of the Unauthorized Immigrant Population Residing in the United States.*

A. *How Could Legal Immigration Become More Responsive to the Economic Cycle?*

These facts suggest that legal immigration should also be made to respond to labor-market conditions. How can this be done? One principle would be to allow the number of employer visa applications to serve as the main indicator of how strong labor demand is under current economic conditions. This obviates the need for the government to undertake the very difficult task of determining labor demand using incomplete and often outdated statistical sources. For instance, suppose firms were able to apply and bid one quarter in advance for foreign workers' permits in programs such as the H-1B, in an auction. While the government could set the total number of permits, employers who bid the most for visas would receive them, ensuring that visas are allocated efficiently. Moreover a high winning price would signal high demand and could prompt a larger number of permits in the following quarter. In order to implement this policy, one would need to determine several details of the auction; some economists have spelled out how such a system could work.[25] An independent government agency or commission could be called upon to determine the number of permits issued and the details of implementation.[26]

How much would net immigration ideally vary over the economic cycle? As a thought experiment, let us present here a few simple reference calculations. The current foreign-born population in the United States is about 40 million people (according to data from the 2010 ACS).[27] Over the past 20 years the return migration rate has been about 1.5 percent of the stock each year.[28] On average, therefore, if 600,000 new immigrants arrived each year, the size of the foreign-born population would remain unchanged (resulting in zero net immigration). While the number of returnees should be calculated more carefully if one would really like to implement immigration policies based on it, the basic point here is the following: as it is net immigration that affects the labor market and the productive outcomes of the US economy, we should think of 600,000 new immigrants as "the floor" that produces no changes at all in the current US labor market.

Allowing new entries through work-related visas in years of economic expansion on top of the 600,000 needed to maintain the stock would

---

25 See Pia Orrenius and Madeline Zavodny, *Beside the Golden Door: US Immigration Reform in a New Era of Globalization* (Washington, DC: American Enterprise Institute, 2010).
26 Demetrios G. Papademetriou, Doris Meissner, Marc Rosenblum, and Madeleine Sumption, *Harnessing the Advantages of Immigration for a 21st Century Economy: A Standing Commission on Labor Markets, Economic Competitiveness, and Immigration* (Washington, DC: Migration Policy Institute, 2009), www.migrationpolicy.org/pubs/StandingCommission_May09.pdf.
27 United States Census Bureau, *2010 American Community Survey Highlights* (Washington, DC: US Census Bureau, 2011), www.census.gov/newsroom/releases/pdf/acs_2010_highlights.pdf.
28 I use here the implicit return rate adopted in the study of Hoefer, Rytina, and Baker, *Estimates of the Unauthorized Immigrant Population*, to calculate the reduction of unauthorized immigrants due to return.

allow the United States to retain the positive long-run effects of immigration while minimizing the negative short-run effects. Implementing this policy would, of course, require careful consideration of which types of visas should be encouraged to respond to the economic cycle. While I will not go into detail here, the basic principle is that new labor-demand-driven visas can simply reinforce the natural cyclicality of immigration and speed up the capital and technology adjustment in the face of immigration. For instance, if we assume that gross inflows of workers on employment-based visas of some kind (temporary or permanent) were allowed to increase by 300,000 during economic expansion in addition to the baseline of 600,000, and if we assume that in a given decade half of the years, on average, have strong economic growth, this would imply 1.5 million net new immigrants per decade, representing about 1 percent of the labor force of 150 million people. This, in turn, would imply a net increase of 0.26 percent of income per native worker over that period, and no job losses either in the short or in the long run for native workers of high or low skill levels. These numbers are quite small, and the US economy could easily adjust to such an inflow of immigrant workers in the expansionary years.

B. Legal Immigration for Less-Skilled Foreign Workers

Another interesting fact emerging from the empirical analysis is that while immigration during downturns seems to hurt less-educated natives, in the long run immigration affects neither their employment nor their income negatively. The productivity gains that result from less-skilled immigration are likely to benefit the highly educated more, since these workers do not compete for the same jobs, but even less-educated natives do not seem to suffer significant wage losses in the long run. Since less-skilled immigration appears to bring benefits for the aggregate economy without harming the wages of less-educated natives in the long run (and previous work suggests that there is also little effect on the relative wage distribution),[29] this implies that the US immigration system should find a way to admit a certain number of less-educated immigrants legally each year. Currently very little of the demand for these less-skilled workers can be satisfied legally, unless the workers have a close relative in the United States (or classify under special rules).

In other words, a share of work visas should be reserved for occupations typically performed by less-educated workers (including those predominantly handling manual and physical tasks, such as construction workers, janitorial workers, household cleaners, gardeners, and so on). Those types of jobs are the ones that US-born workers are increasingly shunning (at the current wage) and in which immigration has brought large benefits in terms of complementing native workers and

---

29 Ottaviano and Peri, "Immigration and National Wages;" David Card, "Immigration and Inequality."

allowing firms to expand. Approximately how many visas should be available for these less-skilled workers? Suppose one designed a system to admit workers legally to perform less-skilled work. In order to leave relative wages unchanged, the share of new inflows into less-skilled occupations would need roughly to mirror the occupational composition of foreign workers already in the United States. Over the past 15 years, approximately 46 percent of foreign-born workers have had a high school diploma or less — the typical education level of workers doing this type of job. If a total of 900,000 new arrivals were allowed in a given year (as in the previous example), this would imply that about 40 percent should be workers in low-skill occupations (360,000 of the 900,000)[30] and 60 percent in high-skill occupations. This division by skill level would only mildly recalibrate the actual flows, but would allow less-skilled immigrants to come in as authorized workers, possibly reducing significantly the pressure to enter the United States illegally.

V. Conclusion

Let me add two more general considerations on the topic of employment-based visas. In general, given the economic effects of immigration and its positive productive contribution to the US economy, I would be in favor of shifting the balance of new permanent resident visas toward those that are employment based and away from those that are selected by family sponsorship. While this provision could be politically controversial, and while the unity of the immediate family (spouse and minor children) has to be preserved, the economic benefits of immigrants to the US economy should be one consideration when admitting other family members (such as adult siblings). The second consideration is that temporary visa programs such as H-1B, which allow holders to transition to permanent residence, may allow the adjustment of immigration to labor-demand fluctuations. This analysis emphasizes that given the average tendency for immigrants to return to their country of origin, visa policy can produce the desired variation in net immigration simply by making new visa issuance respond to labor demand.

Let me conclude that the economic impact of immigrants on the US economy and on the employment and average wage of US native workers should be one — but cannot be the only — criterion to guide immigration policies. The analysis in this chapter dispels some myths

---

30 This number is more than five times as large as the current cap of H2-B visas for nonagricultural temporary/seasonal workers, which is currently at 66,000 per year, and is the only category for less-skilled workers to enter the country for jobs outside of agriculture. It is lower, however, than the peak inflows of unauthorized immigrants during the economic expansion. In addition to these temporary visas, 5,000 green cards per year are reserved for less-skilled workers.

about long-run economic costs, emphasizes the cost-benefit trade-offs, and suggests a strategy to best absorb immigrants in the US productive structure. Currently these considerations are completely absent in the determination of quotas and new resident permits. The present analysis and some of its implications could be kept in mind when the current immigration system is reformed.

Appendices

Appendix A. Methodology and Data

The data sources and the methodology to construct each component of gross state product are described in detail in an earlier paper.[31] Here, I briefly review the methodology.

A useful starting point to evaluate the aggregate economic impact of net immigration (equal to the inflow of immigrants minus the outflow of returnees and remigrants) is to identify its effect on total employment and on output per worker. The total effect of immigrants on US gross domestic product (GDP) is the product of those two effects. So, any percentage change of US GDP can be decomposed into the sum of the percentage change in employment and the percentage change in output per worker. In turn a change in output per worker can be decomposed into four parts: A change in the intensity of physical capital per worker (more machinery, structure, and equipments), a change in the skill-intensity of workers (the share of workers with some college education), a change in hours worked per worker, and a change in technological productivity/efficiency per worker (called total factor productivity). Each of these components can be measured, provided we have data on gross product, employment, hours worked, workers' skills, and the value of physical capital. So in compact notation (and using the expression GSP to denote gross state product) we can observe each term of the following expression in each US state and year:

(% Change of GSP) =

(% Change of employment) + (% Change of GSP per worker) =

(% Change of employment) + (% Change of capital intensity) + (% Change of skill intensity) + (% Change of hours per worker) + (% Change of factor productivity)

Immigration may affect each term of this decomposition in the short and long run. Our goal is to estimate the response of each of those terms to the net immigration rate (i.e., to the inflow of working immigrants as a percentage of initial employment) in the short and long run. The estimated effects indicate the percentage impact of an increase of immigrants equal to 1 percent of initial employment on the corresponding variable.

The results presented in this chapter come from a series of two-stage least squares (2SLS) regressions. For each term representing the percentage change of a component of output we identify the response within one year, two years, four years, seven years, and ten years to a 1

---

31 Peri, "The Effect of Immigration on Productivity."

percent net change of employment due to immigration. We use a panel of 50 US states plus the District of Columbia. To identify the short-run effects up to seven years, we use data from the Current Population Survey for employment, population, and labor market variables together with data from the National Accounts and State Gross Domestic Product from the Bureau of Economic Analysis for capital and output over the period 1994-2008. For the long-run effect (ten-year changes), we use Census data on population and employment for every ten years over the period 1960-2008 and the same sources for data on gross product and capital.

The responses of each component of income to net immigration are captured by the estimated coefficient βC in the following type of regression:

(% Change of component)$_{s,t}$ = f_t + b_C (Net immigration rate)$_{s,t}$ +$e_{s,t}$

where s indicates states; t indicates time intervals of (alternatively) one, two, four, seven, and ten years; and the percentage changes and net immigration rates are calculated relative to those intervals. The dependent variable is alternatively each of the terms in expression (1), ft is a set of dummy variables capturing year-specific common effects, and es,t is a zero-mean random variable.

In order to interpret the estimated coefficients βC as the impact of net immigration on the corresponding economic variable, we need to make sure that the variation of immigration rates over time and across states is not driven by changes of those variables themselves (reverse causality). The presence of unobservable changes that would affect the economic variables as well as the immigration rates would also bias the coefficient estimates. In particular, the cycles of economic expansion and recession would affect employment and productivity and also the net inflow of immigrants. A positive correlation between immigrants and native employment, can be driven by the creation of native and immigrant jobs during expansions. To solve this problem we use an instrumental variable strategy.[32] As immigrants of a certain nationality tend to locate near communities of other immigrants of the same nationality, the cross-state variation of net immigration is affected by the preexisting distribution of immigrants of each nationality. During years (or decades) of large total inflows of some national groups, the states where their preexisting presence is large will receive large net inflow of immigrants for reasons unrelated to productivity and labor demand. Hence, by interacting the initial size of immigrant communities (or simply the distance of the state from the place of entry of immigrants) with the total yearly inflow of immigrants by nationality produces a predicted inflow of immigrants by state. Such prediction

---

[32] This strategy has been used to identify long-run effects of immigrants in several papers beginning with Card, "Immigrant Inflows, Native Outflows." We extend it to the estimates of short-run effects.

is purely driven by the revealed preferences of immigrants for locations as existing in the first year considered and not by the economic conditions of the state and their changes over the sample. We also use the distance of a state from the main ports of entry of immigrants (New York and Los Angeles) and from the border interacted with year dummies as a predictor of the supply-driven inflow of immigrants in states more easily accessible to them. The prediction obtained using these instruments is correlated with the actual inflow of migrants in a state and should proxy for the supply-driven part of immigration. Therefore, it should not be correlated with other factors affecting productivity (labor demand) of a state and hence it would be a valid instrument.[33]

Appendix B. Response to Net Immigration Rates over Different Time Intervals, US States

The estimated effects indicate the percentage impact of an increase of immigrants equal to 1 percent of initial employment on the corresponding variable. For example, after one year, a 1 percent increase in the labor supply due to immigrants leads to a 0.98 percent increase in total employment, or a 0.02 percent decrease in native employment. Asterisks indicate whether the estimate is statistically significant. For example, the 0.02 percent change in native employment is not statistically different from zero. For the total employment estimates, a response of total employment smaller than 1 implies that some native jobs are lost when immigrants enter employment (crowding out). An estimated response larger than 1 implies that some natives would gain jobs as a consequence of immigration (crowding in).

---

[33] As we use the distance-based instruments and the imputed immigrant instrument together, we can test the exogeneity of instrument hypothesis. The Sargan test never rejects the null of exogenous instrument at the 1 percent significance level.

Dependent Variable:	1-year 1994-2008	2-year 1994-2008	4-year 1994-2008	7-year 1994-2008	10-year interval 1960-2008
% response of total employment	0.98* (0.39)	1.69** (0.63)	0.85 (0.57)	1.18** (0.38)	1.10** (0.50)
% response of native employment	-0.02 (0.39)	0.69 (0.63)	-0.15 (0.57)	0.18 (0.38)	0.10 (0.50)
% response of GDP per worker	0.01 (0.32)	0.05 (0.54)	0.83** (0.31)	0.63* (0.36)	0.26** (0.11)
Components of GDP per worker					
% response of capital intensity	-0.30* (0.15)	-0.99* (0.40)	-0.61 (0.61)	-0.22 (0.42)	-0.02 (0.05)
% response of skill per worker	-0.07 (0.15)	-0.02 (0.22)	-0.13 (0.10)	-0.12 (0.17)	-0.21** (0.03)
% response of hours per worker	-0.05 (0.12)	0.04 (0.12)	0.11 (0.08)	0.15** (0.07)	0.07* (0.02)
% response of total factor productivity	0.11 (0.47)	0.48 (0.62)	1.01** (0.57)	0.51 (0.58)	0.43** (0.12)
Observations	714	357	204	102	255

Source: Author's analysis.

Moving from column 1 to 5 we can track the total response over one, two, four, seven, and ten years. The top row shows the impact on total employment, while the second row isolates the impact on native employment. The third row shows the total effect on output per worker. The other four rows show the effects on individual components of output per worker which are, respectively, capital intensity, skill per worker, hours per workers, and total factor productivity.[34]

---

34 Each coefficient is estimated using two-stage least squares (2SLS) from a separate regression. The dependent variable in each regression is the net change in foreign-born employment relative to employment at the beginning of the period. The units of observations are US states (plus DC) over the time interval. Instruments are the imputed immigrants from their national 1990 distribution and distance from ports of entry interacted with time dummies. Heteroskedasticity and cluster-robust standard errors are in parenthesis. Each regression includes time-fixed effects.

Appendix C. Response to Net Immigration Rates in Periods of Expansion and Downturn[35]

	1-year differences 1994-2008		2-year differences 1994-2008		4-year differences 1994-2008		7-year differences 1994-2008	
Dependent Variable:	Effect if output gap<0	Effect if output gap>=0	Effect if output average gap<0,	Effect if output average gap>=0,	Effect if output average gap<0,	Effect if output average gap>=0,	Effect if output average gap<0,	Effect if output average gap>=0,
% response of total employment	0.57** (0.17)	0.63** (0.12)	0.63** (0.26)	0.95** (0.15)	0.73 (0.50)	1.07** (0.26)	1.50** (0.25)	1.21** (0.34)
% response of native employment	-0.43** (0.17)	-0.37** (0.12)	-0.37 (0.26)	0.05 (0.15)	-0.27 (0.50)	0.07 (0.26)	0.50 (0.25)	0.21 (0.34)
% response of GDP per worker	-0.59** (0.18)	-0.17 (0.12)	-0.55** (0.22)	-0.05 (0.28)	-0.17 (0.30)	0.36 (0.31)	0.08 (0.39)	0.36 (0.31)
Components of GDP per worker								
% response of capital intensity	-0.07 (0.09)	-0.03 (0.05)	-0.32 (0.22)	0.07 (0.09)	-0.33** (0.11)	-0.17* (0.08)	-0.12 (0.28)	-0.15 (0.10)
% response of skill per worker	0.07 (0.12)	-0.07 (0.09)	-0.34* (0.14)	-0.03 (0.09)	-0.34 (0.29)	0.11 (0.13)	0.15 (0.10)	0.11 (0.28)
% response of hours per worker	-0.02 (0.06)	-0.03 (0.05)	0.01 (0.08)	0.07 (0.08)	0.05 (0.10)	0.09 (0.07)	0.09 (0.06)	0.02 (0.11)
% response of total factor productivity	-0.57** (0.22)	0.01 (0.17)	-0.21 (0.38)	0.29 (0.43)	0.20 (0.48)	0.47 (0.40)	0.24 (0.37)	0.47 (0.45)
Observations	714	714	357	357	204	204	102	102

Source: Author's analysis.

---

35 Each couple of coefficients (for Output Gap>, =, and < 0) is estimated within the same regression allowing differential response to the immigration rate. The method of estimation is 2SLS. The dependent variable in each regression is the net change in foreign-born employment relative to employment at the beginning of the period. The units of observations are US states (plus DC) over the time interval. Instruments are the imputed immigrants from their national 1990 distribution and distance from ports of entry interacted with time dummies. Heteroskedasticity- and cluster-robust standard errors are reported in parenthesis. Each regression includes time-fixed effects.

Appendix D. Response to Net Immigration Rates of Employment of Less-Educated Natives[36]

% Effect on less-educated native workers	1 year Downturn	1 year Expansion	2 years Downturn	2 years Expansion	4 years Downturn	4 years Expansion	7 years Downturn	7 years Expansion
average	-0.32* (0.19)		-0.38 (0.28)		0.54* (0.33)		0.54* (0.33)	
Separating downturns and expansions	-0.51** (0.23)	-0.16 (0.23)	-0.81** (0.30)	-0.03 (0.35)	-0.75** (0.36)	0.44 (0.36)	0.70 (0.44)	0.34 (0.36)
Observations	714		357		153		102	

Source: Author's analysis.

---

[36] The specifications are as in Appendices B and C. The method of estimation is 2SLS regression with time-fixed effects. The dependent variable is the change in employment of native workers with high school degree or less relative to initial employment in that group and the explanatory variable is the net change in foreign born as a percentage of initial employment. Heteroskedasticity- and cluster-robust standard errors are reported in parenthesis. Each regression includes time-fixed effects.

Works Cited

Barcellos, Silvia. 2010. The Dynamics of Immigration and Wages. RAND working paper WR-755. www.rand.org/pubs/working_papers/2010/RAND_WR755.pdf.

Bureau of Labor Statistics (BLS). E-1 Employment Status of the Civilian Noninstitutional Population by Sex and Age, Seasonally Adjusted. www.bls.gov/web/empsit/cpsee_e01.pdf.

Card, David. 2001. Immigrant Inflows, Native Outflows, and the Local Labor Market Impacts of Higher Immigration. *Journal of Labor Economics* 19 (1): 22–64.

———. 2009. Immigration and Inequality. NBER Working Paper no. 14683, National Bureau of Economic Research, Cambridge, MA.

Cortes, Patricia. 2008. The Effect of Low-Skilled Immigration on U.S. Prices: Evidence from CPI Data. *Journal of Political Economy* 116 (3): 381–422.

Department of Homeland Security (DHS). 2008. *Yearbook of Immigration Statistics.* Washington, DC: DHS.

Gauthier-Loiselle, Marjolaine and Jennifer Hunt. 2010. How Much Does Immigration Boost Innovation? *American Economic Journal: Macroeconomics* 2 (2): 31–56.

Hatton, Timothy J. and Jeffery G. Williamson. 2005. *Global Migration and the World Economy: Two Centuries of Policy and Performance.* Cambridge, MA: MIT Press.

Hoefer, Michael, Nancy Rytina, and Bryan Baker. 2011. *Estimates of the Unauthorized Immigrant Population Residing in the United States: January 2010.* Washington, DC: Office of Immigration Statistics, DHS. www.dhs.gov/xlibrary/assets/statistics/publications/ois_ill_pe_2010.pdf.

Kerr, William R. and William F. Lincoln. 2010. The Supply Side of Innovation: H-1B Visa Reforms and U.S. Ethnic Invention. *Journal of Labor Economics* 28 (3): 473–508.

Lewis, Ethan. 2005. Immigration, Skill Mix, and the Choice of Technique. Federal Reserve Bank of Philadelphia Working Paper 05-08, Philadelphia.

Neumark, David and Francesca Mazzolari. 2009. Beyond Wages: The Effect of Immigration on the Scale and Composition of Output. NBER Working Paper 14900, National Bureau of Economic Research, Cambridge, MA. .

Orrenius, Pia and Madeline Zavodny. 2010. *Beside the Golden Door: US Immigration Reform in a New Era of Globalization.* Washington, DC: American Enterprise Institute.

Ottaviano, Gianmarco and Giovanni Peri. 2008. Immigration and National Wages: Clarifying the Theory and the Empirics. NBER Working Paper 14188, National Bureau of Economic Research, Cambridge, MA. www.nber.org/papers/w14188.

Papademetriou, Demetrios G., Doris Meissner, Marc Rosenblum, and Madeleine Sumption. 2009. *Harnessing the Advantages of Immigration for a 21st Century Economy: A Standing Commission on Labor Markets, Economic Competitiveness, and Immigration.* Washington, DC: Migration Policy Institute. www.migrationpolicy.org/pubs/StandingCommission_May09.pdf.

Peri, Giovanni. 2009. The Effect of Immigration on Productivity: Evidence from U.S. States. NBER Working Paper 15507, National Bureau of Economic Research, Cambridge, MA.

Peri, Giovanni and Chad Sparber. 2009. Task Specialization, Immigration and Wages. *American Economic Journal: Applied Economics* 1 (3): 135–69.

United States Census Bureau. 2011. *2010 American Community Survey Highlights.* Washington, DC: US Census Bureau. www.census.gov/newsroom/releases/pdf/acs_2010_highlights.pdf.

Yang, Dean. 2006. Why Do Migrants Return to Poor Countries? Evidence from Philippines' Migrants Response to Exchange Rate Shocks. *Review of Economics and Statistics* 88 (4): 715–35.

CHAPTER 4

THE ELUSIVE IDEA OF LABOR-MARKET 'SHORTAGES' AND THE US APPROACH TO EMPLOYMENT-BASED IMMIGRATION POLICY

Madeleine Sumption

Migration Policy Institute

Introduction[1]

Labor or skill "shortages" are a recurrent theme in debates on employment-based immigration. The basic idea that work visas should attract workers with the most needed skills into jobs for which an insufficient number of local workers are available enjoys widespread support. On the one hand, immigrant workers whose skills are in high demand are thought to make a disproportionate contribution to economic growth, complementing the skills of the existing labor force. On the other, if certain skills are *not* particularly scarce, employers are expected to find them with ease in the local labor force instead of hiring foreign workers.[2]

This thinking has created an impetus, both in the United States and in

---

1 This chapter is an updated and expanded version of a report that initially was produced for the International Organization for Migration's (IOM's) Independent Network of Labour Migration and Integration Experts (LINET) project "Identifying Labour and Skill Shortages and Migration Policy."
2 In particular, there is a concern that unless there is a lack of resident workers, immigrants may undermine the opportunities of existing workforce members who would otherwise have taken the work. In practice, the empirical evidence for this is mixed. Immigrants to the United States are thought to create at least as many jobs as they occupy, even if for the most part they work in the same occupations as natives. However, this may not be true when the labor market is weak, for example, during periods of high unemployment. See Giovanni Peri, in Chapter 3 of this volume.

other immigrant-receiving countries, to identify systematically what the labor force "needs" and to target immigration accordingly. Labor shortages are an elusive concept with no straightforward definition, however. The simplest definition of a labor shortage is that demand for a given type of worker exceeds the number of willing candidates at the prevailing wage and working conditions. Economists disagree as to whether shortages should exist at all, since if employers find it difficult to recruit at the prevailing wage, they could simply raise wages to encourage more workers to apply or seek training to join the occupation. As a result, economists tend to see rising wages as the most convincing evidence that a specific skill is scarce, although they disagree as to whether high wages are the problem, or the solution to the problem.[3]

Some "shortages" are transient and disappear when the market has had time to adjust to high demand. Others persist because wages cannot or do not rise, or because rising wages do not solve the underlying reasons for labor scarcity. This could be because demand for a given skill rises faster than supply can catch up (especially in occupations that require several years of training or in which training is difficult or costly to acquire) or because consumers' sensitivity to prices and/or competition from other producers at home or abroad make it difficult for employers to raise wages. Meanwhile, some occupations are considered socially valuable (such as those of teachers or nurses), but must be financed by taxpayers and price-sensitive consumers who are not willing or able to pay the price necessary to attract more or better-qualified workers into the profession. In these cases, one might argue that there is a shortage of workers relative to the number policymakers might consider optimal from a social perspective.

More generally, the word "shortage" is itself somewhat problematic. First, it suggests an empirically verifiable and binary state of the world — that employers either find it difficult to recruit a particular skill or that they do not. It also implies a normative judgment to the effect that there are "not enough" workers in a given field, whereas in practice employers' recruiting difficulties can result not just from a simple lack of skills, but also from a failure to use available skills to their full potential or pay market-clearing wages. As a result, it is perhaps more useful to talk about cases in which skills are scarce or recruiting is difficult. Some skills are more difficult to recruit than others, and some vacancies harder to fill than others. But there is clearly no objective, absolute threshold beyond which we can say with confidence that recruiting is "difficult" or "not difficult," nor is there a single response

---

3   Rising wages indicate the labor market is adjusting to the limited supply of a certain skill by remunerating it accordingly. From an economic perspective, higher wages address a shortage of workers both by encouraging more workers to enter the occupation but also by reducing employers' willingness to hire them. From the employers' perspective, however, the process of "reducing their demand" for workers may look and feel exactly like a shortage — they would have liked to hire a given number of workers, but cannot.

that is appropriate in cases where recruiting problems are identified.

When analyzing whether employers find it difficult to recruit a sufficient number of workers, and especially when devising immigration policies to address this problem, it matters not just *whether* employers face hiring difficulties, but also *why*. (For example, increasing immigration may not be the most effective solution if the primary problem is employers' difficulties in retaining qualified workers.) Other considerations include whether the market is likely to adjust of its own accord and what the economic or social consequences would be of either intervening or not intervening through immigration policy. Answering these questions can require substantial occupation-by-occupation investigation, qualitative analysis, and a series of relatively subjective judgments — processes that are often difficult to incorporate effectively or transparently into immigration policies.

Despite these difficulties, the need to create immigration policies that are sensitive to labor-market demand generates continuing interest. This chapter examines the different tools that policymakers have used to identify and fill specific skills needs through the immigration system. It concludes that despite the political allure of fine-tuning the immigration system by introducing more occupation-specific policies, these policies would not necessarily have the desired effect and would do little to resolve the real dilemmas faced by the US immigration system.

I. Assessing the Extent of Labor Shortages

Most of the employment-based immigration systems of the Organization for Economic Cooperation and Development (OECD) countries accommodate one or more of three mechanisms designed to match prospective employment-based immigrants' skills or abilities with the perceived needs of the economy. The first is to assess the need for workers on a case-by-case basis when employers apply to bring foreign workers from abroad, requiring them to "test" the labor market by advertising locally for workers. The second is to ease the eligibility criteria for workers with skills or training (such as advanced degrees in certain fields) that are considered to be in particularly high demand, economically beneficial, or likely to facilitate immigrants' rapid labor-market integration. The third is to vary visa-eligibility criteria by occupation. Dedicated visa programs for specific occupations or sectors in which host countries wish to increase labor supply (for example, in agriculture or health) are common, and some countries have created detailed lists of "shortage occupations" for which immigration regulations may be relaxed or additional visas provided.

A. Shortage Lists and Statistical Measures of Labor-Market Demand

How do immigration policies differentiate between occupations with higher and lower levels of demand? The decision-making process can be political, relying on policymakers' or legislators' subjective judgments about which areas of the economy require special rules. Since this process is not transparent or systematic, some countries have tried to create more objective, data-driven measures of occupational shortage. Today, this approach is best known through the work of the United Kingdom's Migration Advisory Committee, which monitors labor-market statistics, collects qualitative evidence about potential occupational shortages, and publishes a regularly updated list of jobs into which the Committee deems it "sensible" to facilitate immigration.[4]

Similar exercises have been conducted with US labor-market data, and are worth reviewing to illustrate how the statistical approach works. One of the first attempts to measure shortages for immigration purposes was published by economist Malcolm Cohen in the mid-1990s.[5] (An earlier version of the same work had been commissioned by the US Department of Labor in the early 1980s to inform discussions at the time about the potential for creating a systematic analysis of occupational "shortages" for immigration purposes.) This analysis assessed occupations according to a series of statistical indicators, such as unemployment rates for individuals who recently worked in the occupation, recent changes in employment levels, changes in wages, employment growth as predicted by the US Bureau of Labor Statistics, and the number of months of specific vocational training.[6] Occupations received a score for each indicator; these scores were aggregated and the occupations ranked in order. Cohen then designated the highest-ranked occupations as shortage occupations. These were primarily medical, scientific, and technical jobs, including those of natural

---

4 Madeleine Sumption, "Filling Labor Shortages through Immigration: An Overview of Shortage Lists and their Implications," *Migration Information Source*, February 2011, www.migrationinformation.org/Feature/display.cfm?ID=828.

5 Malcolm Cohen, *Labor Shortages as America Approaches the Twenty-first Century* (Ann Arbor, MI: University of Michigan Press, 1995). Note that the United Kingdom also does substantial qualitative analysis that was not a feature of Malcolm Cohen's work.

6 Since the early 1970s, the US Bureau of Labor Statistics (BLS) has produced regular ten-year-forward projections of occupational employment. These data do not attempt to identify future shortages or surpluses of workers, but rather describe where job growth is most likely to occur. (High job growth does not necessarily mean shortages will occur if the supply of qualified workers is sufficiently high.) Moreover, the forecasts are not always accurate, especially at the detailed occupational level, and are subject to unpredictable developments that affect the distribution of growth across industries. For an evaluation of BLS projections, see, for example, Andrew Alpert and Jill Auyer, *The 1988-2000 Employment Projections: How Accurate Were They?* (Washington, DC: Bureau of Labor Statistics, 2003), www.bls.gov/opub/ooq/2003/spring/art01.pdf.

scientists, physical therapists, nurses, chemists, and computer programmers.[7]

A similar analysis using 1992-97 data took a slightly different approach. Instead of designating the highest-ranked occupations as shortage occupations, it sought to determine the number of occupations that met a predetermined set of criteria described by the author as "somewhat arbitrary": employment growth of 50 percent faster than average, wage increases of 30 percent faster than average, and unemployment rates at least 30 percent below average.[8] Out of 68 occupations analyzed, seven met this threshold: management analysts, special education teachers, dental hygienists, marketing managers, airplane pilots, purchasing agents, and mechanical engineers. The author argued that in all but one of these occupations (special education teachers) no anecdotal or qualitative information existed to confirm the existence of shortages, while other occupations in which complaints of shortages were routine (including some skilled trades such as plumbers, electricians, and carpenters) found no support of labor-market tightness in the data. The author concluded that statistical analysis alone was insufficient to gauge with confidence the existence of a shortage or the lack of one.

These exercises illustrate some of the difficulties that arise when analyzing occupational shortages with labor-market statistics. The methodologies typically appeal because they appear to be both objective and robust. In practice, however, a number of problems arise for reasons much more profound than a lack of good data.[9] First, the criteria used to determine whether a labor shortage exists are plausible but arbitrary. Employers' recruiting difficulties may manifest themselves in various ways in the data, and this is why the studies described use a combination of indicators rather than one single measure. However, there is no obvious or theoretically defensible way to decide which indicators should be given most weight or which methodology to choose over another. Should the increase in an occupation's wages be 50 percent greater than average in the exercise described above, or would 40 percent have been sufficient? Does past employment growth in an occupation show that shortages are occurring or, on the contrary, that demand for workers is being met? Questions of this nature abound. The result is that the number of occupations found to be in shortage is,

---

7   In order, the top ten occupations according to the baseline methodology variant used in the study were: (1) other natural scientists, (2) veterinarians, (3) physical therapists, (4) physicians, (5) registered nurses, (6) speech therapists, (7) chemists except biologists, (8) biological and life scientists, (9) computer programmers, and (10) computer systems analysts and scientists. Cohen, *Labor Shortages as America Approaches the Twenty-First Century.*
8   Carolyn Veneri, "Can Occupational Labor Shortages Be Identified Using Available Data," *Monthly Labor Review*, March 1999, www.bls.gov/opub/mlr/1999/03/art2full.pdf.
9   The United States has relatively good labor market data, in the form of the Current Population Survey (CPS), American Community Survey (ACS), and the Job Openings and Labor Turnover Survey. However, the sample sizes are not always sufficient to disaggregate the data by region.

more or less, whatever the analyst would like it to be, making the objectivity and transparency of the process highly questionable.

Second, analysis of this kind relies on occupational data to group together workers who perform similar tasks. The occupation an individual practices provides information about both the broad levels of human capital and specialized knowledge required for a particular kind of work, but remains a relatively crude measure of the skill a specific job requires.[10] Occupational categories fail to account for a huge variety of required experience, qualifications, or abilities; earnings within a single occupation can vary quite substantially, suggesting that not all workers are equivalent or make good substitutes.[11] Even within small occupational groups, substantial differences in the required knowledge will arise depending on the idiosyncrasies of the work in question — especially in more highly skilled occupations. As a result, unemployment might be high in a given occupation, but if an employer requires a very specific expertise, he or she might still not be able to find a worker with the right skills.

Third, occupational analysis is both a backward-looking and fundamentally static way of approaching the question of labor and skill "needs." Labor-market statistics typically become available a few or even several months after they are collected and must then be analyzed and used to update assessments about labor needs. As a result, there may be a substantial time lag between the data collection and the policy adjustment, not to mention between the data collection and the arrival of immigrants themselves. When using this analysis to inform immigration or other policy areas, policymakers implicitly rely on the assumption that past trends will continue to hold in future. This is often not true: labor markets can adjust in unpredictable ways depending on the economic cycle, technological developments (including the arrival of labor-saving technologies), trade and outsourcing (which affect the demand for specific goods and services in the host country), trends in education and training provisions, and employers' efforts to recruit more effectively, restructure jobs, or improve wages and working conditions.

These analytical problems are compounded by a set of operational ones. Even if areas of labor scarcity could be identified with reasonable accuracy, it is not clear whether governments have the means and ability to appropriately adjust the number of immigrants arriving in those occupations. Not only is the timing difficult to fine-tune (governments must wait for data to become available, be analyzed, be translated into immigration policies, and then lead to immigrant arrivals — by which point employers may already have changed their behavior in

---

10 Researchers disagree about the extent to which occupation is a good indicator of human capital. Sociologists have typically focused on occupation as the standard unit of analysis, while economists tend to focus on education (such as years of schooling or diplomas received).
11 Ted Mouw and Arne Kalleberg, "Occupations and the Structure of Wage Inequality in the United States, 1980s to 2000s," *American Sociological Review* 75, no. 3 (2010): 402–31.

response to recruiting difficulties); the duration of recruiting problems is not usually known in advance, nor is the size of the flow that would best remedy them in a sensible and proportionate manner.

In practice, information about shortages can be incorporated into the immigration system in a limited number of ways. In the US employer-driven system, the two main options are to exempt employers from certain immigration regulations if the occupation into which they are hiring faces a shortage, to provide additional visas for certain occupations, or to restrict the number of visas in "nonshortage" occupations. As discussed later in this chapter, the more the immigration system prioritizes occupations that are supposed to face shortages at the expense of those that do not, the greater the impact of the policy *and* greater the cost of inevitable inaccuracies. These costs include the risk of preventing a legitimate and economically beneficial use of the immigration system in cases where employers face genuine recruiting difficulties, as well as overcorrecting for the problem and sending disproportionate numbers of immigrants to some occupations at the expense of others.

B. Examples of Shortages in the US Labor Market

Before discussing how US immigration policies have sought to accommodate varying demand for different types of skills, it is worth reviewing some cases that have dominated the public debate about the country's need for skills and in which the US labor market is thought to have experienced shortages in the recent past.

1. Nursing

Nursing shortages are perhaps the most persistent and widely recognized in the recent history of the US labor market.[12] In recent years, demand for nurses has grown inexorably alongside the growing and aging US population. Employment in the nursing and residential care industry grew by 41 percent from 1990 to 2000, when total nonfarm employment in the United States rose by about 20 percent; it grew by 21 percent from 2000 to 2010, a period during which total US employment fell by just over 1 percent largely due to the devastating economic crisis of the late 2000s.[13] Even with employment increases of this scale, many analysts predict that nursing employment will not be enough to meet the enormous expected growth in demand, especially if more robust economic growth reverses the recent rise in young people

---

12   Incidentally, registered nurses were ranked among the occupations most likely to face a shortage in Malcolm Cohen's statistical analyses for both the 1980s and 1990s.
13   US Bureau of Labor Statistics (BLS), "Employment, Hours, and Earnings from the Current Employment Statistics survey (National). Nursing and Residential Care Facilities," www.bls.gov/ces/#data; BLS, "Employment, Hours, and Earnings from the Current Employment Statistics survey (National). Total Nonfarm Employment," www.bls.gov/ces/#data.

entering the profession and the lower number of unfilled vacancies during the economic crisis.[14]

Public policies designed to address these concerns face some rather complex challenges. First, the nursing profession is heterogeneous and the types of vacancies employers find hard to fill shift continuously. The need for nursing aides, licensed practical nurses, registered nurses, and nurse practitioners (in ascending order of educational level and credentials) varies over time and between hospitals. For example, financially constrained hospitals (such as Veterans Affairs [VA] hospitals or those with larger proportions of uninsured or Medicaid patients) tend to experience more systematic recruiting difficulties than their better-funded counterparts.[15] Nurses who move up the career ladder into more desirable shifts or more qualified positions may leave hard-to-fill vacancies behind, especially in undesirable "graveyard" shifts. Geography compounds some of these problems. Because health care is needed all across the country, providers cannot simply relocate to areas where skills or labor are more readily available, as if they were regular private-sector providers of a tradable good. Despite advances in communication technologies that have increased the potential for providing medical services remotely,[16] most health services must be provided in person (at a local clinic or hospital, or even in the home), thus creating the risk of geographic mismatches and persistent recruitment problems in rural and other "underserved" areas such as inner cities.

Second, while the labor market for nurses has traditionally responded to increasing demand with higher wages and rising enrollments in training, the response has typically been slow. The resulting time lags have created something of a "feast or famine" labor market in which concerns about shortages are interspersed with periods of oversupply and stagnating wages.[17] This disequilibrium in the nursing labor market has proved persistent, prompting sporadic government interventions to subsidize training, regulate employment practices, or temporarily boost supply through immigration.[18] Recent studies of the labor market for nurses have identified several causes of recruiting difficulties, of which the most significant is a lack of clinical placements

---

14   See, for example, Peter Buerhaus, David Auerbach, and Douglas Staiger, "The Recent Surge in Nurse Employment: Causes and Implications," *Health Affairs* 28, no. 4 (2009): 657–68, www.healthstaff.org/documents/surgeinnurseemployment.pdf.
15   For a more detailed analysis, see Mark C. Long, Marsha G. Goldfarb, and Robert S. Goldfarb, "Explanations for Persistent Nursing Shortages," *Forum for Health Economics and Policy* 11, no. 2 (2008): article 10, https://digital.lib.washington.edu/researchworks/bitstream/handle/1773/15547/Long1.pdf?sequence=1.
16   Alan Blinder, "Offshoring: The Next Industrial Revolution?" *Foreign Affairs* 85 (2): 113–28.
17   Long, Goldfarb, and Goldfarb, "Explanations for Persistent Nursing Shortages;" and Craig J. Newschaffer and Julie A. Schoenman, "Registered Nurse Shortages: The Road to Appropriate Public Policy," *Health Affairs* 9, no. 1 (1990): 98–106, www.foreignaffairs.com/articles/61514/alan-s-blinder/offshoring-the-next-industrial-revolution.
18   Newschaffer and Schoenman, "Registered Nurse Shortages."

and faculty to train new nurses, as a result of which qualified candidates are turned away. Other ongoing causes include high turnover rates, especially among newly graduated nurses, and the ongoing retirement of many of the profession's most experienced workers.[19] In less-skilled nursing-related positions (such as health aides and assistants and health home attendants), low wages are also a barrier to recruiting and retaining staff, even as the aging population increases the demand for their services.

The policy implications of these trends are complicated by the fact that the health sector has a strong social function in addition to its commercial role. As a result, prices matter, and higher wages could mean less widely available and affordable health care.[20] This makes the argument for intervening through immigration policy more compelling. However, immigration is unlikely to solve the underlying problems of recruitment and retention; in the long run the supply of nurses is likely to rely on measures to make the occupation more attractive to existing workers and to bring those who have left the nursing workforce back into it.

2. Science, Technology, Engineering, and Math (STEM)

Another focal point in the debate about occupational shortages is the STEM fields. STEM skills are considered central to US economic growth and competitiveness, particularly in advanced manufacturing and knowledge industries, and employer surveys have consistently ranked positions requiring technical skills among the hardest-to-fill vacancies.[21] Moreover, demand for these workers remains high despite the economic crisis. Unemployment in May 2012 was 3.5 percent for workers in computer and mathematical occupations and 3.9 percent for all workers with a bachelor's degree or higher compared to a rate of 8.2

---

19 Institute of Medicine, *The Future of Nursing: Leading Change, Advancing Health* (Washington, DC: The National Academies Press, 2011), https://folio.iupui.edu/bitstream/handle/10244/911/Future%20of%20Nursing_Leading%20Change%20Advancing%20Health.pdf?sequence=1; and Linda Aiken and Robyn Cheung, "Nurse Workforce Challenges in the United States: Implications for Policy" (OECD health working paper 35, Organization for Economic Cooperation and Development, Paris, 2008), www.oecd.org/dataoecd/34/9/41431864.pdf.
20 Moreover, medical practitioners may define shortages not as an imbalance of supply and demand, but as a situation in which the provision of care falls short of what they believe to be ideal or acceptable standards (these situations have been referred to as "professional standards shortages"). Long, Goldfarb, and Goldfarb, "Explanations for Persistent Nursing Shortages."
21 An annual employer survey by the employment agency, Manpower, for example, listed engineers in top place for employer recruitment difficulties in the United States in 2008 and 2009, eighth place in 2010, and third place in 2011. Manpower, "Talent Shortage Survey" (various years), http://us.manpower.com/us/en/multimedia/Global-Shortage-Survey-Results.pdf.

percent nationwide,[22] a phenomenon that has been referred to in the tech industry as the "dual unemployment rate."[23]

Establishing whether tech occupations meet formal definitions of shortage is difficult, since different analysts interpret the data in different ways. On the one hand, the number of people graduating from US universities in science and engineering fields has not kept pace with perceived demand. Degrees granted in engineering grew at half the average rate between 2000 and 2009 (from 73,000 to 85,000).[24] Both bachelor's and master's graduates in computer science have fallen since a 2004 peak that followed the dotcom crash,[25] although an IT major is just one of several routes into computer-related jobs and large IT firms often train workers in-house rather than expecting new hires to have the full range of technical skills they need.[26] Across STEM fields, foreign-born students have made up a large and growing share of graduates, especially in advanced and doctoral education,[27] fuelling concerns that US students have lost interest in the hard sciences or that too many arrive at US universities without the strong mathematics background that study and work in STEM fields typically require.

Meanwhile, one cannot neatly match the supply of people with STEM skills to employers' demand in jobs requiring these skills, since a STEM education can be used in a variety of productive ways, many of which are not in formally classified STEM occupations. According to the National Science Foundation, 64 percent of those with their highest degree in engineering and 56 percent of those in computer science work in a science or engineering job (the shares are substantially higher at the master's and doctoral levels). Significantly higher shares of science and engineering graduates, however, report that their jobs are "related" to their studies, including 96 percent of doctoral graduates, 92 percent of master's, and 75 percent of bachelor's degree holders

---

22 BLS, "Table A-30. Unemployed Persons by Industry and Sex," www.bls.gov/web/empsit/cpseea30.pdf; BLS, "Table A-5. Employment Status of the Civilian Noninstitutional Population 25 Years and Older by Educational Attainment, Seasonally Adjusted," www.bls.gov/web/empsit/cpseea05.pdf.
23 Testimony of Brad Smith, General Counsel and Senior Vice President, Legal Corporate Affairs, Microsoft, before the US Senate Committee on the Judiciary, Subcommittee on Immigration, Refugees, and Border Security, *The Economic Imperative for Immigration Reform: High-Skilled Immigration as a Driver of Economic Growth*, 112th Cong., 1st sess., July 26, 2011, www.judiciary.senate.gov/pdf/11-7-26%20Smith%20Testimony.pdf.
24 Includes engineering and engineering technologies. US Census Bureau, "Table 298, Bachelor's Degrees Earned by Field," 2011, www.census.gov/compendia/statab/cats/education/higher_education_degrees.html.
25 Ibid; US Census Bureau, "Table 302, Master's and Doctorate Degrees Earned by Field," 2011, www.census.gov/compendia/statab/cats/education/higher_education_degrees.html.
26 In addition to gaining bachelor's degrees in information technology (IT), students can take IT courses as part of other degrees, study for a range of nondegree credentials and qualifications, or learn IT skills on the job after demonstrating their potential aptitude through another quantitative degree such as mathematics or engineering.
27 National Science Foundation (NSF), *Science and Engineering Indicators 2012* (Arlington, VA: National Science Foundation, January 2012), www.nsf.gov/statistics/seind12/.

when surveyed up to five years after graduation.[28] Some of these workers hold managerial, business-development, and sales roles that require technical knowledge. Indeed, research shows that demand for the abilities associated with a science or engineering education (such as problem solving and mathematical reasoning) has grown across the economy, and not just in formally classified STEM occupations.[29]

Remuneration in STEM occupations remains high and STEM workers have received a growing wage premium relative to all other workers with similar levels of education,[30] although earnings have risen faster in a few other highly skilled occupational clusters, such as health professionals, potentially making the field less attractive.[31] As a result, it is not clear to what extent STEM-trained individuals are wasting their skills or leaving their fields in favor of more attractive or better-paid occupations — a concern that is exacerbated by the fact that once a worker has left the field their skills can become outdated quite quickly as technologies change.

The debates that took place during the dotcom boom of the late 1990s illustrate particularly well the difficulty in providing a simple characterization of whether or not an occupation faces a skill shortage. Rapidly rising IT employment and growing entry-level wages during the boom period prompted a flurry of studies on the subject of IT skill shortages, several arguing that hundreds of thousands of IT vacancies were going unfilled.[32] Other analysts, however, argued that employers complaining of shortages were simply not willing to pay the wages that experienced IT professionals command,[33] or that perceived competition for workers in fact focused on a relatively small group of the top individuals, rather than on IT professionals across the board.[34] In some cases, IT personnel problems may also have stemmed in part from managerial failures. For example, one report argues that fragmented projects, limited opportunities for systematic training and learning from others, punishing hours, and employers' difficulty in identifying

---

28 Ibid.
29 Anthony Carnevale, Nicole Smith, and Michelle Melton, *STEM* (Washington, DC: Center on Education and the Workforce, October 2011), www9.georgetown.edu/grad/gppi/hpi/cew/pdfs/stem-complete.pdf.
30 Ibid.
31 Lindsay B. Lowell, Hal Salzman, and Hamutal Bernstein, *Steady as She Goes? Three Generations of Students through the Science and Engineering Pipeline* (Washington, DC: Institute for the Study of International Migration, October 2009), http://policy.rutgers.edu/faculty/salzman/steadyasshegoes.pdf.
32 These studies are elegantly summarized in Peter Cappelli, *Is There a Shortage of Information Technology Workers?* (Report to McKinsey and Company for the "War for Technical Talent" Project, Wharton School, University of Pennsylvania, June 2000), http://knowledge.wharton.upenn.edu/papers/979.pdf.
33 For the latter view, see, for example, Peter Freeman and William Aspray, *The Supply of Information Technology Workers in the United States* (Washington, DC: Computing Research Organization, 1999), http://archive.cra.org/reports/wits/charts_figs_boxes_tables.pdf.
34 Capelli, *Is There a Shortage of Information Technology Workers?*

good performance and rewarding it meant that for many, an occupation such as computer programming was simply a "lousy job," putting off potential entrants and pushing substantial numbers of workers with IT skills out of the industry.[35]

In both IT and engineering, concerns about labor scarcity emerge not just from evidence of employers' recruiting difficulties, but also from the fact that regardless of whether employers *can* adjust to lower numbers of workers or higher wages, these workers are thought to have beneficial effects for the rest of the economy. In other words, if science and technology workers help to fuel innovation and technological advances, increasing the competitiveness of the US economy, it could be a good idea to admit more workers with these skills even if formal indicators do not point to a particular malaise in the market. An extension of this argument is that increasing the supply of workers in science and technology fields makes sense because it allows the United States to develop its human capital pool and thus build or maintain a competitive advantage relative to other countries that have been rapidly developing scientific expertise. These arguments have gained particular traction in light of concerns about the outsourcing of skilled work that has traditionally been considered a US comparative advantage.[36]

3. Low-Wage and Seasonal Jobs?

Finally, US employers have also periodically complained of recruitment difficulties at the low-wage end of the labor market — for example, in hospitality, construction, and various service occupations — especially in times of low unemployment and robust economic growth. One of the main arguments supporting this position is that a progressively more skilled workforce and the retirement of elderly cohorts of workers with lower levels of formal education are leaving behind a smaller share of workers available for less-skilled jobs. On the other side of the ledger, formal indicators of demand for less-skilled workers are not favorable. The real earnings of less-educated workers relative to those with at least some postsecondary education are as low as ever,[37] and unemployment is typically high among many of the traditional candidates for low-wage jobs. Even when national unemployment dipped below 4 percent in 2000, for example, it exceeded 9 percent for workers in their early 20s, and 15 percent for 20- to 24-year-old African Americans.[38]

---

35   Ibid.
36   By contrast, it has also been argued that the outsourcing of technical jobs will reduce the demand for workers and hence makes immigration *less* necessary. See Clair Brown and Greg Linden, "Is There a Shortage of Engineering Talent in the U.S.?" (working paper, Center for Work, Technology, and Society, IRLE, University of California, Berkeley, February 2008), http://escholarship.org/uc/item/86w3r3w5.
37   Anthony Carnevale, Nicole Smith, and Jeff Strohl, *Help Wanted: Projections of Jobs and Education Requirements Through 2018* (Washington, DC: Center on Education and the Workforce, June 2010), www9.georgetown.edu/grad/gppi/hpi/cew/pdfs/FullReport.pdf.
38   CPS data from BLS, "Databases, Tables, and Calculators by Subject," www.bls.gov/data/#unemployment.

Most of the jobs do not require formal qualifications, suggesting that they should be easily accessible to new entrants without experience in the field — although this argument ignores the sometimes significant skills acquired through long-term on-the-job training and experience.

However, various factors make it difficult to match unemployed workers to the jobs that are available. Employers may be unable to raise wages to attract prospective employees while remaining commercially viable. Barriers to work arise from child-care obligations, long commuting times or relocation costs (often known as "spatial mismatches"), or the need to find full-time, year-round work (especially since welfare systems tend to penalize part-time employment). Indeed, some of the low- and middle-skilled occupations in which immigrants are concentrated have a strong cyclical or seasonal character that leads to large fluctuations in demand over the course of the year or the business cycle, making it difficult for employers to meet peak demand from the local labor force.[39]

C. Summary: Assessing the Extent of Labor Shortages

As the previous examples show, behind each occupation lies a complicated story about supply and demand; reward structures that attract the most talented students to certain occupations (and away from others); incentives for training, retention and turnover; and employer recruitment practices, wages, or working conditions. This information can help to explain not just *whether* skills are hard to come by, but also *why*, and how policymakers should respond.

Even when this analytical information is of high quality, however, selecting the right response is not straightforward. The long-run impact of increasing immigration in a given occupation will depend in part on the extent to which immigration either gives employers breathing space to make necessary adjustments, or simply delays the adjustment process by reducing their need to undertake more fundamental changes to employment and training practices. In several highly skilled occupations, meanwhile, there is a strong argument that even substantial adjustments to increase the domestic production and use of skills would still leave immigration an important role. This is especially the case in highly skilled occupations where the role of immigration is not just to fill immediate skills deficits but to build the country's talent pool over time. As a result, deciding on the best response to specific occupational problems — and especially whether increasing immigration in a given case is desirable and sensible — will in many cases be a

---

39 For example, construction-industry unemployment reached a low of 4.5 percent in October 2006 during the US construction boom, before skyrocketing to 18.7 percent in October 2009 with the housing collapse and economic crisis. Even during boom years, seasonal variations meant that occupational unemployment often doubled from peak to trough over a 12-month period. BLS, "Unemployment Rate — Construction Industry, Private and Salary Workers," 2011, http://data.bls.gov/pdq/SurveyOutputServlet?series_id=LNU04032231&-data_tool=XGtable.

qualitative decision requiring subjective judgments on which reasonable analysts will not necessarily agree.

II. The Current US Policy Approach toward Shortages

US policymakers have for the most part remained skeptical about the value of relying on statistical measures of labor needs or scarcity for employment-based immigration.[40] The idea of attempting to identify shortages has recurred periodically in the immigration debate, and the *Immigration Act of 1990* in fact mandated a pilot program within the US Department of Labor to test the idea. But it has never been considered sufficiently palatable or feasible to make its way into law.

However, the goal of meeting specific labor needs is nonetheless built into the design of work visas in the form of the principle of employer selection. For almost all economic-stream flows, employers identify the individual candidates and then sponsor them for admission (in some cases, especially for low-wage jobs, they may delegate this task to recruitment agents).[41] As a result, employment-based immigrants cannot enter unless there is proven demand for their skills, in the form of a job offer from an employer.[42]

Given the difficultly in creating objective or reliable assessments of an economy's labor needs that can match demand with supply in an efficient and timely manner, this mechanism represents one means of "aggregating" diffuse information that individual employers hold about their labor needs. Employer selection alone is not necessarily sufficient to determine that an employer faces recruitment difficulties or that immigration is a sensible response, as discussed shortly. But it does have the overwhelming advantage of removing the need for policymakers to decide, on the basis of highly flawed data and techniques, how to allocate immigration flows across the economy. Equally

---

40 Note, of course, that most immigration to the United States is not explicitly designed to meet labor market needs, but instead to enable family unification. Two-thirds of permanent immigration comes via family routes, and just 6 percent comes as economic-stream principal applicants. Department of Homeland Security (DHS), *Yearbook of Immigration Statistics 2009* (Washington, DC: DHS, 2010), www.dhs.gov/xlibrary/assets/statistics/yearbook/2009/ois_yb_2009.pdf.
41 The exception to this rule is for permanent immigrants with "extraordinary ability" in the arts or sciences, who enter on EB-1(a) visas and do not require an employer sponsor.
42 Within each category, visas are considered in the order received, on a first-come, first-served basis. Processing times for temporary work authorization varies from one to three months, and workers coming from abroad must then apply at a US consulate for a physical visa. Employers with more urgent needs who are willing and able to pay a $1,000 fee for premium processing can have their applications processed within 15 calendar days. US Citizenship and Immigration Services (USCIS), "USCIS Processing Time Information," https://egov.uscis.gov/cris/processTimesDisplayInit.do;jsessionid=cbactdj7Co_zwbb8hNs1s.

importantly, because employers' assessment of skill needs is dynamic and continuously updated, their decisions can react more quickly to changing circumstances than statistical measures relying on past data. (One could even go as far as to say that employer selection is or can be *forward looking*. That is, if any actors are able to *anticipate* skill needs, it is likely to be employers.).

This delegation to employers is not absolute. First, US immigration laws have placed limits on the *number* of immigrants that can be admitted. Periodic adjustments to these numbers have aimed to respond (often unsuccessfully) to evolving or unfolding labor-market needs, although so far the United States has not developed an effective mechanism for doing this systematically.[43] Second, immigration laws and policies still shape and limit immigration flows by imposing criteria on employers, workers, and their jobs. Allowing employers to determine the occupational mix of immigration flows does not eliminate the need to make strategic decisions about the circumstances under which employers should be able to hire foreign workers and the means of prioritizing between large numbers of prospective immigrants seeking admission. However, these strategic choices are much more often made on the basis of workers' human capital than on the specific occupation they will perform in the United States. Still, a limited number of occupation-specific policies have arisen in a few cases in which there has been a specific economic, social, or political rationale for doing so, most notably for agricultural workers, nurses, and a broad set of "high-tech" workers.

A. *Labor Scarcity and the Regulation of Employer Sponsorship*

Employer selection may be essential in selecting workers whose skills are in demand, but it also raises an inevitable question: How can one prevent or at least discourage employers who could have hired locally from hiring foreign workers simply out of preference, in order to pay lower wages, or to avoid training members of the existing labor force?

The US immigration system relies on a number of policies designed to discourage employers from hiring foreign workers unless they face a genuine need, although concrete evidence on their effectiveness is limited.

First, employers may be required to "test" the labor market by advertising vacancies to local workers before hiring workers on temporary visas. This labor-market test is designed to show that no US workers[44]

---

43   Demetrios G. Papademetriou, Doris Meissner, Marc R. Rosenblum, and Madeleine Sumption, *Harnessing the Advantages of Immigration for a Twenty-First Century Economy: A Standing Commission on Labor Markets, Economic Competitiveness, and Immigration* (Washington, DC: Migration Policy Institute, 2009), www.migrationpolicy.org/pubs/StandingCommission_May09.pdf.
44   The term "US workers" is defined as all those authorized to work in the United States (a group that comprises primarily US citizens and green-card holders).

are able, willing, qualified, and available to perform the work — the closest thing to a definition of a shortage in US immigration law.[45] The labor-market test represents a case-by-case determination of labor-market recruiting difficulties, in contrast to the occupation-by-occupation approach described earlier — that is, employers are required to show that they face a shortage in this particular case, but not that there is an occupation-wide recruiting problem.

Labor-market tests are widely used in immigrant-receiving countries, although their impact is uncertain. On the one hand, the process of advertising a vacancy may help to make hiring locally the default option for employers. But if certain employers are determined to hire foreign workers regardless of the state of the local labor market, they may simply reject any candidates who apply on the basis that they are not qualified. For government agencies, determining whether this is true is rather difficult, and active efforts to do so risk becoming overly intrusive and imposing excessive paperwork on employers who play by the rules.

US employers are not required to test the labor market in this way when hiring highly skilled workers for highly skilled H-1B visas, "extraordinary ability" O-1 visas, or permanent residence in the highest skill category (the "first-preference" employment-based green card).[46] This reflects the underlying assumption that skilled immigrants augment the country's human capital pool and do not tend to displace US workers or jeopardize their wages and working conditions — an assumption that receives considerable empirical support.[47] In other words, identifying a "shortage" is less necessary at higher skill levels because the benefits and positive spillovers of these workers are considered significant and the risk of adverse effects on the existing labor force small.

A second mechanism to discourage employers from hiring a foreign worker where they could have recruited locally is to regulate the cost of doing so. This is done in two ways. First, employers are required to

---

45 US House of Representatives, *Admission of Temporary H-2A Workers*, 8 US Code §1188 (2002). For permanent certification, see *Inadmissible Aliens*, 8 US Code §1182 (2001).

46 For various historical reasons, employers who hire workers on temporary visas without the requirement to advertise their job are often required to look for local replacements after the foreign employee has worked with the firm for several years, in order to receive labor certification for a permanent visa. In other words, employers must advertise vacancies that they do not wish to fill. Further complicating the process, they are not allowed to require skills or knowledge that the foreign employee learned on the job. They may also be required to offer prospective "minimally qualified" workers the same salary that their existing, more-experienced employees are *currently* paid. These provisions have received considerable criticism. See Alan Lee, "Important Developments in Labor Certification Applications," *Interpreter Releases* 88, no. 6 (February 2011): 473-9; and Demetrios G. Papademetriou and Stephen Yale-Loehr, *Balancing Interests: Rethinking US Selection of Skilled Immigrants* (Washington, DC: Carnegie Endowment for International Peace, 1996).

47 Will Somerville and Madeleine Sumption, *Immigration and the Labour Market: Theory, Evidence and Policy* (Washington, DC: Migration Policy Institute, 2009), www.migrationpolicy.org/pubs/Immigration-and-the-Labour-Market.pdf.

pay foreign workers the amount that they would pay to other workers in the same position or the regulated "prevailing wage" for their occupation and area (whichever is higher). This requirement was introduced in 1990 to prevent employers from hiring foreign workers simply to pay lower wages. The methodology for determining what the prevailing wage should be has, however, occasionally provoked debate.[48]

Visa fees also increase the cost of hiring foreign workers, making this a less-attractive option in cases in which local workers are, in fact, available. Visa fees have fluctuated over time, although the basic trajectory has been upward. In addition to a processing fee for all temporary visas (currently $325), employers pay separate fees for certain work visas. Most notably, Congress introduced an additional H-1B visa fee of $500 in 1998,[49] increasing it to $1,000 in 2000[50] and to $2,000 in 2004 (the latter included a new $500 fee to fund "fraud detection").[51] In 2010 a further $2,000 was added to these amounts for employers considered "dependent" on temporary foreign workers (defined as employers with more than 50 employees and more than 50 percent of their employees on H-1B or L-1 visas).[52]

In some cases, visa fees have also been used to create an explicit link between immigration and other policies to address labor scarcity, such as workforce development. Most of the additional fees introduced since 1998 for H-1B employers have been earmarked for education and training programs designed to increase the supply of qualified US workers. These fees have been used for a variety of purposes, including scholarships for low-income students in STEM fields and grants for training programs disbursed by the National Science Foundation and the US Department of Labor — although total revenues from the fees are relatively modest.[53] New or increased fees have typically been introduced at the same time as increases in the number of H-1B visas available. (The 1998 and 2000 legislation increased fees and raised the basic H-1B cap, while the 2004 fee increase came at the same time as an extra 20,000 visas for US-educated master's students were added.)

---

48 This is in part because prevailing wages are calculated by occupation, making them subject to the same risks of inaccuracy that plague occupational shortage analysis, described earlier.
49 US House of Representatives, *American Competitiveness and Workforce Improvement Act of 1998*, Public Law 105-277, 112, U.S. Statutes at Large 2681 (1998).
50 US House of Representatives, *American Competitiveness in the Twenty-First Century Act*, Public Law 106-313, 114, U.S. Statutes at Large 1251 (2000).
51 US House of Representatives, *H-1B Visa Reform Act of 2004*, HR 4818, 108th Cong. 2nd sess. This legislation also created a lower fee of $750 for small businesses (those with 25 or fewer employees).
52 L-1 visas are for intracompany transferees moving between offices of a multinational firm.
53 A small proportion of the training fee also went to USCIS to speed up processing times. For more details on the allocation of the fees, see Linda Levine, *Programs Funded by the H-1B Visa Education and Training Fee, and Labor Market Conditions for Information Technology Workers* (Washington, DC: Congressional Research Service, 2007), http://assets.opencrs.com/rpts/RL31973_20071005.pdf.

Finally, US law imposes restrictions on the duration of visaholders' stays. At the highly skilled level, workers receive temporary visas lasting several years and are able to apply for permanent residence if an employer is willing to sponsor them. Employers seeking to hire foreign workers in less-skilled or low-wage jobs (on H-2B visas), however, can retain workers for no more than one year (renewable twice under "extraordinary circumstances"). As part of the application, they must provide evidence that the employee is needed for seasonal, intermittent, peak-load, or one-off work.[54] In practice, this requirement limits the number of occupations in which employers are able to hire less-skilled workers, albeit without specifying particular occupations that are or are not eligible. The economic rationale behind it is that meeting large variations in staffing is difficult when the local labor force is small and its members typically prefer year-round work (this is especially the case in rural areas — for example, in hotels or ski resorts with significant workload fluctuations), and that allowing employers to meet these seasonal variations by hiring foreign workers may allow them to sustain a larger and more-productive, year-round workforce. As a result, temporary seasonal workers are thought less likely to undermine the wages or job prospects of existing workers, although labor unions and groups advocating restricted immigration strongly contest this presumption.

Strictly temporary migration programs at the low-skilled level are partly based on the assumption that at this level "shortages" of labor for ongoing, year-round jobs are rare. As noted in Chapter 1 of this book, economists disagree about the extent to which this is the case (and whether local workers are *willing* to take certain work).[55] In practice, however, the desire to restrict less-skilled migration to temporary jobs stems not just from this type of economic reasoning, but also from uncertainty about less-skilled immigrants' long-term integration prospects.

B. Occupation-Specific Immigration Policies

For the most part, the US system does not attempt to channel immigration into specific types of jobs, but relies on employer sponsorship to determine the occupational mix.[56] Some notable exceptions to this principle exist, however.

---

54 H-2B visas are for nonagricultural work. As discussed earlier, a separate temporary visa exists for agricultural workers. For more details on H-2B visas, see the US Department of Labor (DOL), "H-2B Certification for Temporary Non-Agricultural Work," 2011, www.foreignlaborcert.doleta.gov/h-2b.cfm.

55 See Chapter 1 of this volume by Harry J. Holzer, "Immigration Policy and Less-Skilled Workers in the United States: Reflections on Future Directions for Reform."

56 A distinction is made between the skill levels required for specific jobs. In order to qualify for an H-1B visa (designed to bring skilled workers into areas of strong employer demand) workers must work in a "professional" occupation; however, these occupations are defined broadly and justified on a case-by-case basis, rather than through a specific list of "approved" occupations.

Like most immigrant-receiving countries, the United States recognizes the specific circumstances of certain components of the agricultural sector in its work authorization laws.[57] A dedicated temporary agricultural visa (the H-2A visa) was carved out of the existing H-2 visa (whose origins go back to the 1952 legislation) as part of a 1986 law that legalized 2.6 million unauthorized workers, including 1.1 million agricultural workers.[58] This "new" visa program was in large part designed to allay concerns about a potential reduction in the numbers of agricultural laborers if the legalized population took advantage of their new status to leave for other, more attractive occupations. The same law also foresaw an additional "replenishment agricultural worker" program, which would be activated during the 1990-93 period if it was determined that an agricultural labor shortage existed (this determination would take place according to a complicated formula comparing projected supply and demand, laid out in detail in the legislation).[59] No such shortage was ever identified.[60] The basic H-2A visa for temporary agricultural workers, however, remains in place today.

The nursing profession has also been the subject of periodic occupation-specific visa arrangements. In 1989 the *Immigration Nursing Relief Act* (INRA) responded to widespread concerns about an inadequate nursing workforce by creating a dedicated temporary visa for registered nurses (RNs). This provision was allowed to expire in 1995, but a similar visa (known as the H-1C) was created in 1999, albeit limited to 500 places per year and reserved exclusively for nurses working in disadvantaged areas.[61] Authorization for this visa was renewed once, in 2005,[62] before expiring in 2009.[63] A bill to extend the visa further was introduced in the House of Representatives in 2010 but died in committee.[64] While no longer in force, one interesting feature of these nursing provisions is that the conditions attached to the visas created an explicit link between immigration and other policies to address labor supply problems. Employers hiring nurses under the H-1A or H-1C were required to attest that they had made efforts to develop the nursing workforce, such as by operating or financing a training program for

---

57 See Demetrios G. Papademetriou and Monica L. Heppel, *Balancing Acts: Toward a Fair Bargain on Seasonal Agricultural Workers* (Washington, DC: Brookings Institution Press, 1999).
58 Donald M. Kerwin, *More than IRCA: US Legalization Programs and the Current Policy Debate* (Washington, DC: Migration Policy Institute, 2010), www.migrationpolicy.org/pubs/legalization-historical.pdf.
59 *Immigration and Nationality Act*, US Code 8 § 201(a).
60 Government Printing Office, *Federal Register* vol. 61, no. 19, January 29, 1996, www.gpo.gov/fdsys/pkg/FR-1996-01-29/pdf/96-1294.pdf.
61 US House of Representatives, *Nursing Relief for Disadvantaged Areas Act of 1999* (NRDAA), HR 441, 106th Cong., 1st sess.
62 US House of Representatives, *Nursing Relief for Disadvantaged Areas Reauthorization Act of 2005* (NRDARA), HR 1285, 109th Cong. 2nd sess.
63 DOL, "H-1C Nurses for Disadvantaged Areas," http://webapps.dol.gov/libraryforms/go-us-dol-form.asp?FormNumber=4.
64 US House of Representatives, *Underserved Area Nursing Relief Restoration Act*, H.R. 5687, 111th Congress, 2nd sess.

RNs, providing career development to prospective nurses, restructuring work schedules or workloads, and various other activities.[65] In practice, however, many immigration policy practitioners believe that these provisions have had little impact, serving primarily to raise the barriers to recruiting foreign workers rather than to make a genuine impact on the supply of trained nurses.

Currently, nurses must typically enter on permanent visas since most do not meet the skill criteria for the H-1B temporary visa, which requires a bachelor's degree or higher and work in a job that demands this level of education (for example, they might work in a specialism within the nursing profession, such as acute care).[66] The numbers entering on H-1B visas are therefore quite small.[67] A pathway also exists for Mexican and Canadian nurses, who can enter on the TN visa created as part of the North American Free Trade Agreement (NAFTA). However, the majority of employment-based immigrants in nursing must wait for a permanent visa, and waiting times can be quite substantial (often several years). As a result, employment-based immigration is not the main route for foreign health professionals to enter the country.[68] Instead, health-care employers rely more heavily on immigrants already in the country who arrived through other routes: family unification, humanitarian migrants, or the unauthorized (the latter especially in occupations that require little training or few credentials, such as home health aides and attendants).[69]

Finally, STEM occupations receive special treatment in various ways. For student visaholders with a US education in STEM subjects, post-study work authorization is extended from the standard 12 months

---

65 *Code of Federal Regulations*, "Employees' Benefits," title 20, sec 655.3.
66 DOL, "H-1C Nurses in Disadvantaged Areas."
67 In fiscal year 2010, just over 1,000 H-1B labor condition applications were approved for registered nurses, the vast majority of which were for a specific nursing specialization. A much smaller number is likely to have entered on H-1B visas, since fewer than half of all labor condition applications lead to an employer visa petition and subsequently to a worker entering the United States. MPI calculations from the Foreign Labor Certification (FLC) Data Center, "H-1B Program Data," http://flcdatacenter.com/CaseH1B.aspx.
68 Randy Capps, Michael Fix, and Serena Yi-Ying Lin, *Still an Hourglass? Immigrant Workers in Middle-Skilled Jobs* (Washington, DC: Migration Policy Institute, September 2010); and Demetrios G. Papademetriou and Madeleine Sumption, *The Role of Immigration in Fostering Competitiveness in the United States* (Washington, DC: Migration Policy Institute, 2011), www.migrationpolicy.org/pubs/competitiveness-US.pdf.
69 Note that US law also includes some limited provisions exempting employers from the labor market test when sponsoring immigrants for permanent residence in occupations deemed to face a shortage. These occupations are known as "Schedule A" occupations, in which the DOL has "determined that there are not sufficient United States workers who are able, willing, qualified, and available." Only physical therapists and nurses are included on Schedule A. See DOL, "Permanent Labor Certification," www.foreignlaborcert.doleta.gov/perm.cfm.

to a total of 29 months.[70] This makes it easier for US employers to hire science and technology graduates and to sponsor them for permanent residence. Over the past few years, several legislative proposals aiming to retain STEM graduates or increase their flows have attracted attention. These proposals would either raise numerical limits on green cards or H-1B visas for advanced STEM degree graduates from US universities, or exempt these individuals from numerical limits entirely.[71]

III. Conclusion

US employment-based immigration rules are designed to meet labor or skill shortages by relying on employer selection and an accompanying set of regulatory requirements. With some important exceptions in the health-care and STEM fields, the system does not isolate specific occupational skills for preferential treatment, in contrast to the approach used in some other countries, such as the United Kingdom.

Should the US system do more to fine-tune immigration by occupation? Any attempt to do this would likely rely on one of two approaches. First, employers hiring in certain occupations could receive exemptions from regulatory requirements such as the labor-market test (a policy designed to ascertain whether a shortage exists) or from visa fees. Absent any change in regulatory requirements and fees, the impact of this policy would probably not be dramatic: all employers would still have the ability to sponsor workers but the cost of doing so would vary somewhat by occupation.

Second, some might propose that occupation-based policy should be used to make more visas available to shortage occupations and/or fewer available to those in which shortages have *not* been identified. This option presents a host of analytical and operational difficulties, the scale of which would depend on how significantly it changed the distribution of visas (and in particular, whether and how substantially it would reduce the number of visas available to occupations not deemed to face a shortage). Using occupational analysis to restrict immigration into some jobs at the expense of others is problematic in light of the impossibility of creating a uniformly accurate and reliable measure of skill shortfalls, as well as the difficulty in identifying the root causes of any shortages and responding to evolving labor-market data in a timely manner. Most importantly, employers might face recruiting difficulties regardless of

---

70 This extension took effect in April 2008 and employers can only take advantage if they are signed up to participate in E-Verify, a program for verifying employees' work authorization status. See Government Printing Office, *Federal Register* 73, no. 68 (April 8, 2008), www.gpo.gov/fdsys/pkg/FR-2008-04-08/pdf/E8-7427.pdf.

71 See, for example, US House of Representatives, *Staple Act*, HR 1791, 111th Cong., 1st sess., www.gpo.gov/fdsys/pkg/BILLS-111hr1791ih/pdf/BILLS-111hr1791ih.pdf; and US House of Representatives, *Comprehensive Immigration Reform Act*, S 3932, 111th Cong., 2nd sess., www.gpo.gov/fdsys/pkg/BILLS-111s3932is/pdf/BILLS-111s3932is.pdf.

whether their occupation is on a shortage list. Relative to systems that rely on shortage lists, therefore, the current case-by-case approach has the advantage of vastly superior information.

A problem that arises when considering ways to align immigration policy to occupational demand is that the concept of occupational shortages is both most useful and most difficult to apply in the case of low- and middle-skilled jobs. In highly skilled or highly paid jobs (especially at the very top of the skill spectrum), there is often little need for governments to identify particular occupational skills to prioritize in the immigration system. Immigrants with the skills required to secure a job in a well-paying occupation tend to qualify for immigration on the basis of their human capital and present fewer concerns about competition for jobs. At the same time, statistical analysis is likely to be less accurate in identifying shortages in highly skilled occupations and more likely to ignore subtle distinctions in the knowledge and experience required for a particular position.[72]

It is at the low-skilled level that the drive to prevent the displacement of US workers by ensuring that foreign workers only fill jobs that face shortages is most acute. Even if many economists agree that at least some employment-based immigration into these jobs can be beneficial, deciding which workers to admit for which jobs is much more difficult. One cannot, by definition, require high wages or high levels of human capital, and the vocational skills these jobs may require are often difficult to capture in the simplistic ways that immigration policies tend to demand. Meanwhile, substantially raising employer fees could help to screen out some employers who could have hired locally, but it might also simply reduce firms' ability to operate on US soil or encourage them to opt out of the legal immigration system and hire unauthorized workers. At the same time, decisions about the less-skilled occupations in which immigration is most necessary depend in large part on subjective judgments. For example, one could argue that poultry processing is an inherently unattractive occupation to which native-born workers are unlikely to aspire, while some other initially low-wage jobs in construction or manufacturing are both more appealing and offer better opportunities for long-term wage and skill growth. Does this mean that low-wage or low-skilled immigration should only be allowed into "undesirable" occupations? If so, how would policymakers possibly distinguish systematically between the two?

At the low-skilled level, the US response to this dilemma has been to restrict immigration to seasonal, one-off, or otherwise temporary work. This position has some theoretical appeal and is common among immigrant-receiving countries. However, the presence of a large unau-

---

72 Even if the average accuracy of the shortage list can be increased using subjective information and judgments specific to each occupation (as in the United Kingdom, for example), this does not remove the underlying need to group jobs into a manageable number of occupations.

thorized workforce in the United States suggests that the current range of strictly temporary foreign worker programs alone has not been able to meet strong demand for immigration into less-skilled occupations. This raises the difficult question to what extent immigration policy should accommodate employer demand even in the absence of objective evidence of recruiting difficulties.

Finally, many workers admitted for employment ultimately gain permanent residence. If workers are brought to the country to perform specific tasks or occupations, it matters whether that demand is transient or persistent. Complaints about the insufficient pipeline workers in some occupations, particularly in health care, are expected to be relatively persistent; but some specialized and relatively well-paid construction jobs that experienced extremely high demand just a few years ago now have been decimated in the wake of the housing crash, deep economic crisis, and slow recovery. Indeed, the recent economic turmoil in the United States has underscored the dramatic and unpredictable instability of certain occupations compared to others.[73]

As a result, employment-based immigration systems that allow a transition to long-term or permanent residence must not only admit workers who meet current labor demand, but also select and retain those with the potential to integrate and find sustainable employment opportunities in the long run.[74] Ultimately, this ability is likely to rest on language proficiency, human capital, and the ability to learn and adapt to a changing labor market, and not just from specific occupational skills. ⤴

---

[73] Large numbers of young immigrant men from Latin America, for example, flocked to the country during the economic boom and worked their way up career ladders in construction, but have subsequently faced soaring rates of unemployment. Of course, most of the immigrant construction workforce did not come on employment-based visas (more than half — an estimated 1.7 million individuals — were unauthorized in 2008 and most of the rest would have come through family unification provisions). Jeff Passel and D'Vera Cohn, *A Portrait of Unauthorized Immigrants in the United States* (Washington, DC: Pew Hispanic Center, 2009), http://pewhispanic.org/files/reports/107.pdf. For a broader discussion of the economic crisis and its effects on immigrant employment in the United States, see Demetrios G. Papademetriou and Aaron Terrazas, "Immigrants and the US Economic Crisis: From Recession to Recovery," in *Migration and Immigrants Two Years After the Financial Collapse: Where Do We Stand*, eds., Demetrios G. Papademetriou, Madeleine Sumption, and Aaron Terrazas (Washington, DC: Migration Policy Institute and BBC World Service, 2010), www.migrationpolicy.org/pubs/MPI-BBCreport-2010.pdf; and Capps, Fix, and Lin, *Still an Hourglass?*

[74] Demetrios G. Papademetriou, Doris Meissner, Marc R. Rosenblum, and Madeleine Sumption, *Aligning Temporary Immigration Visas with US Labor Market Needs: The Case for a New System of Provisional Visas* (Washington, DC: Migration Policy Institute, 2009), www.migrationpolicy.org/pubs/Provisional_visas.pdf.

Works Cited

Aiken, Linda and Robyn Cheung. 2008. Nurse Workforce Challenges in the United States: Implications for Policy. OECD Health Working Papers No. 35, Organization for Economic Cooperation and Development, Paris. www.oecd.org/dataoecd/34/9/41431864.pdf.

Alpert, Andrew and Jill Auyer. 2003. *The 1988-2000 Employment Projections: How Accurate Were They?* Washington, DC: Bureau of Labor Statistics. www.bls.gov/opub/ooq/2003/spring/art01.pdf.

Blinder, Alan. 2006. Offshoring: The Next Industrial Revolution? *Foreign Affairs* 85 (2): 113–28.

Brown, Clair and Greg Linden. 2008. Is There a Shortage of Engineering Talent in the U.S.? Working Paper, Center for Work, Technology, and Society, IRLE, University of California, Berkeley, February 2008. http://escholarship.org/uc/item/86w3r3w5.

Buerhaus, Peter, David Auerbach, and Douglas Staiger. 2009. The Recent Surge in Nurse Employment: Causes and Implications. *Health Affairs* 28 (4): 657–68. www.healthstaff.org/documents/surgeinnurseemployment.pdf.

Cappelli, Peter. 2000. *Is There a Shortage of Information Technology Workers?* A Report to McKinsey and Company for the "War for Technical Talent" Project, Wharton School, University of Pennsylvania. http://knowledge.wharton.upenn.edu/papers/979.pdf.

Capps, Randy, Michael Fix, and Serena Yi-Ying Lin. 2010. *Still an Hourglass? Immigrant Workers in Middle-Skilled Jobs.* Washington, DC: Migration Policy Institute.

Carnevale, Anthony, Nicole Smith, and Jeff Strohl. 2010. *Help Wanted: Projections of Jobs and Education Requirements through 2018.* Washington, DC: Center on Education and the Workforce. www9.georgetown.edu/grad/gppi/hpi/cew/pdfs/FullReport.pdf.

Carnevale, Anthony, Nicole Smith, and Michelle Melton. 2011. *STEM*. Washington, DC: Center on Education and the Workforce. www9.georgetown.edu/grad/gppi/hpi/cew/pdfs/stem-complete.pdf.

Code of Federal Regulations. Title 20. Employees' Benefits.

Cohen, Malcolm. 1995. *Labor Shortages as America Approaches the Twenty-first Century*. Ann Arbor, MI: University of Michigan Press.

Freeman, Peter and William Aspray. 1999. *The Supply of Information Technology Workers in the United States.* Washington, DC: Computing Research Organization. http://archive.cra.org/reports/wits/charts_figs_boxes_tables.pdf.

Foreign Labor Certification (FLC) Data Center. H-1B Program Data. http://flcdatacenter.com/CaseH1B.aspx.

Government Printing Office. 1996. *Federal Register* 61 (19), January 29, 1996. www.gpo.gov/fdsys/pkg/FR-1996-01-29/pdf/96-1294.pdf.

———. 2008. *Federal Register* 73 (68), April 8, 2008. www.gpo.gov/fdsys/pkg/FR-2008-04-08/pdf/E8-7427.pdf.

Holzer, Harry. 2013. Immigration Policy and Less Skilled Workers in the United States. In *Immigrants in a Changing Labor Market: Responding to Economic Needs*, eds. Michael Fix, Demetrios G. Papademetriou, and Madeleine Sumption. Washington, DC: Migration Policy Institute.

Institute of Medicine. 2011. *The Future of Nursing: Leading Change, Advancing Health.* Washington, DC: The National Academies Press. https://folio.iupui.edu/bitstream/handle/10244/911/Future%20of%20Nursing_Leading%20Change%20Advancing%20Health.pdf?sequence=1.

Kerwin, Donald M. 2010. *More than IRCA: US Legalization Programs and the Current Policy Debate*. Washington, DC: Migration Policy Institute. www.migrationpolicy.org/pubs/legalization-historical.pdf.

Lee, Alan. 2011. Important Developments in Labor Certification Applications. *Interpreter Releases* 88 (6): 473-9.

Levine, Linda. 2007. *Programs Funded by the H-1B Visa Education and Training Fee, and Labor Market Conditions for Information Technology Workers*. Washington, DC: Congressional Research Service. http://assets.opencrs.com/rpts/RL31973_20071005.pdf.

Long, Mark C., Marsha G. Goldfarb, and Robert S. Goldfarb. 2008. Explanations for Persistent Nursing Shortages. *Forum for Health Economics and Policy* 11 (2): Article 10.

Lowell, Lindsay B., Hal Salzman, and Hamutal Bernstein. 2009. *Steady as She Goes? Three Generations of Students through the Science and Engineering Pipeline*. Washington, DC: Institute for the Study of International Migration. http://policy.rutgers.edu/faculty/salzman/steadyasshegoes.pdf.

Manpower. Various years. Talent Shortage Survey. http://us.manpower.com/us/en/multimedia/Global-Shortage-Survey-Results.pdf.

Mouw, Ted and Arne Kalleberg. 2010. Occupations and the Structure of Wage Inequality in the United States, 1980s to 2000s. *American Sociological Review* 75 (3): 402–31.

National Science Foundation (NSF). 2012. *Science and Engineering Indicators 2012*. Arlington, VA: National Science Foundation. www.nsf.gov/statistics/seind12/.

Newschaffer, Craig J. and Julie A Schoenman. 1990. Registered Nurse Shortages: The Road to Appropriate Public Policy. *Health Affairs* 9 (1): 98–106.

Papademetriou, Demetrios G. and Aaron Terrazas. 2010. Immigrants and the US Economic Crisis: From Recession to Recovery. In *Migration and Immigrants Two Years After the Financial Collapse: Where Do We Stand*, eds. Demetrios G. Papademetriou, Madeleine Sumption, and Aaron Terrazas. Washington, DC: Migration Policy Institute and BBC World Service. www.migrationpolicy.org/pubs/MPI-BBCreport-2010.pdf.

Papademetriou, Demetrios G. and Madeleine Sumption. 2011. *The Role of Immigration in Fostering Competitiveness in the United States*. Washington, DC: Migration Policy Institute. www.migrationpolicy.org/pubs/competitiveness-US.pdf.

Papademetriou, Demetrios G. and Monica L. Heppel. 1999. *Balancing Acts: Toward a Fair Bargain on Seasonal Agricultural Workers*. Washington, DC: Brookings Institution Press.

Papademetriou, Demetrios G. and Stephen Yale-Loehr. 1996. *Balancing Interests: Rethinking US Selection of Skilled Immigrants.* Washington, DC: Carnegie Endowment for International Peace.

Papademetriou, Demetrios G., Doris Meissner, Marc R. Rosenblum, and Madeleine Sumption. 2009. *Aligning Temporary Immigration Visas with US Labor Market Needs: The Case for a New System of Provisional Visas.* Washington, DC: Migration Policy Institute. www.migrationpolicy.org/pubs/Provisional_visas.pdf.

———. 2009. *Harnessing the Advantages of Immigration for a Twenty-First Century Economy: A Standing Commission on Labor Markets, Economic Competitiveness, and Immigration.* Washington, DC: Migration Policy Institute. www.migrationpolicy.org/pubs/StandingCommission_May09.pdf.

Passel, Jeff and D'Vera Cohn. 2009. *A Portrait of Unauthorized Immigrants in the United States.* Washington, DC: Pew Hispanic Center. http://pewhispanic.org/files/reports/107.pdf.

Peri, Giovanni. 2009. The Impact of Immigrants in Recession and Expansion. In *Immigrants in a Changing Labor Market: Responding to Economic Needs,* eds. Michael Fix, Demetrios G. Papademetriou, and Madeleine Sumption. Washington, DC: Migration Policy Institute.

Smith, Brad. 2011. Testimony of General Counsel and Senior Vice President, Legal Corporate Affairs, Microsoft, before the US Senate Committee on the Judiciary, Subcommittee on Immigration, Refugees, and Border Security. *The Economic Imperative for Immigration Reform: High-Skilled Immigration as a Driver of Economic Growth,* 112th Cong., 1st sess., July 26, 2011. www.judiciary.senate.gov/pdf/11-7-26%20Smith%20Testimony.pdf.

Somerville, Will and Madeleine Sumption. 2009. *Immigration and the Labour Market: Theory, Evidence and Policy.* Washington, DC: Migration Policy Institute. www.migrationpolicy.org/pubs/Immigration-and-the-Labour-Market.pdf.

Sumption, Madeleine. 2011. Filling Labor Shortages through Immigration: An Overview of Shortage Lists and their Implications. *Migration Information Source,* February 2011. www.migrationinformation.org/Feature/display.cfm?ID=828.

US Bureau of Labor Statistics (BLS). Databases, Tables, and Calculators by Subject. www.bls.gov/data/#unemployment.

———. Table A-5. Employment Status of the Civilian Noninstitutional Population 25 Years and Older by Educational Attainment, Seasonally Adjusted. www.bls.gov/web/empsit/cpseea05.pdf.

———. Table A-30. Unemployed Persons by Industry and Sex. www.bls.gov/web/empsit/cpseea30.pdf.

———. 2010. Employment, Hours, and Earnings from the Current Employment Statistics survey (National). Nursing and Residential Care Facilities. www.bls.gov/ces/#data.

———. 2010. Employment, Hours, and Earnings from the Current Employment Statistics survey (National). Total Nonfarm Employment. www.bls.gov/ces/#data.

———. 2011. Current Population Survey. www.bls.gov/data/#unemployment.

———. 2011. Unemployment Rate — Construction Industry, Private and Salary Workers. http://data.bls.gov/pdq/SurveyOutputServlet?series_id=L-NU04032231&data_tool=XGtable.

US Census Bureau. 2011. Table 302. Bachelor's Degrees Earned by Field. www.census.gov/compendia/statab/cats/education/higher_education_degrees.html.

———. 2011. Table 303. Master's and Doctorate's Degrees Earned by Field. www.census.gov/compendia/statab/cats/education/higher_education_degrees.html.

US Citizenship and Immigration Services (USCIS). USCIS Processing Time Information. https://egov.uscis.gov/cris/processTimesDisplayInit.do;jsessionid=cbactdj7Co_zwbb8hNs1s.

US Congress. House of Representatives. *Admission of Temporary H-2A Workers*. 8 U.S. Code §1188 (2002).

———. *American Competitiveness and Workforce Improvement Act of 1998*. Public Law 105-277, 112. U.S. Statutes at Large 2681 (1998).

———. *American Competitiveness in the Twenty-First Century Act of 2000*. Public Law 106-313, 114. U.S. Statutes at Large 1251 (2000).

———. *Comprehensive Immigration Reform Act*. S 3932. 111th Cong., 2nd sess. www.gpo.gov/fdsys/pkg/BILLS-111s3932is/pdf/BILLS-111s3932is.pdf.

———. *H-1B Visa Reform Act of 2004*. HR 4818. 108th Cong. 2nd sess.

———. *Immigration and Nationality Act*. US Code. Title 8, sec. 201(a)

———. *Inadmissible Aliens*. 8 U.S. Code §1182 (2001).

———. *Nursing Relief for Disadvantaged Areas Act of 1999 (NRDAA)*. HR 441. 106th Cong. 1st sess.

———. *Nursing Relief for Disadvantaged Areas Reauthorization Act of 2005 (NRDARA)*. HR 1285. 109th Cong. 2nd sess.

———. *Staple Act*. HR 1791. 111th Cong., 1st sess. www.gpo.gov/fdsys/pkg/BILLS-111hr1791ih/pdf/BILLS-111hr1791ih.pdf.

———. *Underserved Area Nursing Relief Restoration Act*. HR 5687, 111th Cong., 2nd sess. www.gpo.gov/fdsys/pkg/BILLS-111hr5687ih/pdf/BILLS-111hr5687ih.pdf.

US Department of Homeland Security (DHS). 2010. *Yearbook of Immigration Statistics 2009*. Washington, DC: Department of Homeland Security. www.dhs.gov/xlibrary/assets/statistics/yearbook/2009/ois_yb_2009.pdf.

US Department of Labor. 2010. H-1C Nurses in Disadvantaged Areas. www.foreignlaborcert.doleta.gov/h-1c.cfm.

———. 2011. H-2B Certification for Temporary Non-Agricultural Work. www.foreignlaborcert.doleta.gov/h-2b.cfm.

———. 2011. Permanent Labor Certification. www.foreignlaborcert.doleta.gov/perm.cfm.

Veneri, Carolyn. 1999. Can Occupational Labor Shortages Be Identified Using Available Data. *Monthly Labor Review*, March 1999. www.bls.gov/opub/mlr/1999/03/art2full.pdf.

PART TWO

NEW BARRIERS TO IMMIGRANT INTEGRATION IN A WEAK ECONOMY

CHAPTER 5

HOW IMMIGRANTS AND US NATIVES FARE DURING RECESSIONS AND RECOVERIES

By Pia M. Orrenius
Federal Reserve Bank of Dallas and Institute for the Study of Labor (IZA)

Madeline Zavodny
Agnes Scott College and IZA

Introduction[1]

Employment plunged and unemployment surged for native and immigrants alike during the Great Recession. The recession officially began in December 2007 and ended in June 2009, but the labor market has remained weak and the recovery sluggish. As of mid-2012, employment was still almost 5 million below its level at the start of the recession. All demographic groups experienced job losses, but some groups were more adversely affected than others. Repeating the pattern of most previous downturns, the recession's impact was felt most by less-educated and minority workers.[2]

Immigrants were particularly hard hit during the recession, especially during its early phases. Immigrants also saw their employment rebound more strongly than natives during the early part of the recovery.[3] The large size of the immigrant population makes it important

---

[1] The views expressed herein do not necessarily reflect the views of the Federal Reserve Bank of Dallas or the Federal Reserve System. This chapter is a revised and updated version of the 2009 report, *Tied to the Business Cycle: How Immigrants Fare in Good and Bad Economic Times*, available at www.migrationpolicy.org/pubs/orrenius-Nov09.pdf.

[2] See Hilary W. Hoynes, Douglas L. Miller, and Jessamyn Schaller, "Who Suffers During Recessions?" (NBER working paper 17951, National Bureau of Economic Research, Cambridge, MA, 2012), http://nber.org/papers/w17951.

[3] Rakesh Kochhar with C. Soledad Espinoza and Rebecca Hinze-Pifer, *After the Great Recession: Foreign Born Gain Jobs; Native Born Lose Jobs* (Washington, DC: Pew Hispanic Center, 2010), www.pewhispanic.org/files/reports/129.pdf.

to understand the extent and causes of differences in the recession's impact on the foreign born versus US natives. Immigrants comprise 13 percent of the US population and an even larger share — over 16 percent — of the labor force.[4] Immigrants are overrepresented in the labor force mainly because they are more likely to be of working age and less likely to be enrolled in school than the general population.

By almost any measure, immigrants fared poorly during the recession. Among immigrant-headed households, real median household income in 2008 was 5.3 percent lower than in 2007, and the poverty rate among immigrants rose to 17.8 percent from 16.5 percent.[5] Before the recession, the unemployment rate among immigrants had hit a low of 3.4 percent. It then rose to a high of 10.2 percent. In contrast, natives' unemployment rate increased from a low of 4.3 percent to a high of 9.7 percent.[6]

Immigrants are vulnerable to economic downturns in large part because of their relatively low average education levels. While immigrants account for about one-sixth of all workers, they make up two-fifths of workers who do not have a high school diploma or equivalent and three-quarters of workers who have completed at most eighth grade.[7] Employment tends to be very cyclical among low-skilled workers. When the economy slows, employers look to shed their least productive employees first. Employers tend to invest less in training low-skilled workers and therefore have less incentive to try to keep them during layoffs. Less-skilled workers may also be displaced by high-skilled workers who move down the skill chain during a recession.[8]

Low-skilled immigrants, particularly recent arrivals, face additional difficulties. Over half of all immigrants and three-quarters of those who have not completed high school report that they cannot speak English very well.[9] In addition, immigrants tend to have less social capital, meaning fewer connections and less knowledge about labor markets, than low-skilled natives. Such difficulties are compounded by a lack of legal status for some 8 million unauthorized immigrant

---

4   Authors' calculations from 2010 American Community Survey (ACS) data from the Integrated Public Use Microdata Series (IPUMS), www.ipums.umn.edu.

5   See US Census Bureau, "Income, Poverty, and Health Insurance Coverage in the United States: 2008," www.census.gov/prod/2009pubs/p60-236.pdf.

6   Immigrant unemployment bottomed out in the fourth quarter of 2006 and native unemployment in the second quarter of 2007. Authors' calculations from the Current Population Survey (CPS) outgoing rotation group data from NBER.

7   Authors' calculations from the 2011 CPS outgoing rotation group data.

8   Paul J. Devereux, "Cyclical Quality Adjustment in the Labor Market," *Southern Economic Journal* 70, no. 3 (2004): 600–15.

9   Authors' calculations from 2010 ACS data among immigrants aged 16 and older. Over 80 percent of immigrants aged 25 and older who have not completed high school report that they cannot speak English very well.

workers.[10] Discrimination against immigrants, many of whom are racial or ethnic minorities, may be greater during downturns, when employers have more potential employees to choose from when hiring.[11]

Although immigrants' relatively low average skill levels make this group particularly vulnerable during recessions, other factors may partly offset this effect. Immigrants tend to be more mobile than natives, both geographically and across industries and occupations.[12] If immigrants are quicker to search for and find alternative employment than natives, their unemployment spells may be shorter. Immigrant inflows may slow during recessions, particularly among unauthorized and employment-based legal immigrants, and some immigrants may even return home as their economic prospects worsen during a downturn. Both behaviors reduce the competition for jobs. In addition, if immigrants who lose their jobs leave, the employment rate among remaining immigrants will be higher. Similarly, larger influxes of immigrants into the United States in search of jobs during recoveries would dampen the cyclicality of immigrants' labor-market outcomes.

Immigrants' vulnerabilities appear to have outweighed these advantages during the Great Recession, which disproportionately hurt their labor-market prospects. Job losses were larger among immigrants than among natives, and their unemployment rate rose more.[13] The impact was exacerbated by immigrants' overrepresentation in certain sectors, such as construction, that experienced the brunt of the downturn.[14] Among immigrants in the construction sector, the unemployment rate was over 17 percent in the first half of 2009.[15]

In sum, largely due to their lower skill levels, immigrants saw a larger overall decline in employment and a correspondingly larger increase in unemployment than natives during the recession. In other words, immigrants' labor-market outcomes deteriorated more than natives' outcomes during the recession primarily because immigrants were

---

10 Jeffrey Passel and D'Vera Cohn, *A Portrait of Unauthorized Immigrants in the United States* (Washington, DC: Pew Hispanic Center, 2009), http://pewhispanic.org/files/reports/107.pdf.
11 Recent research finds that discrimination against women and Hispanics, although not African Americans, increases during downturns. See Jeff E. Biddle and Daniel S. Hamermesh, "Wage Discrimination over the Business Cycle" (IZA discussion paper 6445, IZA, Bonn, Germany, 2012), http://ftp.iza.org/dp6445.pdf.
12 See George J. Borjas, "Does Immigration Grease the Wheels of the Labor Market?" *Brookings Papers on Economic Activity*, no. 1 (2001): 69–119.
13 See Steven A. Camarota and Karen Jensenius, *Trends in Immigrant and Native Employment* (Washington, DC: Center for Immigration Studies, 2009), www.cis.org/articles/2009/back509.pdf; Rakesh Kochhar, *Latino Workers in the Ongoing Recession: 2007 to 2008* (Washington, DC: Pew Hispanic Center, 2008), http://pewhispanic.org/files/reports/99.pdf; and Kochhar, Espinoza and Hinze-Pifer, *After the Great Recession*.
14 See Rakesh Kochhar, *Latino Labor Report, 2008: Construction Reverses Job Growth for Latinos* (Washington, DC: Pew Hispanic Center, 2008), http://pewhispanic.org/files/reports/99.pdf.
15 Authors' calculations from January to June 2009 CPS outgoing rotation group data. Over 10 percent of immigrants in the labor force reported their industry as construction versus 7 percent of natives. Section III further discusses the role of the construction sector.

overrepresented in education groups and sectors that experienced large job losses. Within most education groups, however, immigrants still tend to outperform comparably educated natives. One exception is the college-educated group: here, immigrants have consistently lower employment rates and higher unemployment rates than their native counterparts.

How best to assist immigrants during downturns presents a conundrum for policymakers. Many immigrant households are ineligible for government transfer programs that help families during recessions, such as food stamps and cash welfare. Immigrants may lack legal or permanent resident status or be barred from receiving benefits that require US citizenship. And those who are eligible may be reluctant to apply for benefits for fear of revealing relatives' unauthorized status or of jeopardizing their own or a relative's green-card application. This is a reasonable concern. Sponsoring a relative for a green card requires meeting an income threshold, and applying for a green card requires showing one is not likely to become a "public charge" — that is, dependent on the government for income.[16] It therefore may be relatively difficult for policymakers to aid impoverished immigrant households through traditional transfer programs.

This chapter provides an updated analysis of the economic status of immigrants, how they progressed during the 1990s and 2000s, and how they fared in the recession and its aftermath. It examines not only employment trends but also earnings and poverty. We then step back to provide a broader view of why immigrants tend to be more vulnerable to the business cycle. The chapter addresses the following questions:

- How do labor-market outcomes and poverty rates compare between immigrants and natives over the long run and over the business cycle?

- Why are immigrants more vulnerable to business-cycle downturns than natives?

- What can public policy do to reduce the disparate impact of business-cycle downturns on immigrant households?

A few clarifications should be noted before proceeding. Unless indicated otherwise, this chapter uses the terms *immigrant* and *foreign born* interchangeably to refer to people born outside the United States to parents who are not US citizens. This group includes naturalized US citizens, legal permanent residents, temporary migrants, and unauthorized immigrants. The data analyzed below do not include respondents'

---

16 See US Citizenship and Immigration Services (USCIS), "Public Charge Fact Sheet," 2009, www.uscis.gov/portal/site/uscis/menuitem.5af9bb95919f35e66f614176543f6d1a/?vgne xtoid=354fb2a3fffb4210VgnVCM100000082ca60aRCRD&vgnextchannel=68439c7755cb90 10VgnVCM10000045f3d6a1RCRD.

legal or visa status. The data may underrepresent some immigrant groups, particularly the unauthorized.[17] Caution needs to be exercised in drawing conclusions about relatively small groups, as changes over time and differences from other groups may not always be statistically significant.[18]

I. How Do Labor-Market Outcomes and Poverty Rates Compare between Immigrants and Natives over the Business Cycle?

Until recently, there was limited opportunity to study the business-cycle performance of US immigrants. The necessary data — monthly surveys that ask individuals about economic outcomes and foreign birth — only began to become available as of 1994. Economists then had to wait until 2001 to observe a recession, which was relatively mild. After the recent severe and prolonged downturn, economists now can provide additional insight on how immigrants fare over the business cycle.

This section first examines the long-run trends in immigrant employment and unemployment, earnings, and poverty rates during 1994-2011. It then explores how business cycles have influenced short-run volatility in these same measures. We provide a statistical analysis that separates the changes in native and immigrant employment and unemployment into two components. The first component describes long-run trends over the entire 18-year period; the second describes short-run

---

17 The US Census Bureau estimates that it undercounts the unauthorized population by 15 percent, while the former Immigration and Naturalization Service (INS) assumes a 10 percent undercount. See Gordon H. Hanson, "Illegal Migration from Mexico to the United States," *Journal of Economic Literature* 44, no. 4 (2008): 869–924.

18 We also caution that the comparability of the data over time is affected slightly by periodic revisions in CPS methodology. We focus on rates instead of levels (number of people employed, unemployed, etc.) because CPS is not retrospectively revised to reflect changes in population counts (see www.bls.gov/cps/cps09adj.pdf). Although it is possible to adjust the data to reflect updated counts by age, sex, and race/ethnicity, we opted not to do so here because the Bureau of Labor Statistics (BLS) does not publish updated counts by nativity status. BLS notes that adjustments for updated population counts have a negligible effect on percentages, such as the unemployment rate.

fluctuations around the long-run trend. These short-run movements are due in part to the business cycle.[19]

The data presented here are quarterly averages and are seasonally adjusted, except for the poverty rate data (which are annual and therefore not seasonally adjusted). Earnings data are adjusted for inflation using the Bureau of Labor Statistics (BLS) Consumer Price Index (CPI) for Urban Wage Earners and Clerical Workers. Unless otherwise indicated, the data are from the Current Population Survey (CPS), a monthly survey of about 50,000 households conducted by the US Census Bureau for BLS.

A. Employment and Unemployment

1. Employment Rates

The employment rate is the share of employed workers in the noninstitutionalized civilian population aged 16 and older. It is a good summary statistic of the extent of economic activity of the total population or of a given group. Figure 1 shows the employment rates for immigrants and natives from the first quarter of 1994 through the fourth quarter of 2011, with the shaded portions indicating the two recessions during this period: the high-tech bust in 2001 and the more recent housing bust/financial crisis.[20]

Employment rates are typically procyclical, which means that they increase during economic expansions and fall during recessions. This is true of both immigrant and native employment rates, but the cyclicality is considerably more pronounced for immigrants. The 1990s boom propelled immigrant employment to new heights, both by increasing employment among immigrants already here and by attracting more migrants with strong labor-force attachment.

---

19 We use the Hodrick-Prescott (HP) filter to decompose employment and unemployment rates into a trend and a residual component. The HP filter is a data-smoothing technique that is commonly applied to remove short-term fluctuations associated with the business cycle, thereby revealing long-term trends. For an explanation, see Walter Enders, *Applied Econometric Time Series*, 2nd ed. (Hoboken, NJ: John Wiley and Sons, 2004), 223–5.

20 A recession is often defined in the popular press as two consecutive quarters of negative gross domestic product (GDP) growth. However, NBER's Business Cycle Dating Committee defines a recession more loosely as a "significant decline in economic activity spread across the economy, lasting more than a few months, normally visible in real GDP, real income, employment, industrial production, and wholesale-retail sales." Two economic events date a recession: a peak in activity signals the beginning of the downturn, and a trough in activity marks the end. See NBER, "The NBER's Recession Dating Procedure," www.nber.org/cycles/recessions.html. Because we use quarterly data, the figures here show the 2001 recession — officially from March 2001 to November 2001 — as occurring from the second through the fourth quarter of that year and the Great Recession as beginning in the first quarter of 2008 (instead of NBER's start date of December 2007) and ending in the second quarter of 2009 (instead of NBER's end date of June 2009).

Figure 1. Employment Rates by Nativity, Ages 16 and Older, First Quarter 1994 to Fourth Quarter 2011

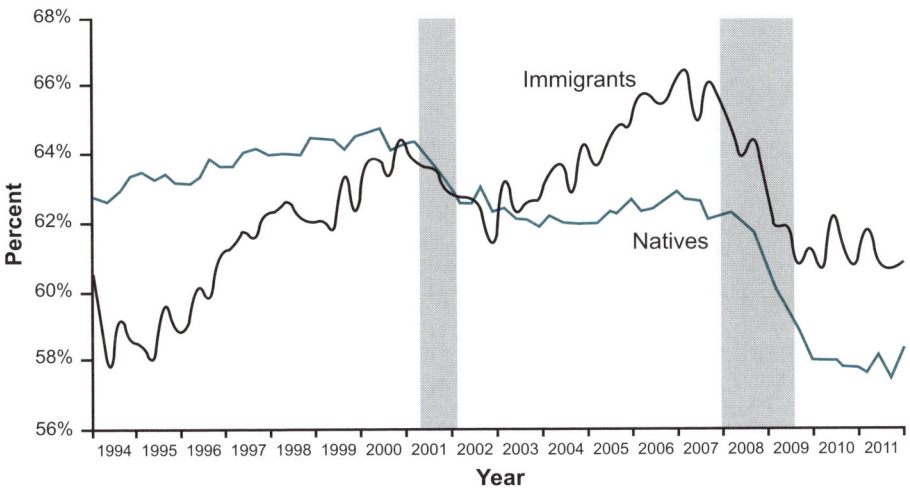

Note: Data are seasonally adjusted. Recessions are shown as shaded areas.
Source: Authors' calculations from US Census Bureau, Current Population Survey, January 1994 to December 2011.

Employment rates for both natives and immigrants fell during the 2001 recession, but the immigrant employment rate recovered sooner and began to increase in 2003, surpassing the native employment rate in every subsequent year. By 2005 the immigrant employment rate exceeded its previous series high of 64.5 percent, reached in 2000. It went on to reach over 66 percent in early 2007. In contrast, the native employment rate never returned to its pre-2000 rates of 63 percent to 64 percent. Instead it remained largely flat in the post-2002 economy and then dropped with the onset of the recession in late 2007.

Employment rates fell precipitously for immigrants and natives alike during the Great Recession. During the nascent recovery, the immigrant employment rate has ranged from 60 to 62 percent, below its level during the 2000s boom but well above its level during the mid-1990s. The native employment rate, in contrast, has remained near 58 percent, well below its level during the mid-1990s. It will be interesting to see if the native employment rate rises above the immigrant employment rate when the recovery strengthens, or if immigrant employment continues to outpace that of natives. One reason that the latter might be a long-term trend is demographic change — in particular, a rapidly aging workforce — among the native population.

2. Unemployment Rates

Unemployment rates are, in a sense, a mirror image of employment rates.[21] Given that these two measures are so closely correlated, albeit inversely, it is no surprise to see a clear countercyclical pattern in both native and immigrant unemployment rates: they rise during downturns and fall during expansions.

Figure 2 suggests a long-run decline in the immigrant unemployment rate from 1994 until about 2006, interrupted briefly by the 2001 recession. In 1994 the immigrant unemployment rate was above 8 percent, compared with around 6 percent for natives. Both rates declined during the 1990s, and the gap between them narrowed. After rising in the early 2000s, immigrant unemployment fell to 3.4 percent in late 2006, its lowest point over the 18-year period. The native unemployment rate did not fall as much during the 2000s expansion and actually bottomed out (at 3.8 percent) in the fourth quarter of 2000. Meanwhile, the immigrant unemployment rate fell below the native rate in the fourth quarter of 2004 and stayed there until 2008.

Unemployment skyrocketed for immigrants and natives alike during the Great Recession and has subsequently fallen only a little. The unemployment rate remains far above the post-2001 recession level for both nativity groups. Both unemployment rates have fallen by only about 1.5 percentage points from their highs. A sizable portion of the decline among natives appears to be due to labor-force withdrawal, not increased employment, given natives' fairly flat employment rate. The decline in the immigrant unemployment rate is partly due to increased employment but also may reflect people leaving the labor force or even the country.

---

21 Unlike employment rates, unemployment rates measure the unemployed as a share of the labor force, not of the entire adult population.

Figure 2. Unemployment Rates by Nativity, Ages 16 and Older, First Quarter 1994 to Fourth Quarter 2011

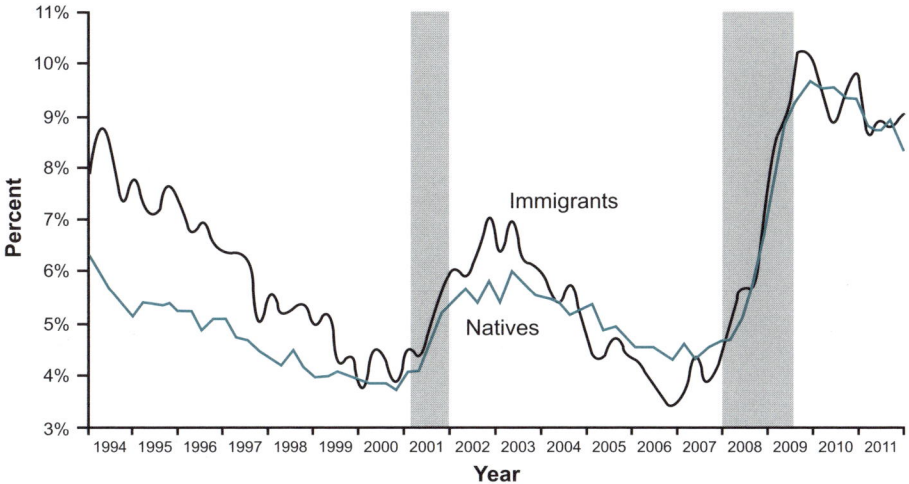

Note: Data are seasonally adjusted. Recessions are shown as shaded areas.
Source: Authors' calculations from US Census Bureau, Current Population Survey, January 1994 to December 2011.

3. Long-Run Trends

a) Employment

Figure 3 shows the trends in employment rates after removing short-run fluctuations from the series. The immigrant trend line suggests that the foreign-born population was becoming more economically active until the Great Recession hit. The long-run trend in the immigrant employment rate remains above its starting level but clearly below its pre-recession peak. In contrast, natives have become less economically active over time. Their employment rate fell almost 6 percentage points over the period as a whole.

Figure 3. Long-Run Trends in Employment Rates by Nativity, Ages 16 and Older, First Quarter 1994 to Fourth Quarter 2011

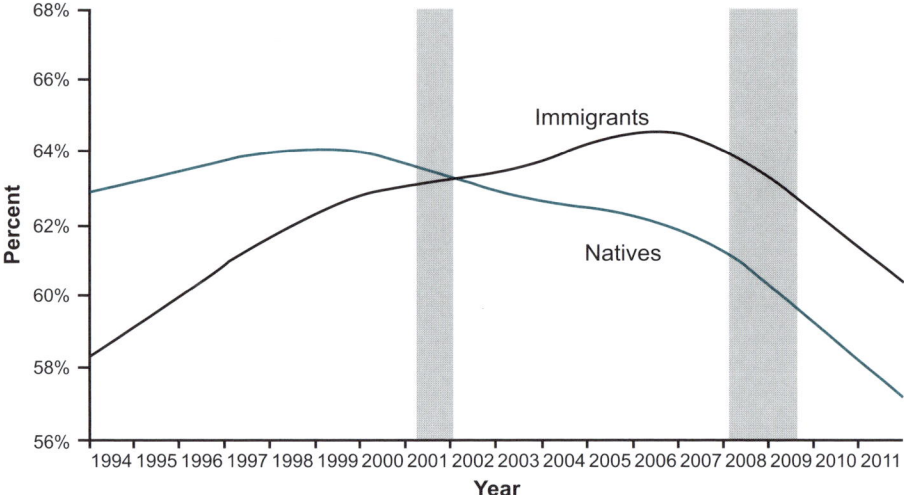

Note: Data are seasonally adjusted. Recessions are shown as shaded areas.
Source: Authors' calculations from US Census Bureau, Current Population Survey, January 1994 to December 2011.

The long-run trends differed between immigrants and natives during the 1990s and 2000s for a number of reasons. One reason is a difference in the age structure of the immigrant and native populations. Most immigrant workers are in their prime working years, when employment and earnings tend to peak. Many native workers, in contrast, are aging out of their prime working years. This means that an increasing number of native workers are leaving the workforce, which partly explains the lower native employment rate after 2001.

Immigrant-native differences in women's labor-force participation also underlie the different trends for immigrants and natives. Among native women, the labor-force participation rate (LFPR) has been largely stagnant for the past 18 years. The female LFPR skyrocketed from 43 percent in 1970 to almost 60 percent in the 1990s as some women joined the workforce for the first time while others returned after exiting to raise children. As this phenomenon slowed and then ended, growth in the native labor force and in the employment rate eased.[22]

---

22 For discussions of changes in women's labor-force participation, see, for example, Francine D. Blau and Lawrence M. Kahn, "Changes in the Labor Supply Behavior of Married Women: 1980-2000," *Journal of Labor Economics* 25, no. 3 (2007): 393–438; and Julie L. Hotchkiss, "Changes in Behavioral and Characteristic Determination of Female Labor Force Participation, 1975-2005," *Federal Reserve Bank of Atlanta Economic Review* 91, no. 2 (2006): 1–20. The statistics presented here on women's labor-force participation are from Francine D. Blau, Marianne A. Ferber, and Anne E. Winkler, *The Economics of Women, Men, and Work*, 5th ed. (Upper Saddle River, NJ: Pearson Prentice Hall, 2006).

In contrast to native women, immigrant women's LFPR rose during the 1990s and 2000s. Comparing 2011 to 1994, the LFPR was almost 5 percentage points higher among foreign-born women but virtually unchanged for native-born women.[23] Possible reasons for the upward trajectory for immigrant women include assimilation among those already here and, as discussed next, a larger percentage of employment-based immigrants among new arrivals.[24]

The changing composition of immigrant inflows has also contributed to the long-run upward trend in the immigrant employment rate. First, the *Immigration Act of 1990* increased the volume of employment-based migration of both temporary immigrants and legal permanent residents. The law raised the number of available employment-based green cards by 160 percent, and created the H-1B visa for temporary skilled workers. As the economy surged during the high-tech boom, demand for H-1B visas exploded. The annual cap on the number of such visas was raised twice, peaking at 195,000 before returning to its original level of 65,000 in 2004. Second, unauthorized immigration also grew during the economic expansions of the 1990s and 2000s. This further boosted the immigrant employment rate because male unauthorized immigrants typically have the highest LFPR of any demographic group, in part because they migrate in order to work and have virtually no access to the government's safety net. They also tend to be of prime working age and are less likely than other groups to be enrolled in school or retired.[25]

Inflows of cyclically sensitive immigrant workers fell during the Great Recession. The annual number of employment-based green cards issued was lower in fiscal years 2009, 2010, and 2011 than in 2008.[26] While the annual caps for H-1B and H-2B visa applications were reached every year, the actual number of visas issued by the US State Department declined during the downturn.[27] Inflows of unauthorized immigrants slowed considerably, and the unauthorized population dipped slightly.[28]

---

23 Immigrant women's labor-force participation rose from 50 percent in 1994 to 55 percent in 2009 and then dropped slightly to 54 percent in 2011. Native women's labor-force participation rate was 60 percent in both 1994 and 2009 and 59 percent in 2011. Authors' calculations from CPS outgoing rotation group data.
24 The increased number of employment-based legal permanent residents after the *Immigration Act of 1990* likely boosted employment not only among principals but also their accompanying spouses because of assortative mating.
25 See Jeffrey S. Passel, *Unauthorized Migrants: Numbers and Characteristics* (Washington, DC: Pew Hispanic Center, 2005), http://pewhispanic.org/files/reports/46.pdf.
26 See US Department of Homeland Security (DHS), "Persons Obtaining Legal Permanent Resident Status by Type and Major Class of Admission: Fiscal Years 2002 to 2011," www.dhs.gov/files/statistics/publications/LPR11.shtm.
27 See US Department of State, "Classes of Nonimmigrants Issued Visas — FY1987-2010 Detail Table," www.travel.state.gov/visa/statistics/nivstats/nivstats_4582.html.
28 See Jeffrey S. Passel and D'Vera Cohn, *Unauthorized Immigrant Population: National and State Trends, 2010* (Washington, DC: Pew Hispanic Center, 2011), www.pewhispanic.org/files/reports/133.pdf.

Whether heightened enforcement and anti-immigrant state initiatives will keep inflows low when the recovery strengthens will be interesting to see.

b) Unemployment

When we remove the short-term fluctuations from the unemployment data, the trends show a striking convergence in the native and immigrant unemployment rates (see Figure 4). The immigrant unemployment rate trend fell more steeply than the native rate during the 1990s, paused, and then resumed its decline for a few years before beginning to rise in mid-2006. The native unemployment trend has been flat or rising for the past 13 years.

Some of the factors that contributed to the trends in the immigrant and native employment rates also contributed to these unemployment rate trends. The increasing proportion of immigrants with strong labor force attachment — namely, employment-based immigrants and the unauthorized — and the shift from seasonal and agricultural work to year-round employment among less-educated immigrants likely underlie much of the long-run decline in the immigrant unemployment rate before the onset of the recession.

Figure 4. Long-Run Trends in Unemployment Rates by Nativity, Age 16 and Older, First Quarter 1994 to Fourth Quarter 2011

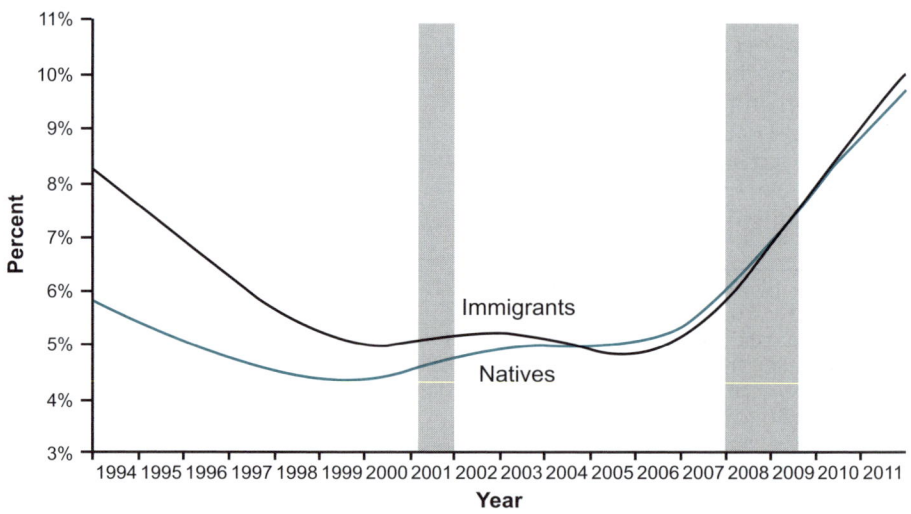

Note: Data are seasonally adjusted. Recessions are shown as shaded areas.
Source: Authors' calculations from US Census Bureau, Current Population Survey, January 1994 to December 2011.

More generally, unemployment-rate trends tend to reflect changes in the age structure and education distribution. As a population enters the prime working ages of 25 to 44 or becomes more educated, its unemployment rate typically trends downward. Although the average age is rising for both the immigrant and native labor forces, immigrants tend to be aging into their prime working years while natives are moving out of those years into retirement or disability. Although the foreign born constitute a growing share of the low-skilled labor force, the education distribution improved slightly among both immigrants and natives during the 1994-2011 period, albeit a bit more among natives. Broad structural changes, such as the shift away from manufacturing toward services, shaped these long-run unemployment trends as well.

4. Immigrant and Native Sensitivity to the Business Cycle

The factors that shape long-run trends in labor-market outcomes also tend to affect short-run fluctuations in those outcomes. For example, younger workers tend to be more vulnerable to economic downturns since they have fewer years of work experience. More educated workers tend to be relatively shielded from the business cycle by virtue of their high skill levels. Since immigrants and natives differ systematically in terms of their age and education distributions, it is likely that they also differ in their vulnerability to business-cycle fluctuations.

Employment

Figure 5 shows the short-run, or "cyclical," component of the immigrant and native employment rates. The figure illustrates the fluctuations above and below the long-term trend discussed earlier, which is represented by the horizontal line at zero. The vertical axis gives the percentage points by which the employment rate in a given quarter was above or below its long-run trend.

Figure 5. Cyclical Fluctuations in Employment Rates by Nativity, Ages 16 and Older, First Quarter 1994 to Fourth Quarter 2011

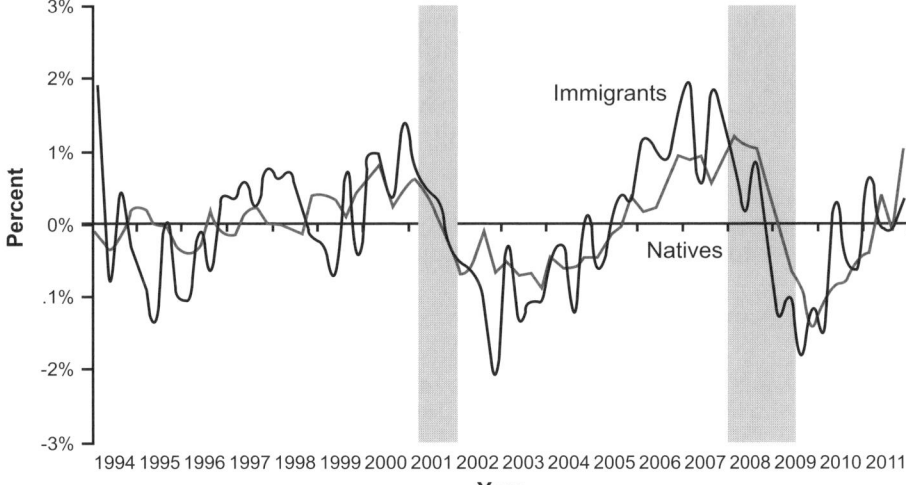

Note: Data are seasonally adjusted. Recessions are shown as shaded areas.
Source: Authors' calculations from US Census Bureau, Current Population Survey,"January 1994 to December 2011.

The impact of the two recessions is apparent. Both native and immigrant employment rates fell below their long-run trends (below the zero line) during the downturns. Employment rates remained low for several years after both recessions ended, periods frequently characterized as a "jobless recovery." The cyclical portion of both the immigrant and native employment rates are now above their long-run trend, which bodes well for the recovery.

Figure 5 also shows that the immigrant employment rate experiences greater volatility, as measured by the magnitude of the swings in the series, than the native employment rate.[29] This greater volatility appears to be caused by greater sensitivity of immigrant employment to the business cycle (smaller sample sizes for immigrants also contribute to higher variance). The immigrant cycle is above the native cycle during booms (1996 to 1998, at the end of 2000, and during 2005 to 2007) and below that of natives during economic troughs (in 2002 and 2008 to 2009). The immigrant employment rate rises higher in booms and sinks lower in busts.

Like the employment rate, the unemployment rate is more volatile among immigrants than natives. Figure 6 shows the short-run, or cyclical, fluctuations in unemployment for natives and immigrants. Again,

---

29   The standard deviation of the cyclical component of the immigrant employment rate is 0.9 percentage points, compared with 0.6 percentage points for natives.

the cyclical portion of the immigrant unemployment rate deviates further from its trend (the zero line) than does the native unemployment rate.[30] These deviations are particularly large before and after recessions, the very high and low points of economic activity.

Figure 6. Cyclical Fluctuations in Unemployment Rates by Nativity, Ages 16 and Older, First Quarter 1994 to Fourth Quarter 2011

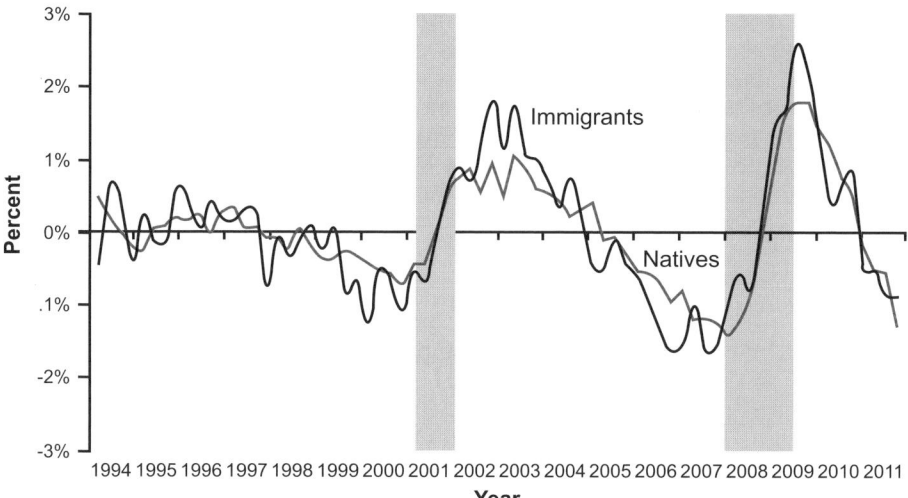

Note: Data are seasonally adjusted. Recessions are shown as shaded areas.
Source: Authors' calculations from US Census Bureau, Current Population Survey, January 1994 to December 2011.

5. Cyclical Fluctuations and GDP

If immigrant economic performance is indeed more sensitive to the fortunes of the macroeconomy, then short-run fluctuations in the immigrant employment rate should be more strongly correlated with the growth rate of the gross domestic product (GDP) than the equivalent fluctuations for natives. Of course, if there are differences among immigrants — for example, if low-education immigrants have more cyclical outcomes than natives but high-education immigrants do not — then comparing aggregate correlations may not reveal that immigrants are much different from natives after all.

Statistical analysis indicates that this is the case. The correlations between the cyclical fluctuations in the employment rate and real GDP

---

[30] The standard deviation of the cyclical component of the unemployment rate is higher for immigrants than for natives (0.9 percentage points for immigrants versus 0.7 percentage points for natives).

are similar for immigrants and natives.[31] As we'll see below, differences in cyclicality arise from differences in education levels.

There is even less difference in the correlations between the cyclical fluctuations in the unemployment rates and real GDP for immigrants and natives.[32] Why isn't this correlation considerably larger for immigrants than for natives? One possible explanation for the pattern is that unemployed immigrants are more likely than natives to move within the United States or even leave the country entirely when jobs are relatively scarce, which dampens the correlation between the immigrant unemployment rate and the business cycle. In addition, the duration of immigrants' unemployment spells may be less variable over the business cycle, both because of greater mobility and because immigrants may search harder for jobs and have lower expectations of job amenities — such as a desirable location, pleasant working conditions, and fringe benefits — than natives do.

B. *Earnings*

Foreign-born workers earn about 20 percent less than US-born workers. In the fourth quarter of 2011, median weekly earnings were $528 for foreign-born workers and $673 for natives (see Figure 7). The gap between immigrants' and natives' earnings changed little between 1994 and 2011; median weekly earnings among immigrants started the period at about 80 percent of natives' earnings and ended up at about 78 percent. The two series have performed similarly over time, rising during the 1990s and largely stagnating since then. Earnings have dipped for both groups since the end of the recession.[33]

Like employment and unemployment, earnings are also affected by both long-run fundamentals and short-run fluctuations. Immigrant earnings are more variable than native earnings (see the jagged line in Figure 7), but the variation appears to be unrelated to the business cycle and could in part be due to smaller sample sizes. Recessions typically reduce individual workers' earnings, but median earnings do not necessarily fall during downturns. Earnings data only include the employed (unemployed workers with zero income are not included in earnings measures). Real median earnings tend to be relatively stable over the business cycle because highly paid workers are more likely

---

31 The correlation between the cyclical components of the employment rate and GDP is 0.70 for immigrants and 0.73 for natives. A correlation ranges between 0 and 1 (in absolute value terms), with larger values indicating a stronger correlation between two variables.
32 These correlations are negative since the unemployment rate is countercyclical. The correlations are -0.86 for immigrants and -0.87 for natives.
33 Immigrants' earnings fell more than natives' during the early phases of the recovery. See Kochhar, Espinoza, and Hinze-Pifer, *After the Great Recession*.

to remain employed in a recession, counteracting the effect of any decreases in earnings among those who remain employed.[34]

Figure 7. Real Median Weekly Earnings by Nativity, Ages 16 and Older, First Quarter 1994 to Fourth Quarter 2011

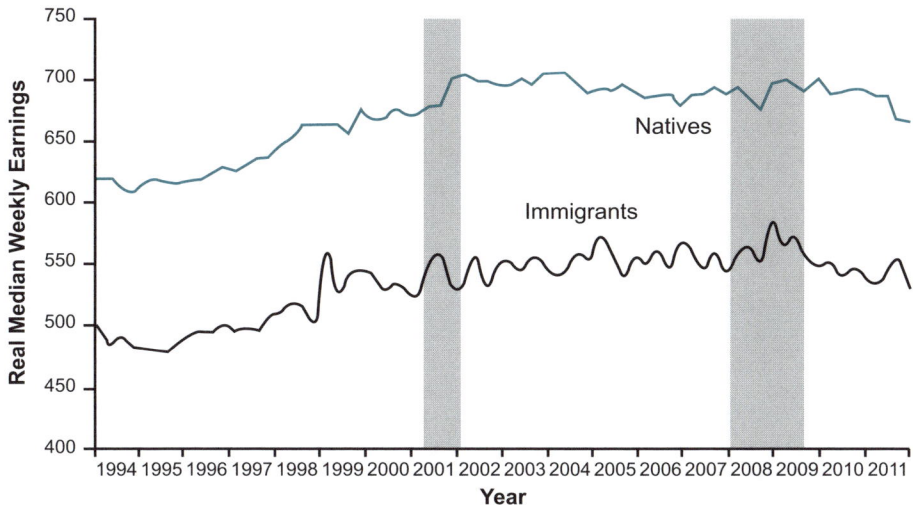

Note: Data are seasonally adjusted. Recessions are shown as shaded areas. Earnings are expressed in December 2011 dollars.
Source: Authors' calculations from US Census Bureau, Current Population Survey, January 1994 to December 2011.

A substantial body of research has looked carefully at the immigrant-native earnings gap, controlling for differences in the two populations, such as age, education, English fluency, and years of work experience. These studies have found that immigrants experience faster earnings growth over their life cycle than natives. Although immigrants initially earn less than natives with similar ages, education levels, and English ability, immigrants' average earnings converge to those of similar natives after 15 to 20 years of US residence. When researchers do not account for differences in education and English fluency, however, less-educated immigrants' average wages typically are predicted to

---

34 More educated, more skilled (and highly paid) workers are more likely to remain employed during a downturn, while the least educated, least skilled (and lowest paid) workers are often the first to be laid off. This compositional change masks the procyclical nature of earnings within workers. See Gary Solon, Robert Barsky, and Jonathan A. Parker, "Measuring the Cyclicality of Real Wages: How Important Is Composition Bias?" *Quarterly Journal of Economics* 109, no. 1 (1994): 1–25.

reach parity with those of natives only after generations.[35] One study notes that the immigrant-native earnings gap declined during the 1990s and attributes this convergence in part to the rise in high-skilled, employment-based immigration, which brought in more high-earning immigrant workers.[36]

C. Poverty

Given that immigrant workers tend to earn substantially less than natives, are immigrants more likely to be poor? Although the earnings gap certainly suggests this would be the case, other factors may intervene. For example, immigrants live in families that include more workers than natives do.[37] For a family to be designated as poor, the family's total money income has to fall below the poverty threshold for a family of that size and age composition; poverty thresholds vary by family size and members' age but not by region of residence. A family with more workers is thus less likely to be defined as poor, all else equal (all members of a family have the same poverty status).[38] The poverty rate is then defined as the proportion of the population living in a family with income below the poverty threshold. In 2011 the poverty threshold for a family of four (two nonelderly adults, two children under age 18) was $22,811 while the threshold for a family of five (three adults, two children) was $27,517.[39]

---

35 "Less educated" here indicates those without a high school diploma. For more on immigrant wages, see, for example, Heather Antecol, Peter Kuhn, and Stephen J. Trejo, "Assimilation via Prices or Quantities? Sources of Immigrant Earnings Growth in Australia, Canada, and the United States," *Journal of Human Resources* 41, no. 4 (2006): 821–40; George J. Borjas, "Assimilation and Changes in Cohort Quality Revisited: What Happened to Immigrant Earnings in the 1980s?" *Journal of Labor Economics* 13, no. 2 (1996): 201–45; and Harriet Orcutt Duleep and Mark C. Regets, "Measuring Immigrant Wage Growth Using Matched CPS Files," *Demography* 34, no. 2 (1997): 239–49. The role of illegal status (which is more prevalent among less-educated immigrants) in the failure of less-educated immigrants to catch up to natives' earnings over their lifetimes is an interesting question and hard to assess absent data on legal status. For a discussion, see Matthew Hall and George Farkas, "Does Human Capital Raise Earnings for Immigrants in the Low-Skill Labor Market?" *Demography* 45, no. 3 (2008): 619–39.
36 See George J. Borjas and Rachel M. Friedberg, "Recent Trends in the Earnings of New Immigrants to the United States" (working paper 15406, National Bureau of Economic Research, Cambridge, MA, 2009), www.nber.org/papers/w15406.
37 During the 1994-2011 period, the average number of labor-force participants in an immigrant-headed household was 1.64 versus 1.46 for natives. Authors' calculations from March CPS data from IPUMS.
38 For an explanation of how the Census Bureau measures poverty and the poverty thresholds, see US Census Bureau, "How the Census Bureau Measures Poverty," www.census. gov/hhes/www/poverty/about/overview/measure.html. The March CPS data used here include family poverty status.
39 US Census Bureau, "Poverty Thresholds for 2011 by Size of Family and Number of Related Children Under 18 Years," www.census.gov/hhes/www/poverty/data/threshld/. A family can include related adults (e.g., an aunt or grandparent), not just married adults. Nonrelatives are considered part of a household but not part of a family.

The poverty rate is indeed much higher among immigrants than natives. In 2010, the most recent year for which poverty data are currently available, 19.9 percent of immigrants lived in families that were in poverty, versus 14.4 percent of natives.[40] These numbers understate the gap between immigrants and natives because they group the US-born children of immigrants, who are more likely to live in impoverished families than other US natives, together with all other US natives. In Figure 8, in contrast, all individuals are assigned the nativity status of the head of the household in order to calculate poverty rates by nativity. This method classifies US-born children as foreign born if they live in a household headed by an immigrant.

Figure 8. Poverty Rates by Nativity of Household Head, 1993 to 2010

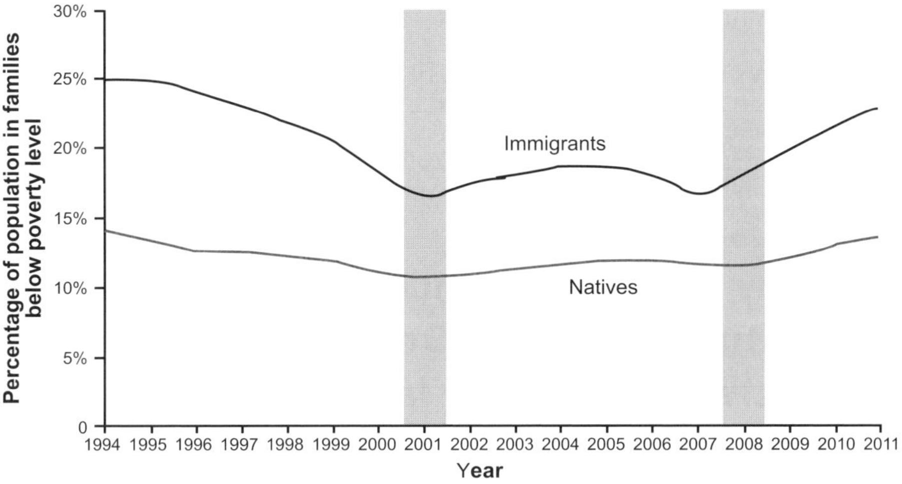

Note: Recessions are shown as shaded areas.
Source: Authors' calculations from US Census Bureau, Annual Social and Economic Supplement, Current Population Survey, March 1994 to 2011.

Poverty rates appear to be quite countercyclical, especially among immigrants. As Figure 8 shows, the 1990s expansion coincided with a drop in the poverty rate for both immigrants and natives. The drop was considerably more pronounced among immigrants. A number of factors contributed to lower poverty rates in general during this time period, including earnings growth, rising employment rates, and tougher work

---

40 US Census Bureau, "Income, Poverty, and Health Insurance Coverage in the United States: 2010," 2011, www.census.gov/prod/2011pubs/p60-239.pdf. For a broader discussion of immigrant-native poverty differences and determinants, see Steven Raphael and Eugene Smolensky, "Immigration and Poverty in the United States," in *Changing Poverty, Changing Policies*, ed. Maria Cancian and Sheldon Danziger (New York: Russell Sage Foundation, 2009).

rules following the 1996 welfare reform.[41] The drop was larger among immigrants partly because the composition of the foreign-born population shifted toward high-skilled, employment-based immigrants and partly because of economic progress of existing immigrant-headed households. Although welfare reform played a role in bringing down poverty rates among immigrants and natives via increased work, legal immigrants faced particularly steep eligibility cuts; they appear to have responded with large increases in work and commensurate declines in poverty.[42]

Poverty rates also fell, although less dramatically, among immigrant-headed households during the 2004-2006 housing boom. Interestingly, the poverty rate was nearly unchanged among native-headed households during that period, mirroring the stagnation in real median earnings among native workers shown in Figure 7.

Poverty rates rise during recessions. In the wake of the 2001 recession, the immigrant poverty rate increased by 1.8 percentage points while the native poverty rate rose by 1.2 percentage points. The sharp spike in the immigrant poverty rate since 2007 provides further evidence of the recession's continuing toll on immigrant families.

II. Why Are Immigrants More Vulnerable to Business-Cycle Downturns than Natives, and which Immigrants Are Most Affected?

The measures examined above show that immigrants experience more volatility in economic outcomes than do natives. Part of this greater volatility appears to be due to greater sensitivity to business-cycle

---

41 For a broader perspective on changes in poverty, see Hilary W. Hoynes, Marianne E. Page, and Ann Huff Stevens, "Poverty in America: Trends and Explanations," *Journal of Economic Perspectives* 20, no. 1 (2006): 47–68.
42 See George J. Borjas, "Welfare Reform, Labor Supply, and Health Insurance in the Immigrant Population," *Journal of Health Economics* 22, no. 6 (2003): 933–58; and Michael Fix, ed., *Immigrants and Welfare: The Impact of Welfare Reform on American's Newcomers* (New York: Russell Sage Foundation, 2009).

fluctuations among certain immigrants, a finding other research has documented.[43]

Which factors contribute to this greater cyclicality? This chapter explores the role of four factors: education, race/ethnicity, industry, and occupation. Research has established that earnings, employment, and incomes tend to be more volatile and cyclical among nonwhites and the less educated than among the population as a whole.[44] Since immigrants are more likely to have low education levels and to belong to racial/ethnic minorities than natives, it is not a surprise that immigrants appear to have more volatile and cyclical economic outcomes. These factors then (combined with others, such as region of residence), may lead to differences in the distribution of immigrants and natives across industries and occupations. Those differences, in turn, reinforce the excess volatility and cyclicality among certain immigrants, while they attenuate it among others.

A. *Education*

Although similar shares of immigrants and natives have at least a college education, a much higher share of immigrants has not completed high school. As Figure 9 shows, immigrants are considerably more likely to have low levels of education — meaning no high school diploma — than natives.[45]

---

43 A study using data from 1979, 1983, 1986, and 1988 reported weak evidence that employment and unemployment are more sensitive among male immigrants than among male natives to the national unemployment rate. See Barry R. Chiswick, Yinon Cohen, and Tzippi Zach, "The Labor Market Status of Immigrants: Effects of the Unemployment Rate at Arrival and Duration of Residence," *Industrial and Labor Relations* 50, no. 2 (1997): 289–303. Another study showed that hourly wages are more sensitive among immigrants than among natives to changes in state-level unemployment rates during the period 1979 to 2003. See Bernt Bratsberg, Erling Barth, and Oddbjørn Raaum, "Local Unemployment and the Relative Wages of Immigrants: Evidence from the Current Population Surveys," *Review of Economics and Statistics* 88, no. 2 (2006): 243–63. Research also shows that unemployment — but not wages — is more cyclical among immigrants than natives in Germany and the United Kingdom, even within skill groups. See Christian Dustmann, Albrecht Glitz, and Thorsten Vogel, "Employment, Wages, and the Economic Cycle: Differences between Immigrants and Natives," *European Economic Review* 54 (2010): 1–17.
44 See, for example, Rebecca M. Blank, "Disaggregating the Effect of the Business Cycle on the Distribution of Income," *Economica* 56, no. 2 (1989): 141–63; Katharine L. Bradbury, "Rising Tide in the Labor Market: To What Degree Do Expansions Benefit the Disadvantaged?" *New England Economic Review* (2000): 3–33; and Hilary W. Hoynes, "The Employment, Earnings, and Income of Less Skilled Workers over the Business Cycle," in *Finding Jobs: Work and Welfare Reform*, eds. David E. Card and Rebecca M. Blank (New York: Russell Sage Foundation, 2000). For a broader discussion of the racial gap in economic outcomes, see, for example, Joseph G. Altonji and Rebecca M. Blank, "Race and Gender in the Labor Market," in *Handbook of Labor Economics*, vol. 3C, eds. Orley Ashenfelter and David Card (Amsterdam: Elsevier, 1999).
45 All data by educational attainment shown here include only individuals aged 25 and older, to capture completed education levels.

Figure 9. Education Distribution among Immigrants and Natives, Ages 25 and Older, 2011

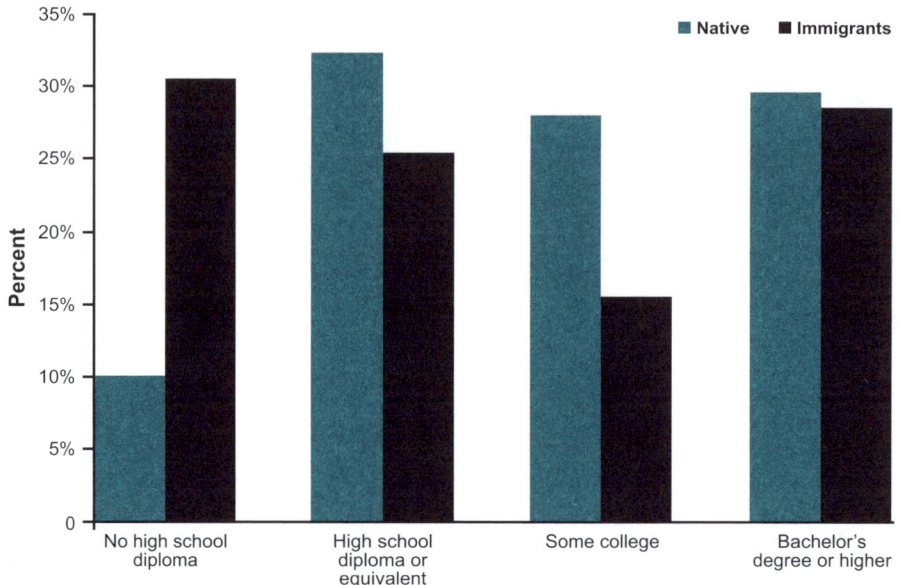

Note: Sample restricted to adults age 25 and older.
Source: Authors' calculations from US Census Bureau, Current Population Survey, 2011.

Natives are concentrated in the middle to high end of the education distribution. Roughly equal shares of adult natives have a high school diploma (32 percent), have attended college (28 percent), and hold a bachelor's degree or higher (31 percent). Less than 10 percent have not completed high school. Immigrants are less likely to be in the middle of the education distribution; about 26 percent have a high school diploma and 16 percent some college education. In contrast, almost 29 percent of immigrants have no high school diploma, and 28 percent have a bachelor's degree or higher. Although educational attainment rose among both immigrants and natives during the past 15 years, it increased slightly faster among natives.

These differences in education largely shape the overall labor-market performance trends for immigrants and natives. It is interesting, therefore, to compare the performance of immigrants and natives *within* education groups, such as among college-educated immigrants and natives or among immigrants and natives without a high school diploma.

In fact, the most dramatic difference in employment and unemployment rates is between immigrants and natives who have not completed high school (see Figures 10 and 11). The employment rate among such immigrants is over 20 percentage points higher than among such natives. Correspondingly, natives who have not completed high school have higher unemployment rates than immigrants. Less-educated immigrants benefited more from the 2000s-era housing boom than less-educated natives, and they are also doing better during the current recovery. The slowdown in unauthorized immigration may have played a key role in this trend.

Figure 10. Employment Rates by Nativity and Education, Ages 25 and Older

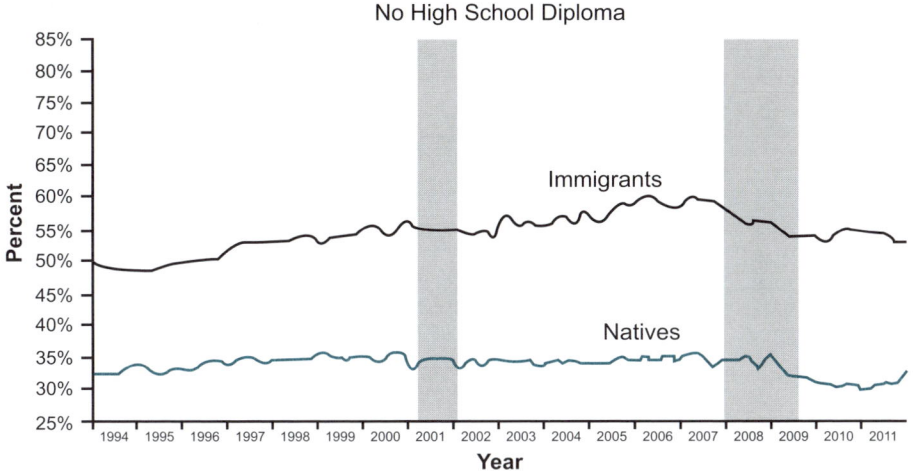

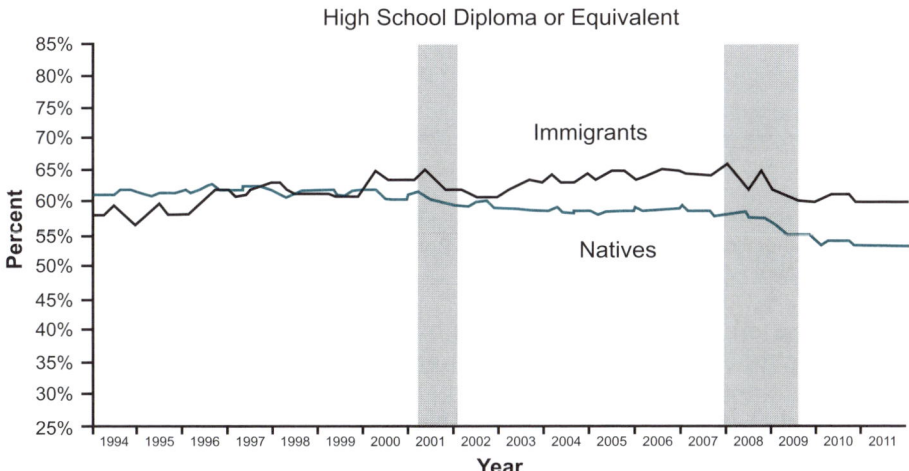

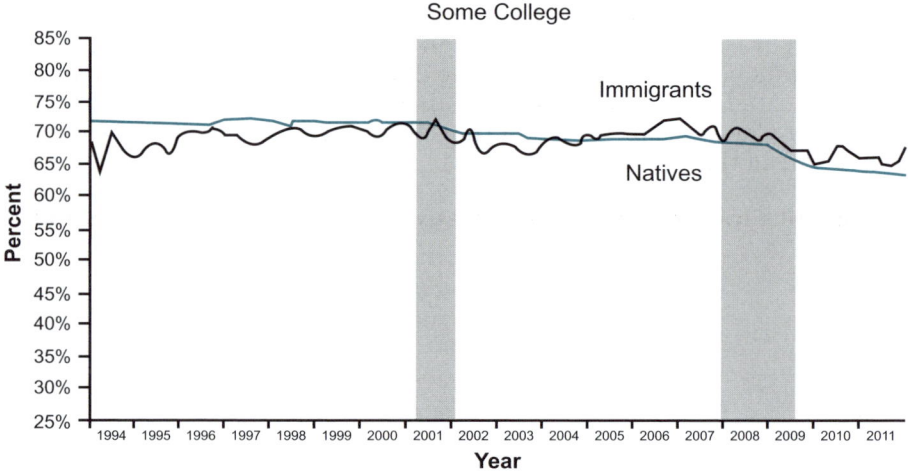

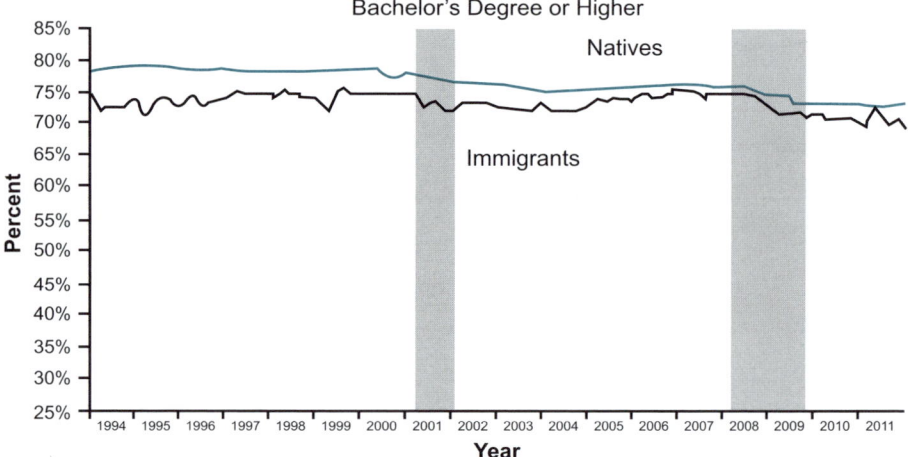

Note: Data are seasonally adjusted. Recessions are shown as shaded areas.
Source: Authors' calculations from US Census Bureau, Current Population Survey, January 1994 to December 2011.

While less-educated immigrants tend to substantially outperform less-educated natives in terms of employment and unemployment, the opposite is the case among the highly educated (although the differences are not as large). College-graduate immigrants tend to have slightly lower employment rates and higher unemployment rates than similarly educated natives.[46] In 2011, for example, college-educated immigrants averaged unemployment rates close to 6 percent, quite a bit higher than the 4 percent rate for college-educated natives.

The factors behind this disparity are likely similar to those affecting underemployment, meaning some well-educated immigrants work in jobs that do not require a college education. Reasons for this include poor fluency in English, lack of legal status, and nonrecognition of foreign credentials, such as professional licenses and university degrees.[47]

Figure 11. Unemployment Rates, by Nativity and Education, Ages 25 and Older

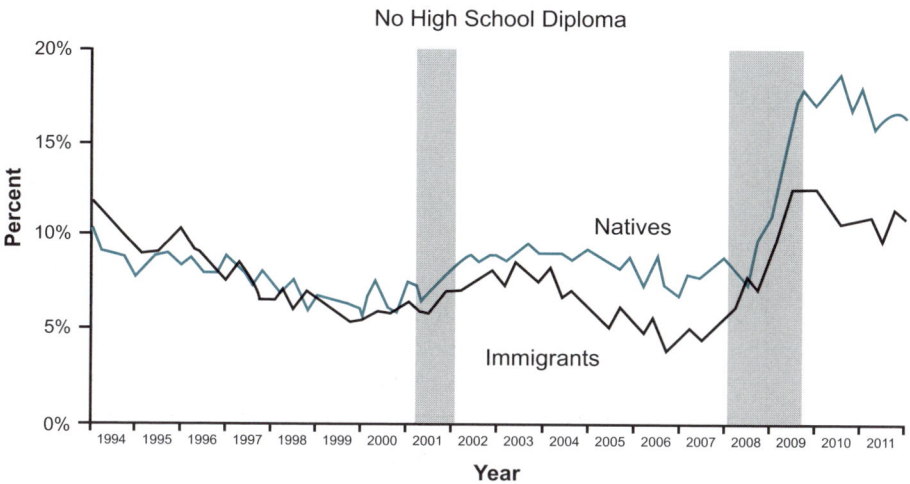

---

46 The pattern is the opposite for the immigrant-native gap in median weekly earnings. Natives earn considerably more than immigrants in all education categories, except for workers with a college degree. From 2005 to 2007, there was virtually no gap in median earnings between immigrants and natives with a college degree, although highly educated immigrants began earning less than natives with the onset of the recession. We do not show figures of median earnings or poverty rates by education since there is less evidence of cyclicality than for employment and unemployment.
47 See Jeanne Batalova and Michael Fix with Peter A. Creticos, *Uneven Progress: The Employment Pathways of Skilled Immigrants in the United States* (Washington, DC: Migration Policy Institute, 2008), www.migrationpolicy.org/pubs/BrainWasteOct08.pdf; and Barry R. Chiswick and Paul W. Miller, "The International Transferability of Immigrants' Human Capital," *Economics of Education Review* 28, no. 2 (2009): 162–9.

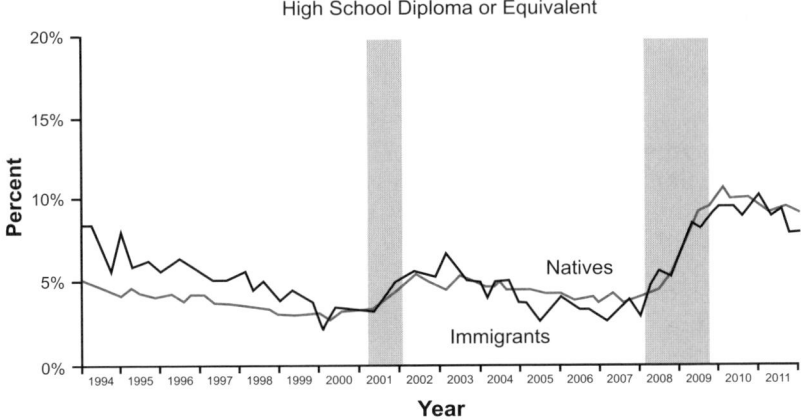

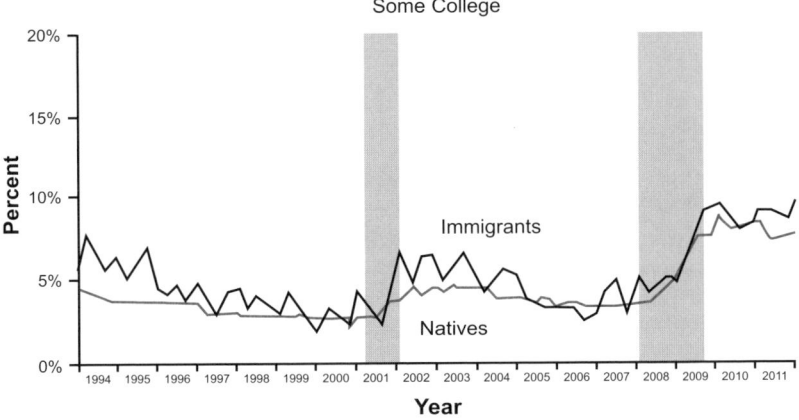

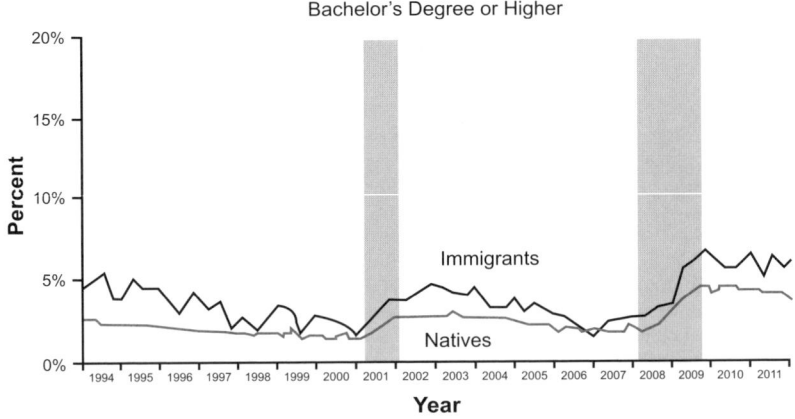

Note: Data are seasonally adjusted. Recessions are shown as shaded areas.
Source: Authors' calculations from US Census Bureau, Current Population Survey, January 1994 to December 2011.

Statistical analysis shows that cyclical changes in employment and unemployment are more pronounced for immigrants than for natives, but only at low levels of education. Short-run, cyclical fluctuations in the employment and unemployment rates of workers without a high school diploma are much more strongly correlated with cyclical changes in GDP for immigrants than for natives.[48] The recession hit the least-educated immigrants especially hard because of their overrepresentation in certain sectors, namely construction and manufacturing. We return to this issue below.

This helps explain how the macroeconomy drives the greater volatility of immigrant employment and unemployment. It also suggests that the business cycle cannot explain changes in low-education natives' employment as well as it can changes in low-education immigrants' employment. Less-educated natives may work in sectors that are not affected as much by the business cycle, or they may have access to public assistance or other aspects of the social safety net that limits their exposure to the business cycle.

B. Race, Ethnicity, and Country of Origin

It is well established that economic outcomes tend to differ between racial and ethnic groups. While some groups do at least as well as the majority group — non-Hispanic whites — others lag behind, particularly blacks and Hispanics. A multitude of factors underlies these differences, from discrimination to geographic isolation to the intergenerational transmission of poverty. As noted above, in addition to having worse economic outcomes, minorities also tend to have more volatile and cyclical economic outcomes. While research has shown such patterns among minorities as a whole, do these patterns hold among immigrants who are racial or ethnic minorities?

Among immigrants, race and ethnicity are closely associated with region of origin. As of 2010 about 47 percent of the foreign born reported being Hispanic, while 26 percent reported being Asian (versus 12 percent and 3 percent of natives, respectively). Correspondingly, about 44 percent of the foreign born were from Latin America and 25 percent

---

[48] The correlation between the short-run components of the employment rate and real GDP among adults who do not have a high school diploma is 0.38 for natives and 0.57 for immigrants; among adults who have a bachelor's degree, the correlation is 0.61 for natives and 0.51 for immigrants. The patterns are similar when it comes to the unemployment rate: cyclical sensitivity is largest among low-educated immigrants and high-educated natives. The correlation between the cyclical component of the unemployment rate and real GDP among adults who do not have a high school diploma is -0.76 for natives and -0.80 for immigrants. Among adults who have a college degree, in contrast, the correlation is -0.85 for natives and -0.71 for immigrants.

from Asia.[49] Because of this nearly one-to-one correspondence between region of origin and race/ethnicity, we focus on economic outcomes among immigrants by region of origin. Immigrants from Latin America and Asia are compared with immigrants from Western Europe and Canada (the "West," henceforth), who are predominantly non-Hispanic whites.[50]

Immigrants from Latin America, Asia, and the West display clear differences in labor-market performance (see Figures 12 and 13). Immigrants from Latin American and Asia have employment rates well above immigrants from the West, although these rates have converged somewhat during the Great Recession and subsequent recovery. On the other hand, Latin Americans are also consistently more likely to be unemployed. Immigrants from Asia and the West have similar unemployment rates, in large part because the groups have relatively similar educational distributions.[51]

---

49 Authors' calculations from 2010 ACS data from IPUMS. Individuals are asked to report their race and (separately) whether they are of Hispanic origin. We do not examine immigrants from Africa or those of African descent (blacks) because their numbers are relatively small.
50 For an examination of the cyclical sensitivity of employment among Mexican immigrants, see Pia M. Orrenius and Madeline Zavodny, "Mexican Immigrant Employment Outcomes over the Business Cycle," *American Economic Review Papers and Proceedings* 100, no. 3 (2010): 316–20.
51 For example, half of the Latin American immigrants aged 25 and older do not have a high school diploma versus 16 percent of immigrants from Asia and the West. Asian immigrants are more highly educated than immigrants from the West; 50 percent of Asian adult immigrants have a bachelor's degree or higher versus 35 percent of Western immigrants. This may be because Asian immigrants tend to be younger and because of cross-country differences in the returns to skill that promote skilled immigration from Asia more so than from the West. Authors' calculations from 2010 ACS data.

Figure 12. Employment Rates among Immigrants by Region of Origin, Ages 16 and Older

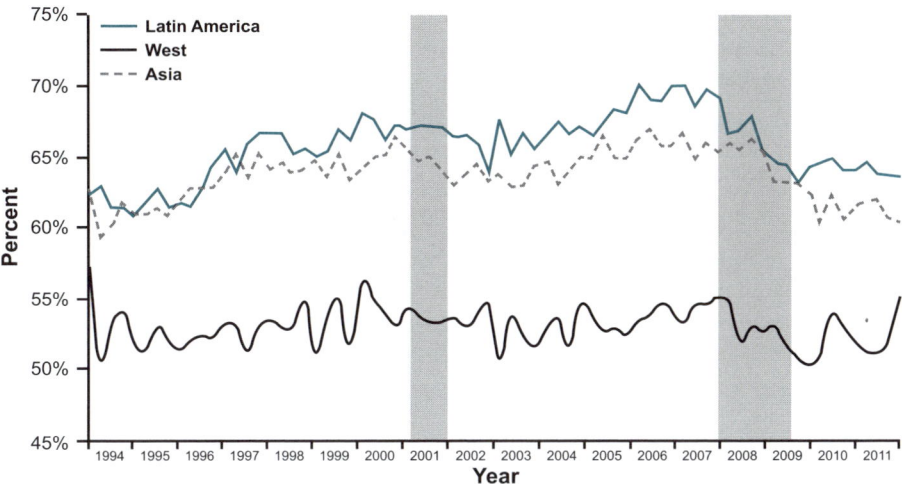

Note: Data are seasonally adjusted. Recessions are shown as shaded areas. The West includes Western Europe and Canada.

Source: Authors' calculations from US Census Bureau, Current Population Survey, January 1994 to December 2011.

Asian immigrants' employment rate dropped more during the 2001 recession than the rates of other groups. This fits with the overrepresentation of Indian and Chinese immigrants in high-tech sectors, which the 2001 recession hit hardest. However, Latin American immigrants display the greatest sensitivity to the business cycle. These immigrants benefited particularly from the 2000s expansion, not surprising given their overrepresentation in construction (industry differences are discussed below). The unemployment rate among Latin Americans converged toward the lower rates among Asian and Western immigrants during the 1990s and 2000s expansions, but the gap widened noticeably with the construction bust and has persisted since. As house prices fell and residential construction employment plummeted starting in late 2006, the unemployment rate among Latin American immigrants began to skyrocket (see Figure 13).

Figure 13. Unemployment Rates among Immigrants by Region of Origin, Ages 16 and Older

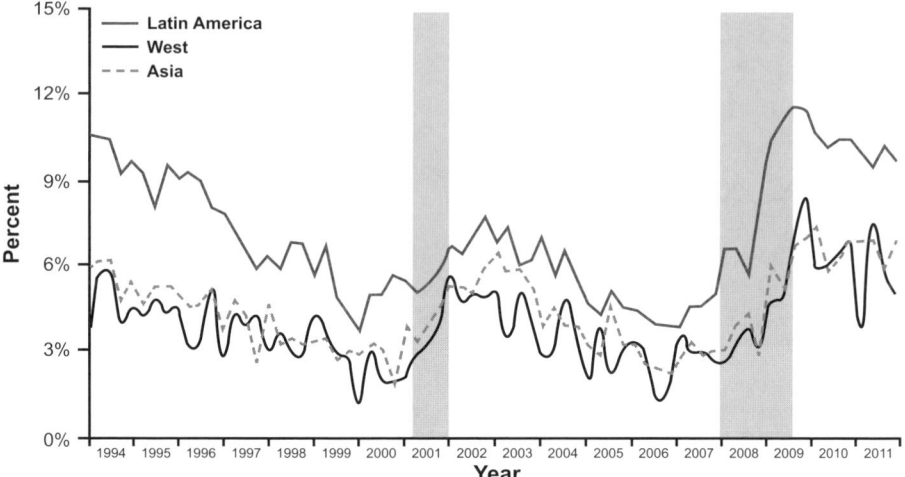

Note: Data are seasonally adjusted. Recessions are shown as shaded areas. The West includes Western Europe and Canada.

Source: Authors' calculations from US Census Bureau, Current Population Survey, January 1994 to December 2011.

Despite these differences, there is no readily visible pattern of differences in employment rate cycles by region of origin (see Appendix). However, more detailed statistical analysis indicates that fluctuations in Latin Americans' employment and unemployment rates are much more closely tied to the business cycle than those of Asian or Western immigrants.[52]

The fact that Latino immigrants have particularly cyclical labor-market outcomes is interesting because several forces exacerbate cyclicality while others smooth outcomes among this group. The relatively low education levels among Latin American immigrants increase their vul-

---

52 The correlation between the short-run components of Latin American immigrant employment rates and real GDP is 0.62, versus 0.41 for Asian immigrants and 0.39 for Western immigrants. In correlations with real GDP, Latino immigrant unemployment rates are also much more cyclical — the correlation is -0.83 for Latin Americans compared with -0.62 and -0.52 for Asian and Western immigrants, respectively.

nerability to the business cycle;[53] unauthorized immigration also plays a role. In 2007 over half of the Mexican immigrants in the United States were here illegally,[54] and the number of workers illegally crossing the US-Mexico border changes quickly in response to shifts in employment conditions in the United States.[55] This unauthorized immigration tends to increase the cyclicality of Latin American immigrants' employment and unemployment rates because many unauthorized immigrants enter only when they can find work. But illegal immigration also dampens the cyclicality of real earnings and poverty rates. The fact that unauthorized migrants may be particularly likely to leave the country when times are bad and they cannot find jobs also acts to reduce the cyclicality of Latino employment and unemployment rates.[56] In addition, Latino workers are typically willing to migrate within the United States or switch industries and occupations in response to changing job opportunities, which also can lessen the cyclicality of their economic outcomes.

C. *Industry and Occupation*

Another reason why immigrants tend to experience more volatile and cyclical labor-market employment outcomes than natives is because they are more likely to work in volatile and cyclical industries. Industries whose fate is tightly linked to overall economic growth include construction and manufacturing, whereas services and the government tend to be relatively shielded from macroeconomic fluctuations. During the period 1994 to 2011 as a whole, 9.2 percent of foreign-born workers were employed in the construction industry, versus 6.6 percent of natives. By the height of the construction boom in 2006, almost 13

---

53 However, a study that used data from the 1980 to 2000 decennial censuses did not find much evidence of excess sensitivity to the business cycle, as measured by state unemployment rates, among minority immigrants. (Notably, the decennial censuses all occurred near business-cycle peaks, so there is little variation in the national business cycle.) Consistent with the findings here, the study found that earnings are more cyclically sensitive for low-skilled immigrant men than for other groups, and that Latin American men tend to have much lower education levels than natives or other immigrants. It concluded that education level matters more than nativity or race/ethnicity. See George J. Borjas, "Wage Trends among Disadvantaged Minorities," in *Working and Poor: How Economic and Policy Changes Are Affecting Low-Wage Workers*, eds. Rebecca M. Blank, Sheldon H. Danziger, and Robert F. Schoeni (New York: Russell Sage Foundation, 2008).

54 See Pew Hispanic Center, *Mexican Immigrants in the United States, 2008* (Washington, DC: Pew Hispanic Center, 2009), http://pewhispanic.org/files/factsheets/47.pdf.

55 Demetrios G. Papademetriou and Aaron Terrazas, *Immigrants and the Current Economic Crisis: Research Evidence, Policy Challenges, and Implications* (Washington, DC: Migration Policy Institute, 2009), www.migrationpolicy.org/pubs/lmi_recessionJan09.pdf.

56 For example, the ACS indicates that the foreign-born population fell by about 100,000 people between 2007 and 2008. The number of Mexicans fell by 300,000, suggesting not only smaller inflows but larger return migration to Mexico. For a more detailed discussion of trends in Mexican migration, see Jeffrey Passel, D'Vera Cohn, and Ana Gonzalez-Barrera, "Net Migration from Mexico Falls to Zero — and Perhaps Less," www.pewhispanic.org/files/2012/04/Mexican-migrants-report_final.pdf.

percent of immigrants were working in that industry (compared with 7 percent of natives) and they accounted for almost one-quarter of all construction workers.[57] Immigrants are also more likely to work in manufacturing industries and agriculture than natives, who are more likely to work in the finance, insurance, and real estate (FIRE) and government sectors. Although the recent recession pummeled the financial sector, the construction industry began shrinking earlier and perhaps more sharply.

Occupation also plays a role in immigrant-native disparities in exposure to the business cycle. Within industries, immigrants are more likely than natives to work in blue-collar and service occupations, and these jobs may be more likely to be cut in downturns. During the period 1994 to 2011, 30 percent of foreign-born workers were employed in blue-collar occupations — as manual laborers, machine operators, and mechanics, for example — compared with 22 percent of natives. Immigrants also were overrepresented in service occupations, such as those of private household and food service workers. By contrast, natives were overrepresented in professional, clerical, and sales occupations.

One study concludes that the unemployment rate was so much higher among immigrants than among natives in 2009 in large part because of these differences in occupations; within occupations, immigrants and natives typically have similar unemployment rates.[58]

III. What Can Public Policy Do to Reduce the Disparate Impact of Business-Cycle Downturns on Immigrant Households?

Numerous programs at the federal, state, and local levels aim to help low-income families. Eligibility for and participation in such programs tend to rise during downturns, although less so for immigrants than natives.[59] This discrepancy is due to many reasons, some of which can be addressed by changes in program design while others reflect more intractable problems. For example, although recessions affect immigrant-headed households more adversely than native-headed households, many immigrant-headed households are ineligible for benefits either because they are unauthorized or have not spent sufficient time in the United States. Also, immigrant-headed households may be reluctant to apply for benefits because they have at least one member who lacks legal status or US citizenship or because they are concerned

---

57 Authors' calculations from the CPS outgoing rotation group data.
58 Camarota and Jensenius, *Trends in Immigrant and Native Employment.*
59 Marianne Bitler and Hilary W. Hoynes, "Immigrants, Welfare Reform, and the US Safety Net" (NBER working paper 17667, National Bureau of Economic Research, Cambridge, MA, 2011), www.nber.org/papers/w17667.

about jeopardizing an application for naturalization or a green card. We leave issues regarding who should be eligible for transfer programs to others. We focus instead on possible program design changes that would better target eligible families in times of need while minimizing any adverse incentives on work effort.

Across the business cycle, immigrant households are more likely to be among the *working* poor than native households, which make them ineligible for many transfer programs. As shown in Figures 10 and 11, less-educated immigrants are much more likely to work and less likely to be unemployed, even during recessions. Some poor immigrant households therefore do not benefit from unemployment insurance during recessions because no one is actually unemployed. In addition, as discussed below, many unemployed immigrants are ineligible for unemployment insurance. Also, many immigrant households do not qualify for means-tested transfer programs, such as cash welfare and food stamps, because their income exceeds the very low income thresholds for those programs. These factors make traditional public assistance programs impractical tools for helping such immigrant families ride out recessions.

We discuss three approaches to helping immigrant families who need assistance during economic downturns: modifying the earned income tax credit to give means-tested benefits to families suffering from unemployment or reduced work hours; targeting children through existing and expanded programs; and providing more financial assistance to local communities. The proposed changes would help natives as well as immigrants. But since immigrants — particularly less-educated and Latin American immigrants — appear to bear the brunt of recessions, they would be among the primary beneficiaries of the proposals discussed below.

The public assistance program most closely tied to the business cycle is unemployment insurance, making it a natural candidate for helping immigrants during economic downturns. However, unemployment insurance programs do not cover many legal immigrants who lose their jobs because they do not meet the minimum earnings requirement. In addition, legal immigrants may work in an uncovered job, a part-time or temporary job, or a job that is off the books, or they may be self-employed or not employed with the same employer long enough to be eligible for benefits. Because of numerous exclusions and benefit time limits, only about 37 percent of all unemployed workers receive unemployment insurance.[60]

---

60   This was the average recipiency rate during the 1980-2007 period. See Howard F. Rosen, "Reforming Unemployment Insurance for the 21st Century Workforce" (testimony before the Income Security and Family Support Subcommittee, House Ways and Means Committee, March 15, 2007).

A modified version of the earned income tax credit (EITC) program might be a more effective way to help legal immigrant and native households during economic downturns.[61] The EITC is a refundable federal income tax credit for low- to moderate-income working individuals and families; many states with income taxes also have an EITC program. The EITC is designed to encourage work and reduce poverty by supplementing low-wage workers' earned income.[62] Tax credits can even be received in advance throughout the year, making them a speedy way to get funds to those who need them. During downturns, the EITC may become less effective because potential recipients might be unable to find work all year, meaning they would have no earned income and hence cannot receive an EITC. To counter this problem, the program could be adapted to channel funds to workers who have suffered a drop in their earnings during a recession. For example, families whose earnings are below their previous-year level because a worker was laid off or had his hours cut might receive a payment equal to part of the lost earnings. This payment would effectively act as unemployment insurance but would be conditioned on meeting the EITC eligibility criteria.

In fact, an adapted EITC program would be even more effective than traditional unemployment insurance for families experiencing economic hardship. First, the EITC is based on family size: families with dependent children receive more credit than childless adults. In contrast, unemployment insurance is tied only to an individual's former earnings — not the family's earnings — and does not vary with the number of dependents. Second, the EITC is based on earnings across all employers, which is important since many low-wage workers switch jobs frequently or work multiple part-time jobs. Unemployment insurance, however, requires a minimum period of work with a single employer.

A modified EITC program could have more impact during a recession than traditional welfare programs. Most importantly, it would reward low-income families with a history of labor-force attachment. Traditional welfare programs tend to penalize work whereas EITC encourages it. EITC already targets low-income working families with children. The modified program for recessions suggested here could be even further targeted, for example at people living in areas with very high unemployment rates or working in certain industries.

---

61 Unauthorized immigrants are not eligible for the earned income tax credit (EITC) since the program requires a valid social security number.
62 Low-wage workers with positive earnings below a certain threshold receive an EITC payment that varies depending on income and family size. In 2008 the upper earnings threshold was approximately $12,800 for single workers with no children, and just over $41,000 for married couples with two or more children filing jointly. The maximum possible EITC credit was $4,824 for a married couple with two children and joint earned income of between $12,050 and $18,750. See Internal Revenue Service, *1040 Instructions* (Washington, DC: Internal Revenue Service, 2009), 53, www.irs.gov/pub/irs-pdf/i1040.pdf.

A second possibility would be to focus on children. Most children of immigrants are US citizens and hence categorically eligible for welfare programs just like the children of natives.[63] However, immigrant-headed households may be reluctant to apply for benefits due to US-citizen children because of confusion or concerns about government involvement, particularly in "mixed-status" families in which at least one person is in the United States illegally. Running public awareness campaigns that emphasize the eligibility of US-citizen children for programs or having schools help immigrants apply for benefits for their children might increase participation. Also, expanding programs that require little to no parental involvement, such as free or reduced-price school meals and after-care or summer school programs, would help ease the financial burden on families during a recession.

Third, the federal government could provide additional resources during downturns to communities with large immigrant populations. For example, public hospitals could receive funding to help defray the costs of charity care to unauthorized immigrants and other uninsured individuals, costs that rise during recessions.[64] Not only would this help families who lose their health insurance along with their jobs, it also would ease the fiscal situation for their communities, which have both greater demands for funds and lower tax revenues during recessions. Federal money for such communities has the added benefit of not tying welfare to individuals, a situation that can create adverse incentives.

The above discussion assumes that policymakers want to use direct transfers to help immigrant families and communities hurt by economic downturns. Funneling more public funds toward low-income immigrants may be controversial. After all, studies suggest that less-educated immigrants already impose a negative fiscal impact on US taxpayers.[65] A more cost-effective alternative would be to encourage

---

63 At least two-thirds of children of unauthorized immigrants — and four-fifths of all children of immigrants — are US citizens by birth. See Urban Institute, *Children of Immigrants: Facts and Figures* (Washington, DC: Urban Institute, 2006), www.urban.org/UploadedPDF/900955_children_of_immigrants.pdf. About 65 percent of immigrant-headed households include minors versus 51 percent of native-headed households

64 About one-third of all immigrants — and 64 percent of unauthorized immigrants — do not have health insurance. See Steven A. Camarota, *Facts on Immigration and Health Insurance* (Washington, DC: Center for Immigration Studies, 2009), www.cis.org/articles/2009/healthcare.pdf. These rates are higher than among natives, but because immigrants are about 13 percent of the population, immigrants comprise about one-fifth of all nonelderly uninsured individuals. See Immigration Policy Center, *Sharing the Costs, Sharing the Benefits* (Washington, DC: Immigration Policy Center, 2009), http://immigrationpolicy.pairsite.com/sites/default/files/docs/Sharing%20the%20Costs%20Sharing%20the%20Benefits%202009.pdf. For a broader discussion of immigrants and health-care reform, see Randy Capps, Marc R. Rosenblum, and Michael Fix, *Immigrants and Health Care Reform: What's Really at Stake?* (Washington, DC: Migration Policy Institute, 2009), www.migrationpolicy.org/pubs/healthcare-Oct09.pdf.

65 See chapters 6 and 7 in James P. Smith and Barry Edmonston, *The New Americans: Economic, Demographic, and Fiscal Effects of Immigration* (Washington, DC: National Academy Press, 1997).

families to save and build up a buffer against future unemployment spells. For example, the federal government could work with community or nonprofit groups to help immigrants and low-income natives get access to banks or other depository institutions and low-cost savings accounts.[66] Savings-incentive programs, where the government provides matching funds to savers, have also proven effective in raising savings rates.[67] The underlying goal is to help all families, both immigrants and natives, smooth their income across time on their own, via savings, instead of relying on public assistance programs in bad economic times. Of course, in a severe recession, these measures alone cannot solve the problems facing families in poverty, but they could certainly help alleviate them.

A different way to reduce immigrants' business-cycle vulnerability in the future would be to restructure immigration policy so that it explicitly takes the business cycle into account. Under current law, Congress sets immigration quotas and changes them very infrequently.[68] Policy could instead tie quotas to changes in the labor market. For example, when the unemployment rate rises, the number of temporary work visas and green cards available could be reduced automatically. Shifting the emphasis from family-based admissions to employment-based admissions also would make immigrant inflows more cyclical, since employment-based immigration is more likely to slow down during a recession.[69] As a result, immigrants and natives would compete with fewer new workers at times when employer demand for workers is relatively low. In addition, reducing immigrant inflows when economic conditions are weak can improve immigrant economic outcomes over the long run. Some previous research suggests that economic conditions at the time of entry have long-term effects on immigrants'

---

66 In 2003, for example, the Mexican Consulate in Chicago partnered with the Federal Deposit Insurance Corporation to provide financial education to immigrants, leading to greater immigrant use of bank accounts. See Dovelyn Ranneveig Agunias, "Committed to the Diaspora: More Developing Countries Setting Up Diaspora Institutions," *Migration Information Source*, November 2009, www.migrationinformation.org/Feature/display.cfm?ID=748.

67 See Esther Duflo, William Gale, Jeffrey Liebman, Peter Orszag, and Emmanuel Saez, "Saving Incentives for Low- and Middle-Income Families: Evidence from a Field Experiment with H&R Block," *Quarterly Journal of Economics* 121, no. 4 (2006): 1311–46.

68 Refugee quotas would not be included in the process described here; they are used to admit immigrants primarily on humanitarian or geopolitical grounds.

69 For a discussion on how legal immigration, particularly family-based immigration, is relatively unresponsive to the business cycle, see Gordon H. Hanson, *The Economic Logic of Illegal Immigration* (Washington, DC: Council on Foreign Relations, 2007), www.cfr.org/publication/12969/economic_logic_of_illegal_immigration.html.

outcomes.[70] Making immigrant policy more responsive to the business cycle requires no outlay of funds and would benefit immigrants already present in the United States and possibly natives as well.

Although most immigration policy is determined at the federal level, states are becoming increasingly involved in immigration. Much state action in recent years has aimed at deterring unauthorized immigrants from settling in a given state. Several states have adopted laws that require employers to use E-Verify and law enforcement agencies to check immigration status during any lawful stop or arrest. Such laws appear to lead to a significant decline in the number of unauthorized Hispanic immigrants likely to be living and working in a state.[71]

Such state actions may cushion competing workers from the business cycle if such laws lead to smaller numbers of immigrants *and* if smaller numbers of immigrants means better labor-market opportunities for natives. However, it is not clear that natives benefit from reductions in the number of immigrants, even during economic downturns. Most economic research does not find that having more immigrants in an area is associated with worse labor-market outcomes for natives.[72] In addition, such laws may only cause immigrants to move to other states rather than leave the United States. Further research on the effect of state immigration laws on both immigrants and natives is needed before clear conclusions can be drawn.

---

70   Immigrants who enter the United States during relatively weak periods appear to have lower earnings not only at entry but also over time. See Barry R. Chiswick and Paul W. Miller, "Immigrant Earnings: Language Skills, Linguistic Concentrations and the Business Cycle," *Journal of Population Economics* 15, no. 1 (2002): 31–57; and Alice Nakamura and Masao Nakamura, "Wage Rates of Immigrant and Native Men in Canada and the United States," in *Immigration, Language, and Ethnicity: Canada and the United States*, ed. Barry R. Chiswick (Washington, DC: AEI Press, 1992). Chiswick and Miller suggest that the effect of the initial unemployment rate on earnings takes 18 years to die out (given mean historical unemployment rates). However, Chiswick, Cohen, and Zach conclude that the unemployment rate at arrival is not associated with employment and unemployment over the long run (see Chiswick, Cohen, and Zach, "The Labor Market Status of Immigrants"). Bratsberg, Barth, and Raaum do not find that the unemployment rate at the time of entry is associated with immigrants' current wages (see Bratsberg, Barth, and Raaum, "Local Unemployment and the Relative Wages of Immigrants").
71   Sarah Bohn, Magnus Lofstrom, and Steven Raphael, "Did the 2007 Legal Arizona Workers Act Reduce the State's Unauthorized Immigrant Population?" (IZA discussion paper 5682, Bonn, Germany, 2011), http://ftp.iza.org/dp5682.pdf; Sarah Bohn, Magnus Lofstrom, and Steven Raphael, *Employment Effects of Arizona's 2007 Legislation Against the Hiring of Unauthorized Immigrants* (San Francisco, CA: Public Policy Institute of California, 2012); and Catalina Amuedo-Dorantes and Cynthia Bansak, "The Labor Market Impacts of Mandated Employment Verification Systems," *American Economic Review* 103, no. 3 (2012): 543-8.
72   See, for example, David Card, "Is the New Immigration Really So Bad?" *Economic Journal* 115 (2005): 300–23; Pia M. Orrenius and Madeline Zavodny, "Does Immigration Affect Wages? A Look at Occupation-Level Evidence," *Labour Economics* 14 (2007): 757–73; and Gianmarco Ottaviano and Giovanni Peri, "Rethinking the Effect of Immigration on Wages," *Journal of the European Economic Association* 10 (2012): 152–97.

IV. Conclusion

The long-run trend over the past 18 years is one of economic progress for immigrants. Economic booms hastened this progress, and the Great Recession slowed it. As the data show, recessions harm employment prospects and raise unemployment and poverty rates. Median earnings are more stable over the business cycle than the other economic variables examined here, and the immigrant-native earnings gap has been largely unchanged since the last recession.

Immigrants' economic outcomes tend to be more sensitive to the business cycle than those of natives. Cyclicality is most pronounced among less-educated immigrants and immigrants from Latin America. This is consistent with two stylized facts. First, many less-educated immigrants take up jobs in sectors that are closely linked to overall economic growth, such as construction and manufacturing. Second, immigrants from Latin America tend to be unauthorized (in addition to being less educated), and illegal migration is closely tied to the business cycle. In good times, when these inflows surge, booming industries disproportionately hire immigrants, who work in jobs with high demand. Meanwhile, many immigrants are blocked from working in the most stable sectors, such as government.

Low-skilled immigrants' greater vulnerability to the business cycle raises an interesting problem for public policy. Existing welfare programs are ill-suited to aid families whose fortunes rise and fall with the macroeconomy. Unemployment insurance, policymakers' main tool during recessions, covers only a minority of unemployed workers and has a large number of exclusions that make it insufficient for helping low-wage workers, who are more likely to move between jobs, hold several part-time jobs, or be self-employed. A modified EITC program that is means-tested, kicks in during recessions, and is triggered by changes in family income — not necessarily by job loss — might be an option for consideration. Another option would be targeting US-citizen children, many of whom have immigrant parents who may not enroll their children in benefits programs for fear of jeopardizing their own immigration paperwork. In addition to informing parents about such programs, governments could increase funding for subsidized school meals, day care, after-school programs, and health care. Finally, funds for communities with large immigrant populations would also help offset recession-induced budget shortfalls for public schools and hospitals.

Lastly, reforming US immigration policy could also help mitigate immigrants' vulnerability to the business cycle, albeit in a more explicit way. By making employment-based flows a larger share of all immigration, inflows would be more cyclical, falling during recessions and rising during expansions. This would better sync immigration with economic growth, lessening the burden on competing workers and reducing the need for expanded safety-net programs during economic downturns.

Appendix

Short-Run Fluctuations in Employment Rates among Immigrants by Region of Origin, Ages 16 and Older, First Quarter 1994 to Fourth Quarter 2011

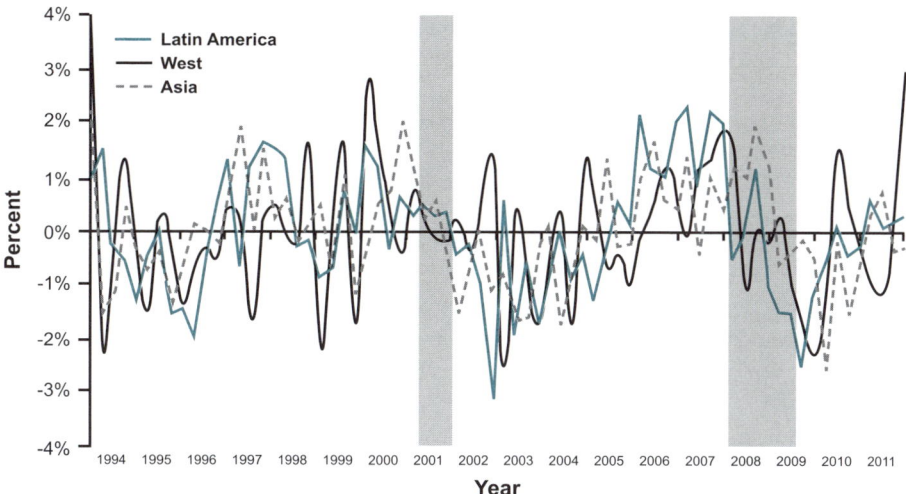

Note: Data are seasonally adjusted. Recessions are shown as shaded areas. The West includes Western Europe and Canada.

Source: Authors' calculations from US Census Bureau, Current Population Survey, January 1994 to December 2011.

Works Cited

Agunias, Dovelyn Ranneveig. 2009. Committed to the Diaspora: More Developing Countries Setting Up Diaspora Institutions. *Migration Information Source*, November 2009. www.migrationinformation.org/Feature/display.cfm?ID=748.

Altonji, Joseph G. and Rebecca M. Blank. 1999. Race and Gender in the Labor Market. In *Handbook of Labor Economics*, vol. 3C, eds. Orley Ashenfelter and David Card. Amsterdam: Elsevier.

Amuedo-Dorantes, Catalina and Cynthia Bansak. 2012. The Labor Market Impacts of Mandated Employment Verification Systems. *American Economic Review* 103 no.3 (2012): 543-8.

Antecol, Heather, Peter Kuhn, and Stephen J. Trejo. 2006. Assimilation via Prices or Quantities? Sources of Immigrant Earnings Growth in Australia, Canada, and the United States. *Journal of Human Resources* 41 (4): 821–40.

Batalova, Jeanne and Michael Fix with Peter A. Creticos. 2008. *Uneven Progress: The Employment Pathways of Skilled Immigrants in the United States.* Washington, DC: Migration Policy Institute. www.migrationpolicy.org/pubs/BrainWasteOct08.pdf.

Biddle, Jeff E. and Daniel S. Hamermesh. 2012. Wage Discrimination over the Business Cycle. IZA Discussion Paper 6445, IZA, Bonn, Germany. http://ftp.iza.org/dp6445.pdf.

Bitler, Marianne and Hilary W. Hoynes. 2011. Immigrants, Welfare Reform, and the US Safety Net. NBER Working Paper 17667, National Bureau of Economic Research, Cambridge, MA. www.nber.org/papers/w17667.

Blank, Rebecca M. 1989. Disaggregating the Effect of the Business Cycle on the Distribution of Income. *Economica* 56 (2): 141–63.

Blau, Francine D. and Lawrence M. Kahn. 2007. Changes in the Labor Supply Behavior of Married Women: 1980-2000. *Journal of Labor Economics* 25 (3): 393–438.

Blau, Francine D., Marianne A. Ferber, and Anne E. Winkler. 2006. *The Economics of Women, Men, and Work*, 5th ed. Upper Saddle River, NJ: Pearson Prentice Hall.

Bohn, Sarah, Magnus Lofstrom, and Steven Raphael. 2012. Did the 2007 Legal Arizona Workers Act Reduce the State's Unauthorized Immigrant Population? IZA Discussion Paper 5682, IZA, Bonn, Germany. http://ftp.iza.org/dp5682.pdf.

———. 2012. *Employment Effects of Arizona's 2007 Legislation Against the Hiring of Unauthorized Immigrants*. San Francisco, CA: Public Policy Institute of California.

Borjas, George J. 1996. Assimilation and Changes in Cohort Quality Revisited: What Happened to Immigrant Earnings in the 1980s? *Journal of Labor Economics* 13 (2): 201–45.

———. 2001. Does Immigration Grease the Wheels of the Labor Market? *Brookings Papers on Economic Activity* (1): 69–119.

———. 2003. Welfare Reform, Labor Supply, and Health Insurance in the Immigrant Population. *Journal of Health Economics* 22 (6): 933–58.

———. 2008. Wage Trends among Disadvantaged Minorities. In *Working and Poor: How Economic and Policy Changes Are Affecting Low-Wage Workers*, ed. Rebecca M. Blank, Sheldon H. Danziger, and Robert F. Schoeni. New York: Russell Sage Foundation.

Borjas, George J. and Rachel M. Friedberg. 2009. Recent Trends in the Earnings of New Immigrants to the United States. NBER Working Paper 15406, National Bureau of Economic Research, Cambridge, MA. www.nber.org/papers/w15406.

Bradbury, Katharine L. 2000. Rising Tide in the Labor Market: To What Degree Do Expansions Benefit the Disadvantaged? *New England Economic Review*: 3–33.

Bratsberg, Bernt, Erling Barth, and Oddbjørn Raaum. 2006. Local Unemployment and the Relative Wages of Immigrants: Evidence from the Current Population Surveys. *Review of Economics and Statistics* 88 (2): 243–63.

Camarota, Steven A. 2009. *Facts on Immigration and Health Insurance.* Washington, DC: Center for Immigration Studies. www.cis.org/articles/2009/healthcare.pdf.

Camarota, Steven A. and Karen Jensenius. 2009. *Trends in Immigrant and Native Employment.* Washington, DC: Center for Immigration Studies. www.cis.org/articles/2009/back509.pdf.

Capps, Randy, Marc R. Rosenblum, and Michael Fix. 2009. *Immigrants and Health Care Reform: What's Really at Stake?* Washington, DC: Migration Policy Institute. www.migrationpolicy.org/pubs/healthcare-Oct09.pdf.

Card, David. 2005. Is the New Immigration Really So Bad? *Economic Journal* 115: 300–23.

Chiswick, Barry R. and Paul W. Miller. 2002. Immigrant Earnings: Language Skills, Linguistic Concentrations and the Business Cycle. *Journal of Population Economics* 15 (1): 31–57.

———. 2009. The International Transferability of Immigrants' Human Capital. *Economics of Education Review* 28 (2): 162–9.

Chiswick, Barry R., Yinon Cohen, and Tzippi Zach. 1997. The Labor Market Status of Immigrants: Effects of the Unemployment Rate at Arrival and Duration of Residence. *Industrial and Labor Relations* 50 (2): 289–303.

DeNavas-Walt, Carmen, Bernadette D. Proctor, and Jessica C. Smith. 2008. *Income, Poverty, and Health Insurance in the Coverage in the United States: 2007.* Washington, DC: US Government Printing Office. www.census.gov/prod/2008pubs/p60-235.pdf.

Devereux, Paul J. 2004. Cyclical Quality Adjustment in the Labor Market. *Southern Economic Journal* 70 (3): 600–15.

Duflo, Esther, William Gale, Jeffrey Liebman, Peter Orszag, and Emmanuel Saez. 2006. Saving Incentives for Low- and Middle-Income Families: Evidence from a Field Experiment with H&R Block. *Quarterly Journal of Economics* 121 (4): 1311–46.

Duleep, Harriet Orcutt and Mark C. Regets. 1997. Measuring Immigrant Wage Growth Using Matched CPS Files. *Demography* 34 (2): 239–49.

Dustmann, Christian, Albrecht Glitz, and Thorsten Vogel. 2010. Employment, Wages, and the Economic Cycle: Differences between Immigrants and Natives. *European Economic Review* 54: 1–17.

Enders, Walter. 2004. *Applied Econometric Time Series*, 2nd ed. Hoboken, NJ: John Wiley and Sons.

Fix, Michael, ed. 2009. *Immigrants and Welfare: The Impact of Welfare Reform on American's Newcomers.* New York: Russell Sage Foundation.

Hall, Matthew and George Farkas. 2008. Does Human Capital Raise Earnings for Immigrants in the Low-Skill Labor Market? *Demography* 45 (3): 619–39.

Hanson, Gordon H. 2007. *The Economic Logic of Illegal Immigration.* Washington, DC: Council on Foreign Relations. www.cfr.org/publication/12969/economic_logic_of_illegal_immigration.html.

———. 2008. Illegal Migration from Mexico to the United States. *Journal of Economic Literature* 44 (4): 869–924.

Hotchkiss, Julie L. 2006. Changes in Behavioral and Characteristic Determination of Female Labor Force Participation, 1975-2005. *Federal Reserve Bank of Atlanta Economic Review* 91 (2): 1–20.

Hoynes, Hilary W. 2000. The Employment, Earnings, and Income of Less Skilled Workers over the Business Cycle. In *Finding Jobs: Work and Welfare Reform*, eds. David E. Card and Rebecca M. Blank. New York: Russell Sage Foundation.

Hoynes, Hilary W., Douglas L. Miller, and Jessamyn Schaller. 2012. Who Suffers During Recessions? NBER Working Paper 17951, National Bureau of Economic Research, Cambridge, MA. http://nber.org/papers/w17951.

Hoynes, Hilary W., Marianne E. Page, and Ann Huff Stevens. 2006. Poverty in America: Trends and Explanations. *Journal of Economic Perspectives* 20 (1): 47–68.

Immigration Policy Center. 2009. *Sharing the Costs, Sharing the Benefits.* Washington, DC: Immigration Policy Center. www.immigrationpolicy.org/images/File/factcheck/Sharing%20the%20Costs%20Sharing%20the%20Benefits%202009.pdf.

Internal Revenue Service. 2009. *1040 Instructions.* Washington, DC: Internal Revenue Service. www.irs.gov/pub/irs-pdf/i1040.pdf.

Kochhar, Rakesh. 2008. *Latino Workers in the Ongoing Recession: 2007 to 2008.* Washington, DC: Pew Hispanic Center. http://pewhispanic.org/files/reports/99.pdf.

———. 2008. *Latino Labor Report 2008: Construction Reverses Job Growth for Latinos.* Washington, DC: Pew Hispanic Center. http://pewhispanic.org/files/reports/99.pdf.

Kochhar, Rakesh, with C. Soledad Espinoza, and Rebecca Hinze-Pifer. 2010. *After the Great Recession: Foreign Born Gain Jobs; Native Born Lose Jobs.* Washington, DC: Pew Hispanic Center. www.pewhispanic.org/files/reports/129.pdf.

Nakamura, Alice and Masao Nakamura. 1992. Wage Rates of Immigrant and Native Men in Canada and the United States. In *Immigration, Language, and Ethnicity: Canada and the United States*, ed. Barry R. Chiswick. Washington, DC: AEI Press.

National Bureau of Economic Research (NBER). The NBER's Recession Dating Procedure. www.nber.org/cycles/recessions.html.

Orrenius, Pia M. and Madeline Zavodny. 2010. Mexican Immigrant Employment Outcomes over the Business Cycle. *American Economic Review Papers and Proceedings* 100 (3): 316–20.

———. 2007. Does Immigration Affect Wages? A Look at Occupation-Level Evidence. *Labour Economics* 14: 757–73.

Ottaviano, Gianmarco and Giovanni Peri. 2012. Rethinking the Effect of Immigration on Wages. *Journal of the European Economic Association* 10: 152–97.

Papademetriou, Demetrios G. and Aaron Terrazas. 2009. *Immigrants and the Current Economic Crisis: Research Evidence, Policy Challenges, and Implications.* Washington, DC: Migration Policy Institute. www.migrationpolicy.org/pubs/lmi_recessionJan09.pdf.

Passel, Jeffrey S. 2005. *Unauthorized Migrants: Numbers and Characteristics.* Washington, DC: Pew Hispanic Center. http://pewhispanic.org/files/reports/46.pdf.

Passel, Jeffery and D'Vera Cohn. 2009. *A Portrait of Unauthorized Immigrants in the United States.* Washington, DC: Pew Hispanic Center. http://pewhispanic.org/files/reports/107.pdf.

———. 2011. *Unauthorized Immigrant Population: National and State Trends, 2010.* Washington, DC: Pew Hispanic Center. www.pewhispanic.org/files/reports/133.pdf.

Jeffrey Passel, D'Vera Cohn, and Ana Gonzalez-Barrera. 2012. *Net Migration from Mexico Falls to Zero—and Perhaps Less.* www.pewhispanic.org/files/2012/04/Mexican-migrants-report_final.pdf.

Pew Hispanic Center. 2009. *Mexican Immigrants in the United States, 2008.* Washington, DC: Pew Hispanic Center. http://pewhispanic.org/files/factsheets/47.pdf.

Raphael, Steven and Eugene Smolensky. 2009. Immigration and Poverty in the United States. In *Changing Poverty, Changing Policies*, eds. Maria Cancian and Sheldon Danziger. New York: Russell Sage Foundation.

Rosen, Howard F. 2007. Reforming Unemployment Insurance for the 21st Century Workforce. Testimony before the Income Security and Family Support Subcommittee, House Ways and Means Committee, March 15, 2007.

Smith, James P. and Barry Edmonston. 1997. *The New Americans: Economic, Demographic, and Fiscal Effects of Immigration.* Washington, DC: National Academy Press.

Solon, Gary, Robert Barsky, and Jonathan A. Parker. 1994. Measuring the Cyclicality of Real Wages: How Important Is Composition Bias? *Quarterly Journal of Economics* 109 (1): 1–25.

Urban Institute. 2006. *Children of Immigrants: Facts and Figures.* Washington, DC: Urban Institute. www.urban.org/UploadedPDF/900955_children_of_immigrants.pdf.

US Census Bureau. 2008. Income, Poverty, and Health Insurance Coverage in the United States: 2008. www.census.gov/prod/2009pubs/p60-236.pdf.

———. 2012. Income, Poverty, and Health Insurance Coverage in the United States: 2010. www.census.gov/prod/2011pubs/p60-239.pdf.

———. How the Census Bureau Measures Poverty. www.census.gov/hhes/www/poverty/about/overview/measure.html.

———. Poverty Thresholds for 2011 by Size of Family and Number of Related Children Under 18 Years. www.census.gov/hhes/www/poverty/data/threshld/.

US Citizenship and Immigration Services (USCIS). 2009. Public Charge Fact Sheet. www.uscis.gov/portal/site/uscis/menuitem.5af9bb95919f35e66f6141765 43f6d1a/?vgnextoid=354fb2a3fffb4210VgnVCM100000082ca60aRCRD&vg nextchannel=68439c7755cb9010VgnVCM10000045f3d6a1RCRD.uscis-menuitem.5af9bb95919f35e66f614176543f6d1a/?vgnextoid=354fb2a3fffb 4210VgnVCM100000082ca60aRCRD&vgnextchannel=68439c7755cb9010V gnVCM10000045f3d6a1RCRD.

US Department of Homeland Security (DHS). Persons Obtaining Legal Permanent Resident Status by Type and Major Class of Admission: Fiscal Years 2002 to 2011. www.dhs.gov/files/statistics/publications/LPR11.shtm.

US Department of State. Classes of Nonimmigrants Issued Visas — FY1987-2010 Detail Table. www.travel.state.gov/visa/statistics/nivstats/nivstats_4582.html.

CHAPTER 6

ERODING GAINS: THE RECESSION'S IMPACT ON IMMIGRANTS IN MIDDLE-SKILLED JOBS

By Jeanne Batalova and Michael Fix

Migration Policy Institute

Introduction

One measure of immigrants' economic incorporation is their expanding employment in a range of occupations, not only low-skilled jobs such as farm and domestic workers, but also middle- and high-skilled ones. High-skilled jobs are those that typically require at least a bachelor's degree, while middle-skilled jobs require more than a high school diploma but less than a four-year college education. Most of these jobs pay a family-sustaining wage, a critical feature of high-quality or "good" jobs.[1]

Immigrant participation in jobs at all skill levels has been increasing rapidly in the 15-year period preceding the 2007-09 Great Recession.[2] We found particularly strong growth in middle-skilled jobs, which, unlike certain high-skilled occupations, are in general *not* supported by a set of dedicated immigrant worker visas, such as H-1B temporary workers in specialty occupations or employer-sponsored visas for permanent immigration.

In this chapter, we carry that work forward, examining the impact of the recession on full-time workers, by skill level, across five sectors that together employ half of the immigrant labor force in the United States: information technology (IT), health care, hospitality, construction, and manufacturing.

---

1   Elizabeth Lower-Basch, *Opportunity at Work: Improving Job Quality* (Washington, DC: Center for Law and Social Policy, 2007), www.clasp.org/admin/site/publications/files/0374.pdf.
2   Randy Capps, Michael Fix, and Serena Yi-Ying Lin, *Still an Hourglass? Immigrant Workers in Middle-Skilled Jobs* (Washington, DC: Migration Policy Institute [MPI], 2010), www.migrationpolicy.org/pubs/sectoralstudy-Sept2010.pdf.

Our analysis takes a sectoral approach, for several reasons. One is that sectors reflect to some degree the ways in which education and training are organized in the United States. Further, as explained in this chapter, immigrants' economic progress and the recession's impacts on it vary widely by sector — variation that is not fully captured by analyses that assess immigrants' progress across the economy as a whole. Finally, most of these sectors have long job ladders (i.e., they have highly differentiated career pathways that provide opportunities for career development and earnings growth) that lend themselves to immigrants' economic progress.

In brief, we find that immigrant workers remained substantially represented in middle-skilled jobs in 2010, with the share of foreign-born workers in middle-skilled jobs exceeding that in high-skilled ones. Nonetheless, the recession prompted a marked decline in immigrants' hold on middle-skill work, largely as a result of trends in the construction and manufacturing sectors. These two sectors were more likely to employ lesser-educated immigrants in middle-skilled jobs than the others examined, underscoring the fact that postrecession the path to good jobs and the middle class increasingly requires higher levels of formal education and greater English language proficiency.[3]

Our results also show that immigrants holding middle-skilled jobs in the health and IT sectors have significantly higher education credentials than their native counterparts. These findings suggest that helping immigrants access these jobs may present less of a policy challenge than "brain waste" — i.e., the underutilization of their education and professional skills.

The sectoral analyses presented also show that immigrant labor force growth following the recession was greatest in the hospitality sector — which involves the shortest job ladders among the industries examined here and offers the fewest pathways to middle- and high-skilled jobs. In contrast, the fastest job growth among native workers took place in the health sector, which promises many more opportunities for good jobs going forward. This trend reinforces the need for English language training and postsecondary credentials for labor market success.

We begin by describing key terms and the analytical approach used in this chapter, and then outline the current state and future prospects of the five sectors and what these trends mean for immigrants' economic participation in them. Using US Census Bureau data, trends are compared in immigrant employment before the Great Recession and in its

---

3 Anthony Carnevale, Nicole Smith, and Jeff Strohl, *Projections of Jobs and Education Requirements through 2018* (Washington, DC: Center on Education and the Workforce, 2010), www9.georgetown.edu/grad/gppi/hpi/cew/pdfs/FullReport.pdf; Stephen Steigleder and Louis Soares, *Let's Get Serious about Our Nation's Human Capital: A Plan to Reform the US Workforce Training System* (Washington, DC: Center for American Progress, 2012), www.americanprogress.org/wp-content/uploads/issues/2012/06/pdf/workforce_training.pdf.

immediate aftermath, with focus on its impact on immigrant workers in high-, middle-, and low-skilled jobs across sectors.

A. Key Definitions and Approach

This chapter builds on the Migration Policy Institute report *Still an Hourglass? Immigrant Workers in Middle-Skilled Jobs,* which examined immigrants' role and penetration in the US labor market prior to the recession. Taking advantage of more recent data that capture immediate postrecession trends, we update this earlier analysis of the role and status of immigrant workers in five sectors. In particular, this chapter looks at workers in jobs that pay family-sustaining earnings, defined here as $34,000 per worker per year.[4]

B. Classifying Occupations into Skill Groups

As in *Still an Hourglass?,* occupations are classified into three major groups — low, middle, and high skilled — based on variables that include education, training, and wages. Here, we adapt the classification of occupations provided by the Occupational Information Network (O*NET),[5] a comprehensive online database of occupational profiles that describe day-to-day work tasks and activities, tools and technologies, and qualifications and skills of the typical worker. The O*NET database is updated regularly from surveys of workers, occupational experts, and occupational analysts. One dimension of the O*NET database is the "job zone": occupations are divided into five zones based on the education, related experience, and job training required (see Box 1).[6]

---

[4] Following recent work of Wider Opportunities for Women, we define "family-sustaining earnings" as $34,000 a year or half of what a dual-earner couple with two young children has to earn annually to cover basic costs such as housing, child care, health care, transportation, savings, and retirement. Wider Opportunities for Women and the Center for Social Development, *Basic Economic Security Tables* (Washington, DC: Wider Opportunities for Women, 2011), www.wowonline.org/documents/BESTIndexforTheUnitedStates2010.pdf.
[5] The development of the Occupational Information Network (O*NET) is supported by the US Department of Labor/Employment and Training Administration (USDOL/ETA). Learn more at: www.onetcenter.org/about.html.
[6] Learn more about these job zones at: www.onetonline.org/help/online/zones.

> **Box 1. Job Zones: Requirements and Examples**
>
> *Zone 1:* Occupations requiring little or no preparation and that may include a high school degree or a General Educational Development (GED) diploma as a requirement (e.g., waiters/waitresses and construction laborers).
>
> *Zone 2:* Occupations generally requiring a high school diploma and some work-related skills and knowledge (e.g., physical therapist aides and cooks).
>
> *Zone 3:* Typically, occupations requiring that workers have trained in vocational schools, have related on-the-job experience, or hold an associate's degree (e.g., registered nurses, teacher assistants, chefs, and carpenters).
>
> *Zone 4:* Occupations usually requiring a four-year bachelor's degree and a substantial amount of work-related skill, knowledge, or experience (e.g., computer programmers, accountants and auditors, elementary and middle school teachers).
>
> *Zone 5:* Occupations requiring a significant amount of academic preparation, typically a master's degree or higher (e.g., physicians and surgeons, lawyers and judges, physical scientists).

Based on comparison of the median annual earnings of occupations in different job zones we combine Zones 1 and 2 as "low skilled" and Zones 4 and 5 as "high skilled." Occupations in Zone 3 are defined as "middle skilled." The low-skilled occupations overwhelmingly pay less than family-sustaining earnings while high-skilled occupations pay significantly more. We find a strong correlation between employment in a middle-skilled job and the earning of family-sustaining income: 58 percent of native workers and 51 percent of immigrant workers in middle-skilled jobs earned $34,000 a year compared to 29 percent of natives and 21 percent of immigrants engaged in low-skilled occupations.

C. Data Employed and Sector Definitions

Data from the Census Bureau's 2000 Decennial Census and various years of the American Community Survey (ACS) are analyzed.[7] For employment trends over time, we use single-year data from the Decen-

---

[7] All data used in the analysis were accessed from Steven Ruggles, Trent Alexander, Katie Genadek, Ronald Goeken, Matthew Schroeder, and Matthew Sobek, *Integrated Public Use Microdata Series: Version 5.0* [Machine-readable database] (Minneapolis: University of Minnesota, 2012), http://usa.ipums.org/usa/index.shtml.

nial Census and 2005-10 ACS; for earnings analysis, pooled 2008-10 data file are used to increase the sample size and improve our estimates' robustness. We disaggregate results by nativity, sector, and skill level. We also restrict our sample to full-time workers with positive earnings. More specifically, we focus on civilian immigrant and native workers (including self-employed but not unpaid family workers) aged 16 to 64 who worked in the year prior to the survey for at least 27 weeks (regardless of hours worked) or, if they were employer for fewer than 27 weeks, only those working at least 35 hours per week were included.

We define four of our study sectors — construction, manufacturing, health care, and hospitality — using industry codes in the ACS and Census data, which are based on the 2007 Census industrial classification system:

- Construction is a single, aggregated sector that comprises all establishments primarily engaged in the construction of building or engineering projects.

- Manufacturing includes a diverse range of durable and nondurable manufacturing subsectors such as electronic component and product manufacturing; animal slaughtering and processing; and apparel manufacturing.

- Health care includes the offices and/or clinics of physicians, dentists, chiropractors, optometrists, and health practitioners; hospitals; nursing and personal care facilities; health services; and residential care services.

- Hospitality includes the industries of hotel and motel services; lodging places; and eating and drinking places.

Because IT jobs are spread across many different industries, occupation codes are primarily relied on to define the IT sector. These codes include those of computer and information systems managers, computer programmers, and network and computer system administrators. (See "Appendix D. Definition of Key Terms" for the complete list of "core" and IT-related occupations.)

I. Sector Profiles and Trends

Many factors affect the kinds of jobs immigrants hold.[8] While education, skills, work experience, and personal drive are important,[9] the characteristics and prospects of the sectors in which immigrants work also shape their employment trajectories. The recent recession affected the economic fortunes of immigrants earlier and more negatively than natives — in part because immigrant workers were younger, had lower levels of education and English skills, and were concentrated in harder-hit sectors.[10] The US Census Bureau's data show that between 2007 and 2008 the size of the immigrant unemployed population grew eight times faster than that of natives (8 percent versus 1 percent).[11] However, the recession's impacts varied across sectors.

A. Construction

Immigrant workers benefited greatly from the sector's expansion prior to 2007. Immigrant employment increased by nearly 300 percent between 1990 and 2006; immigrants constituted one-quarter of all construction workers by the end of the economic expansion.[12] As Jacqueline Hagan and her colleagues argue,[13] many immigrant workers in construction with low formal educations were able to leverage work skills developed informally on the job to improve their economic and wage opportunities both in their home countries and the United States. However, the collapse of housing demand in 2007-08 led to massive job losses. The Bureau of Labor Statistics' (BLS) Current Employment Statistics (CES) recorded a 28 percent drop in construction employment

---

8   Noah Lewin-Epstein, Moshe Semyonov, and Irena Kogan, "Institutional Structure and Immigrant Integration: A Comparative Study of Immigrants' Labor Market Attainment in Canada and Israel," *International Migration Review* 37, no. 2 (2003): 389–420; Ilana Redstone Akresh, "Occupational Trajectories of Legal US Immigrants: Downgrading and Recovery," *Population and Development Review* 34, no. 3 (2008): 435–56.
9   Barry Chiswick and Paul Miller, "Immigrant Earnings: Language Skills, Linguistic Concentrations, and the Business Cycle," *Journal of Population Economics* 15, no. 1 (2002): 31–57; Jacqueline Hagan, "Contextualizing Immigrant Labor Market Incorporation: Legal, Demographic, and Economic Dimensions," *Work and Occupations* 31, no. 4 (2004): 407–23.
10 Demetrios G. Papademetriou, Madeleine Sumption, and Aaron Terrazas with Carola Burkert, Stephen Loyal, and Ruth Ferrero-Turrión, *Migration and Immigrants Two Years after the Financial Collapse: Where Do We Stand?* (Washington, DC: MPI, 2010), www.migrationpolicy.org/pubs/MPI-BBCreport-2010.pdf; See Chapter 5 in this volume by Pia M. Orrenius and Madeline Zavodny, *How Immigrants and Natives Fare During Recessions and Recoveries*.
11 Authors' tabulations of the US Census Bureau's American Community Survey (ACS) 2007 and 2008, "Online Tables: Selected Characteristics of the Native and Foreign-Born Populations," http://factfinder2.census.gov/faces/nav/jsf/pages/index.xhtml.
12 Capps, Fix, and Lin, *Still an Hourglass?*
13 Jacqueline Hagan, Nichola Lowe, and Christian Quingla, "Skills on the Move: Rethinking the Relationship Between Human Capital and Immigrant Economic Mobility," *Work and Occupations* 38, no. 2 (2011): 149–78; Natasha Iskander, Nichola Lowe, and Christine Riordan, "The Rise and Fall of a Micro-Learning Region: Mexican Immigrants and Construction in Center-South Philadelphia," *Environment and Planning A* 42, no. 7 (2010): 1595–612.

between January 2007 and 2010.[14] While total employment remained unchanged between 2010 and 2012, there is little indication of any expanded hiring given the today's uncertainties over future house prices, a large pool of unoccupied and foreclosed houses, and tightened mortgage procedures.[15]

B. Manufacturing

The shift toward a service-driven, knowledge-based economy, coupled with the automation of many manufacturing processes and the outsourcing of manufacturing facilities to China and other countries, has prompted a gradual decline in the sector's share of total US employment. According to CES data, the overall number of employed workers in the industry dropped 34 percent, from 17.3 million to 11.5 million, between January 2000 and 2010.[16] However, the industry's overall employment rebounded between 2010 and 2012, increasing 4 percent. This growth is mostly due to expanded employment in durable goods manufacturing, including the production of machinery, transportation equipment, primary metals, and electrical equipment and appliances. While some types of manufacturing, such as advanced manufacturing that relies on high-tech machines and processes, are expected to grow,[17] lower-skilled workers — nearly one-quarter of whom are immigrants[18] — will likely be excluded from these opportunities without significant improvement in their math and computer skills.

C. Health Care

Health care is one of few sectors that avoided recession-driven employment losses; instead, the number of health-care workers has expanded since 2007.[19] According to BLS and other projections, the sector's prospects remain strong, and added jobs are expected at various skill

---

14 Bureau of Labor Statistics (BLS), "Online Tables: Employment, Hours, and Earnings from the Current Employment Statistics Survey (National) in Construction, 2000 to 2012," www.bls.gov/CES/.

15 Janet Yellen, "The Economic Outlook and Monetary Policy" (speech given at the Money Marketers of New York University, New York, April 11, 2012), www.federalreserve.gov/newsevents/speech/yellen20120411a.htm.

16 BLS, "Online Tables: Employment, Hours, and Earnings from the Current Employment Statistics Survey (National) in Manufacturing, 2000 to 2012," www.bls.gov/CES/.

17 The Toronto-Dominion Bank Group (TD Bank Group), "Caught in the Middle: The Polarization of Skills in the US Labor Market," www.td.com/document/PDF/economics/special/td-economics-special-cj0411_polarization.pdf; Peter Creticos, *Advanced Manufacturing within the Context of México, El Salvador, Guatemala, Honduras and the United States* (Washington, DC: MPI, forthcoming); Stephanie Strom, "For Ohio Pottery, a Small Revival," *New York Times*, June 11, 2012, www.nytimes.com/2012/06/12/business/starbucks-turns-to-ohio-not-china-for-coffee-mugs.html?_r=2.

18 Immigrants were overrepresented among low-skilled manufacturing workers compared to their share of all manufacturing workers in 2010 (23 percent versus 19 percent).

19 BLS, "Online Tables: Employment, Hours, and Earnings from the Current Employment Statistics Survey (National) in Health Care, 2000 to 2012," www.bls.gov/CES/.

levels.[20] Even though the United States does not recruit health-care professionals on employment-based visas at the same rates as other English-speaking countries such as the United Kingdom, Canada, and Australia,[21] immigration has often been viewed as a vehicle to replenish the labor pool across skill levels[22] and to address shortages of medical health-care workers in low-income and rural communities.[23]

Before the recession, 12 percent of all US workers and 10 percent of immigrant workers were employed in health care. Overall, immigrants accounted for 14 percent of the health-care workforce. Immigrants were overrepresented within the sector in both high- and low-skilled occupations: more than one-quarter of all physicians and surgeons and over one-fifth of nursing aids and home-health aides were immigrants. Indeed, the principal problem that immigrant health-care professionals face may not be access to employment *per se* but rather underemployment, resulting in part from foreign credentials going unrecognized by US employers and regulators.[24]

D. Hospitality

Prior to 2007, one-quarter of all hospitality workers were immigrants. As the industry grew rapidly, so did jobs, for both natives and immigrants. The total number of workers employed grew by 15 percent, from 10 million to 11.6 million, between January 2000 and 2008, followed by a drop (almost 5 percent between 2008 and 2010), then a 5-plus percent rebound between 2010 and 2012. Total employment returned to 11.6 million in early 2012. BLS projects a small (1 percent) annual rise in hospitality employment over the next ten years, a rate slightly lower than that of overall employment (1.3 percent).[25]

---

20 BLS, "Employment Projections — 2010-20," News Release, February 1, 2012, www.bls.gov/news.release/pdf/ecopro.pdf.
21 Madeleine Sumption, Michael Fix, Kristen McCabe, and Jeanne Batalova, *Immigration and the Health-Care Workforce since the Global Economic Crisis* (Washington, DC: MPI, forthcoming).
22 Lindsay Lowell and Stefka Gerova, "Immigrants and the Healthcare Workforce Profiles and Shortages," *Work and Occupations* 31, no. 4 (2004): 474–98; Janiszewski Goodin, "The Nursing Shortage in the United States of America: An Integrative Review of the Literature," *Journal of Advanced Nursing* 43, no. 4 (2003): 335–43; Edward Schumacher, "Foreign-Born Nurses in the US Labor Market," *Health Economics* 20, no. 3 (2011): 362–78.
23 Kenneth Fink, Robert Phillips, George Fryer, and Nerissa Koehn, "International Medical Graduates and the Primary Care Workforce for Rural Underserved Areas," *Health Affairs* 22, no. 2 (2003): 255–62, http://content.healthaffairs.org/content/22/2/255.full.pdf.
24 José Ramón Fernández-Peña, "Integrating Immigrant Health Professionals into the US Health Care Workforce: A Report from the Field," *Journal of Immigrant and Minority Health* 14, no. 3, (2012): 441–8; Peggy Chen, Leslie Curry, Susannah Bernheim, David Berg, Aysegul Gozu, and Marcella Nunez-Smith, "Professional Challenges of Non-US-Born International Medical Graduates and Recommendations for Support during Residency Training," *Academic Medicine* 86, no. 11 (2011): 1383–8.
25 BLS, "Employment Projections."

Most hospitality jobs, such as those of maids and janitors, require little training and provide employment in the "back of the house." Thus entry requirements are low, enabling many low-educated, limited English proficient, and recently arrived immigrants to enter the sector. But most such jobs offer little mobility.[26] Workers can advance by acquiring customer service and managerial skills and learning English, however, the number of higher skill positions in hospitality is limited.

E. Information Technology

During the 1990s, the IT sector was the principal engine of US economic growth. Immigrants were an integral part of the sector's success, working as computer programmers and database administrators for established companies and in some cases creating their own start-ups.[27] The expansion of permanent and temporary skilled worker visas by the *Immigration Act of 1990*, combined with increased foreign student enrollment in science, technology, engineering, and math (STEM) programs at US universities, contributed to a surge in the number of immigrants in IT: the share grew from 12 percent to 17 percent between 1990 and 2000. But the bursting of the tech bubble in the late 1990s and a general economic downturn in 2001-02 led to significant job losses among both native and immigrant workers.

As the sector rebounded, employment prospects improved — at least for immigrant workers. By 2006 one in five IT workers was an immigrant. From 2000 to 2007, immigrant employment grew by 26 percent, while that of natives declined slightly (by 3 percent). IT is the most high skilled of the sectors examined here, and immigrants disproportionately work in the high-skilled jobs within it. While IT career pathways offer opportunities for immigrants with college-level degrees, the high entry requirements are barriers for those with less education.

II. Trends in Immigrant Employment before the Recession and in the Early Recovery Period

A. The Recession's Impact by Job Skill Level

Before the recession, the penetration of immigrants in both the overall economy and the sectors examined here was deep, with growth in the

---

26   Katherine Newman, *Chutes and Ladders: Navigating the Low-Wage Labor Market* (Cambridge, MA: Harvard University Press, 2006); Patricia Adler and Peter Adler, *Paradise Laborers: Hotel Work in the Global Economy* (Ithaca, NY: Cornell University Press, 2004).
27   AnnaLee Saxenian, *Silicon Valley's New Immigrant Entrepreneurs* (San Francisco, CA: Public Policy Institute of California, 1999), www.ppic.org/main/publication.asp?i=102.

immigrant full-time workforce significantly outpacing that of natives in percentage terms across all skill levels (see Figure 1, first panel). During the 2000-07 period the number of immigrants in middle-skilled jobs rose 44 percent — a more rapid increase than seen in high-skilled jobs, where immigrant job growth was 36 percent.

Figure 1. Changes in Employment of Full-Time Immigrant and Native Workers, Total and by Job Skill Level

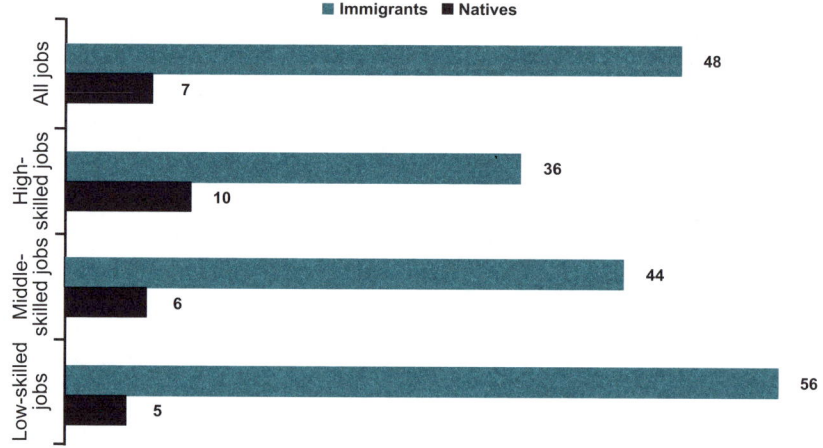

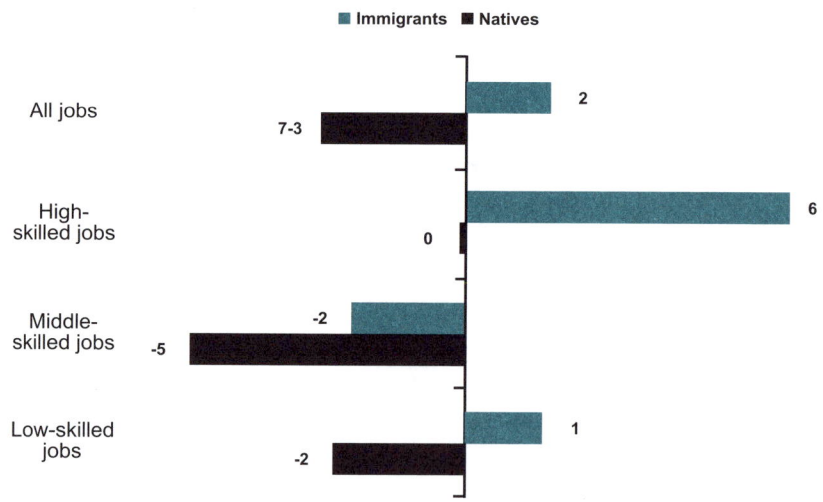

Source: MPI analysis of data from the 2000 Decennial Census, and 2007 ACS and 2010 ACS.

The data also reveal that low-skilled employment grew more rapidly for immigrants (by 56 percent) than did high- or middle-skilled work. At the same time, high-skilled employment grew much more rapidly for native workers (by 10 percent) than did middle- or low-skilled jobs (6 percent and 5 percent, respectively).

The strong pre-recession growth rates for immigrants in middle-skilled jobs reversed following the recession — in large part because of declines in construction and manufacturing (see Figure 1, second panel). We find a modest economy-wide loss of 2 percent in middle-skilled jobs held by immigrants between 2007 and 2010. Natives' middle-skilled-job holdings fell 5 percent over the same period. Nonetheless, both before and after the recession the share of immigrants and natives in middle-skilled jobs exceeded those in high-skilled employment (see Table 1).

Table 1. US Full-Time Workers, by Nativity and Skill Distribution, 2000, 2007, 2010

	Skill Distribution		
	2000	2007	2010
Immigrants (000s)	13,916	20,619	20,932
Employed in (%)	100	100	100
High-skilled jobs	23	21	22
Middle-skilled jobs	26	25	24
Low-skilled jobs	51	54	54
Natives (000s)	100,130	106,879	103,981
Employed in (%)	100	100	100
High-skilled jobs	27	27	28
Middle-skilled jobs	33	33	32
Low-skilled jobs	40	39	39

Source: MPI analysis of data from the 2000 Decennial Census, and 2007 ACS and 2010 ACS.

B. The Recession's Impact, by Industry

During the 2000-07 period, immigrants were major contributors to employment expansion in each of the five sectors examined here. Immigrant employment grew by 119 percent in construction, 64 percent in hospitality, and 47 percent in health care — rates significantly higher than those of natives (see Figure 2, first panel). In two of the sectors examined, immigrant employment grew while native employment declined (IT and manufacturing). These divergent employment trends reflect both the availability of jobs in the sectors as well as changing demographics. We find, for instance, that while the native working-age population (16 to 64) grew by only 7 percent between 2000 and 2007, the immigrant working-age population grew by 24 percent during the same period.

In both 2000 and 2010, the five sectors employed nearly half of all full-time immigrant workers (see Appendix A). Taken together, these sectors' relative importance to immigrant employment changed little over the decade, but the pre-recession growth seen in immigrant employment either slowed or reversed. Figure 2 (bottom panel) highlights notable differences across sectors between 2007 and 2010.

Figure 2. Changes in Employment of Full-Time Immigrant and Native Workers, Total and by Sector

Percent change between 2000 and 2007

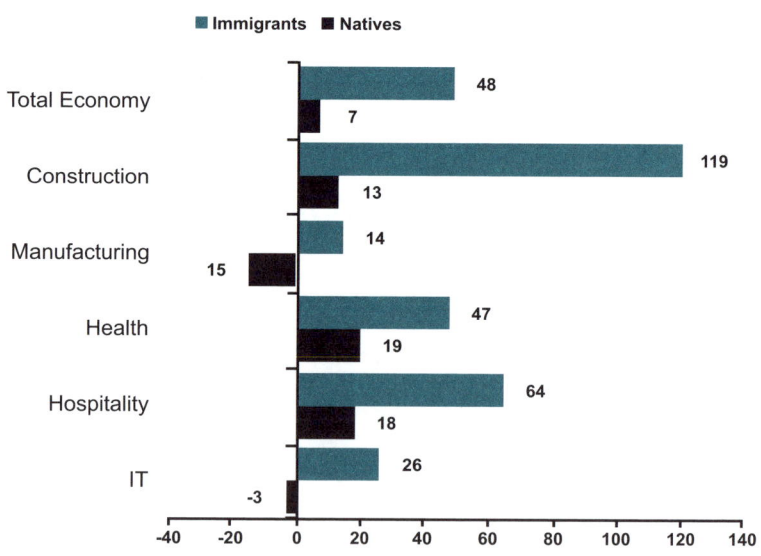

Percent change between 2007 and 2010

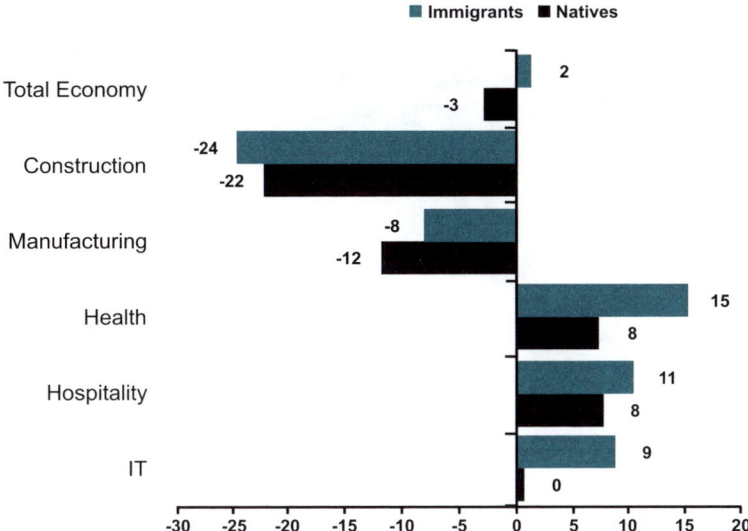

Source: MPI analysis of data from the 2000 Decennial Census and 2007 and 2010 ACSs.

Construction. Between 2007 and 2010, employment decreased 22 percent for natives and 24 percent for immigrants (see Figure 2 and Table 2). Losses were registered across all skill levels, with the sharpest proportional declines occurring in middle-skilled jobs (28 percent for immigrants and 24 percent for natives).

Manufacturing. The 2000-07 pre-recession decline in manufacturing employment among native workers continued through 2010. At the same time, immigrants' earlier employment growth (14 percent between 2000 and 2007) was followed by a decline of 8 percent between 2007 and 2010. Despite losses over the decade, manufacturing continued to employ the largest share of immigrants (12 percent in 2010) of the five sectors.

Table 2. Job Growth and Losses in the US Economy and Five Select Sectors (Percent Change), 2000-07 versus 2007-10

	Immigrants		US born	
	2000-07 (% change)	2007-10 (% change)	2000-07 (% change)	2007-10 (% change)
All workers	48	2	7	(3)
High	36	6	10	(0)
Middle	44	(2)	6	(5)
Low	56	1	5	(2)
Construction workers	119	(24)	13	(22)
High	76	(13)	41	(21)
Middle	111	(28)	9	(24)
Low	130	(24)	8	(20)
Manufacturing workers	14	(8)	(15)	(12)
High	22	7	23	(7)
Middle	5	(11)	53	2
Low	15	(11)	68	13
Health-care workers	47	15	19	8
High	33	14	17	11
Middle	46	15	18	4
Low	61	17	23	9
Hospitality workers	64	11	18	8
High	23	(7)	(10)	2
Middle	53	2	18	3
Low	68	13	19	9
IT workers	26	9	(3)	0
High	27	9	(3)	(0)
Middle	17	13	2	4
Low	12	(19)	(16)	(16)

Source: MPI analysis of data from the 2000 Census, and the 2007 ACS and 2010 ACS.

Health care. The sector continued its pre-recession growth; both immigrant and native workforces expanded across all skill levels between 2007 and 2010. The number of immigrants in health care grew nearly twice as fast as that of natives between 2007 and 2010 (15 versus 8 percent). However, while the fastest growth among natives occurred in high-skilled jobs, low-skilled jobs grew the fastest for immigrants (see Table 2).

Hospitality. While the pre-recession gains in native and immigrant employment slowed, employment across most skill groups increased between 2007 and 2010. Overall, immigrant employment increased by

11 percent during the period, while native employment expanded by 8 percent (see Figure 1). Low-skilled employment grew the fastest for both immigrant and native workers (see Table 2).

Information technology. While immigrants gained jobs in IT in both the 2000-07 and 2007-10 periods (by 26 percent and 9 percent, respectively), native employment was unchanged between 2007 and 2010.

Across the economy as a whole and in all study sectors other than construction, the number of immigrant workers either rose faster or declined more slowly between 2007 and 2010 than did the number of their native counterparts. Our analysis reveals that much of the employment growth occurred at low skill levels, with some erosion in middle-skilled jobs.

III. Trends in Jobs Providing Family-Sustaining Earnings

Middle-skilled jobs are central to economic mobility and to immigrants' economic integration because they represent an important avenue to earning family-sustaining incomes, especially for workers with less than a college degree. Fifty-one percent of immigrants and 58 percent of natives employed in middle-skilled occupations earned a family-sustaining annual income (see Figure 3). In comparison, only one-fifth of immigrant workers and less than one-third of native workers in low-skilled occupations did so. Not surprisingly, almost all high-skilled jobs pay family-sustaining incomes. While the share of natives who earn such incomes exceeds that of immigrants in both middle- and low-skilled jobs, this earnings gap disappears in high-skilled occupations.

Figure 3. Share of Full-Time Workers Earning Family-Sustaining Incomes, by Nativity and Job Skill Level, 2009

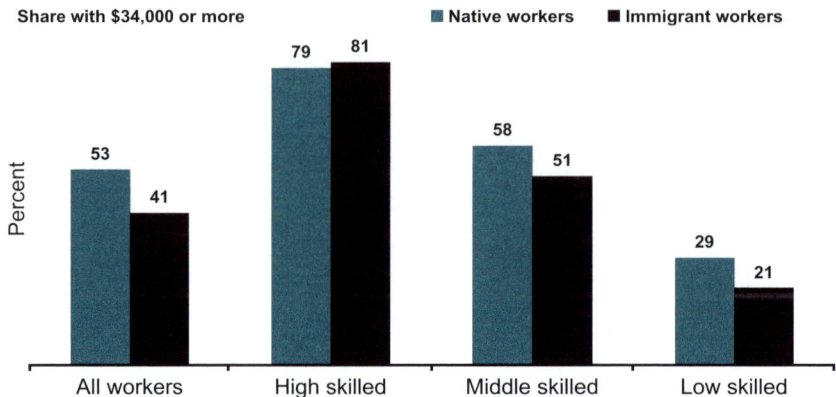

Notes: We define a family-sustaining income as $34,000 a year, or half of what a dual-earner couple with two young children has to earn annually to cover basic costs such as housing, child care, health care, transportation, savings, and retirement.
Source: MPI analysis of data from the pooled 2008-10 ACS.

Workers' opportunities to earn good wages do not just depend on the type of job they hold, but also on the sector in which they work, as Figures 4a through 4c show. Looking again across sectors:

A. Earnings in Construction and Manufacturing

Native workers were much more likely to earn family-sustaining incomes than their immigrant counterparts in *construction* (57 percent versus 33 percent) and in *manufacturing* (62 percent versus 42 percent, respectively) (see Figure 4a). The earnings gap between immigrants and natives was widest in low-skilled occupations: 43 percent of native workers in manufacturing earned family-sustaining incomes versus only 23 percent of immigrants. Immigrants' low earning power owes to their education level: in low-skilled manufacturing jobs, half of immigrants versus 12 percent of natives did not have a high school degree (see Appendix B).

Figure 4a. Share of Full-Time Workers with Family-Sustaining Earnings, by Nativity and Job Skill Level in Construction and Manufacturing, 2009

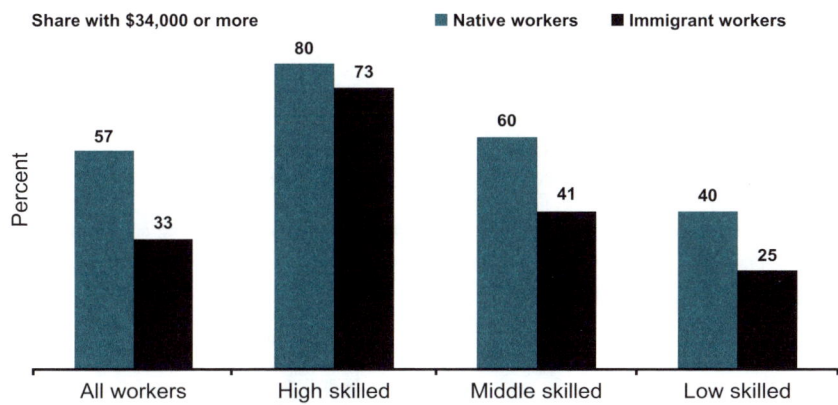

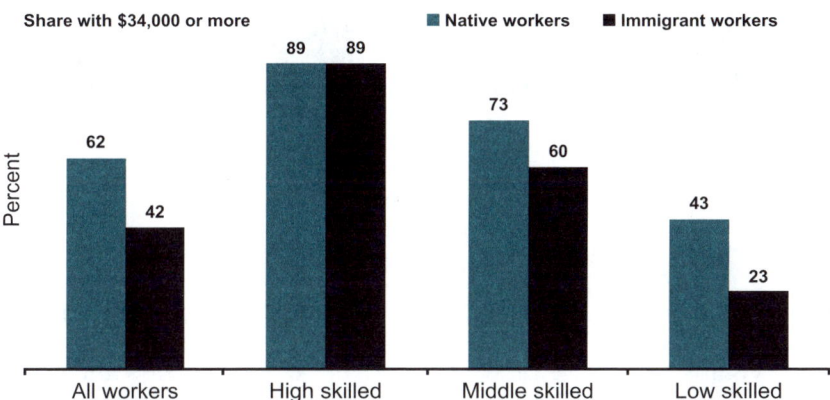

Source: MPI analysis of data from the pooled 2008-10 ACS.

The earnings gap between native and immigrant full-time workers in both manufacturing and construction narrows as skill levels rise. At the high-skill level, close to 90 percent of both immigrant and native workers in manufacturing and more than 75 percent in construction earned family-sustaining incomes.

B. Earnings in Hospitality

In *hospitality*, few immigrant (18 percent) or native (16 percent) workers earned family-sustaining incomes (see Figure 4b). These trends are not surprising given that roughly 80 percent of native and immigrant workers in the sector are employed in low-skilled jobs (Appendix C). While these low-skilled occupations grew both before and after the recession, they provide little occupational mobility.

Figure 4b. Share of Full-Time Workers with Family-Sustaining Earnings, by Nativity and Job Skill Level in Hospitality, 2009

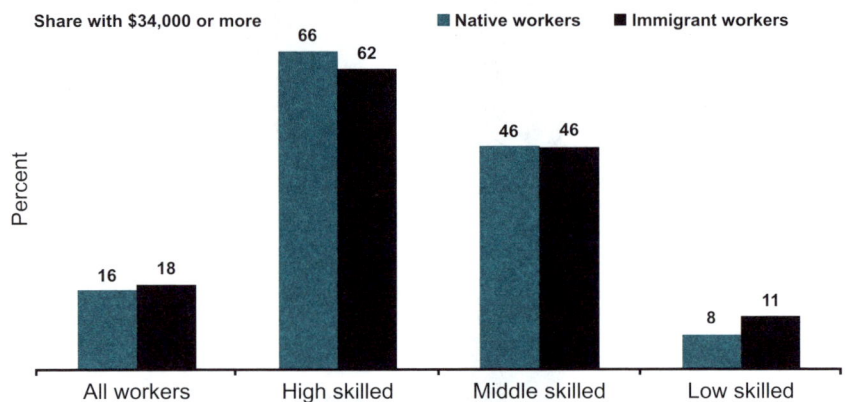

Source: MPI analysis of data from the pooled 2008-10 ACS.

C. Earnings in IT and Health Care

The overwhelming majority of IT workers earn family-sustaining wages (see Figure 4c) owing to the high share of college-educated workers employed in the sector (85 percent of immigrants and 60 percent of natives). Similarly, over half of health-care workers earned family-sustaining incomes. Here again, the share of immigrants earning these incomes slightly exceeded that of natives. Overall the share of health-care workers with college degrees was higher than for the economy as a whole (e.g., 46 percent versus 31 percent).

Figure 4c. Share of Full-Time Workers with Family-Sustaining Earnings, by Nativity and Job Skill Level in IT and Health Care, 2009

Information Technology

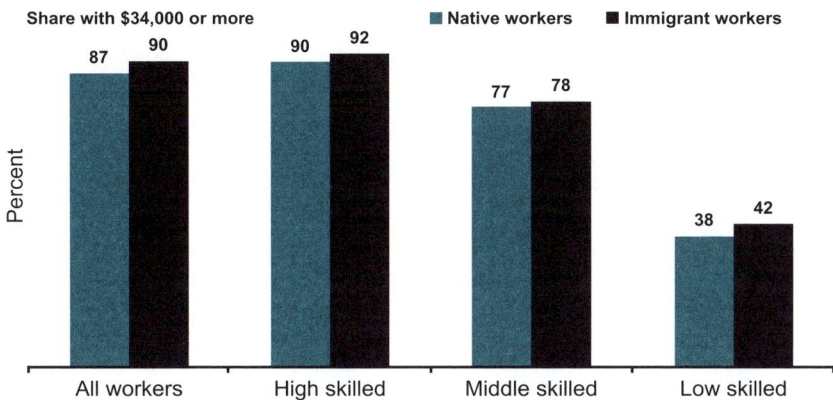

Health Care

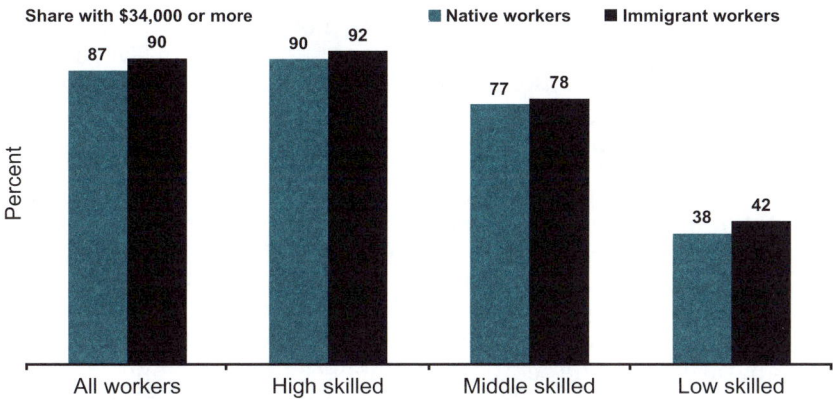

Source: MPI analysis of data from the pooled 2008-10 ACS.

Immigrants were slightly more likely to earn family-sustaining earnings in IT and health care across all skill levels — owing to their higher levels of human capital. We found that 88 percent of immigrants in high-skilled IT jobs had a college degree, versus 65 percent of natives. In the health-care sector immigrants in high-skilled jobs were also more likely than natives to hold a college degree (86 percent versus 76 percent) (see Appendix B). Similarly, in middle-skill jobs that typically require some postsecondary education but not a four-year college degree, immigrants were 20 percentage points more likely than natives to have a bachelor's degree or higher. These findings suggest that while their comparatively higher levels of education may help immigrant workers obtain middle-skilled jobs that pay decently, their skills may often be underutilized, leading to "brain waste."[28]

Overall, workers employed in middle-skilled jobs in the IT, manufacturing, and health-care sectors were more highly educated and better off than their counterparts in construction and hospitality, where less than half of workers in middle-skilled jobs earn family-sustaining incomes.

IV. Conclusion

Immigrants accounted for 5 percent of the US labor force in 1970; by 2010 their share had tripled to 16 percent.[29] Current projections suggest that immigrants and their children will account for almost all labor force growth in the next few decades, helping to finance the expensive retirement and health care of an aging US population. Even in the wake of the Great Recession immigrants have continued to play an important role in the country's labor market, driving sectoral growth and filling occupational gaps.

In this chapter, our primary interest here has been understanding (i) how the recession affected the employment of immigrant workers overall and in middle-skilled jobs in particular, i.e., jobs that typically require more than a high school but less than a four-year college degree and (ii) the role of immigrants' human capital in obtaining jobs that pay family-sustaining incomes.

We find that both immigrant and native employment in middle-skilled jobs slowed relative to the strong growth seen from 1990 to 2006. Further, the two sectors that offered substantial numbers of middle-skilled jobs to foreign-born workers with lower formal education levels — construction and manufacturing — saw declines and face uncertain futures.[30] The sector with the best current economic and mobility prospects — health care — requires more schooling and better English skills.

---

28 Jeanne Batalova and Michael Fix with Peter A. Creticos, *Uneven Progress: The Employment Pathways of Skilled Immigrants in the United States* (Washington, DC: MPI, 2008), www.migrationpolicy.org/pubs/BrainWasteOct08.pdf.
29 Jeanne Batalova and Alicia Lee, "Frequently Requested Statistics on Immigrants and Immigration in the United States," *Migration Information Source*, March 2012, www.migrationinformation.org/USfocus/display.cfm?id=886.
30 The Association of Commercial and Institutional Builders of Massachusetts, "Construction Employment, Spending Drop in Latest Month but Rise from Year Ago," *AGC's Data Digest*, April 2-6, 2012, www.agcmass.org/index.cfm/linkservid/E6FB48E4-D63A-9A68-E115274BA87F9944/showMeta/0/.

While our own and other research[31] do find some erosion in middle-skilled jobs among both natives and immigrants following the recession, it remains the case that immigrants remain well represented among middle-skilled workforce. Interestingly, unlike immigrant entry into some high-skill areas (e.g., IT, academia, and health care), the growth and penetration in middle-skilled job holdings for the most part has not been supported by dedicated high-skilled visas such as the H-1B, pointing to the continuing integration of immigrants who come through family and other immigration channels.

Nonetheless, the recession brought to forefront a worrying development — the narrowing pathway to middle-skilled jobs and good wages for workers with lower levels of human capital. This narrowing means that sustaining immigrants' economic integration will require policies aimed at English language acquisition and postsecondary education that yields credentials with documented labor market value.[32] The prospects of such efforts are uncertain given that the adult basic education, English as a second language (ESL) training, workforce training, and postsecondary education systems charged with these responsibilities are facing substantial fiscal challenges as recession-driven demand for their services rises.

---

31 Annette Bernhardt with Claire McKenna and Mike Evangelist, *The Low-Wage Recovery and Growing Inequality* (New York, National Employment Law Project, 2012), www.nelp.org/page/-/Job_Creation/LowWageRecovery2012.pdf?nocdn=1.
32 Organization for Economic Cooperation and Development (OECD), *Better Skills, Better Jobs, Better Lives: A Strategic Approach to Skills Policies* (Paris: OECD, 2012), http://skills.oecd.org/documents/oecdskillsstrategy.html.

Appendix A. Numbers and Shares of Full-Time Immigrant and Native Workers, by Skill Level and Sector, 2000-10

Immigrant Workers

All full-time workers	2000	2010
Immigrant (000s)	13,916	20,932
Percent		
IT	5	4
Health	9	10
Construction	8	9
Hospitality	9	11
Manufacturing	17	12

Employed in high-skilled jobs	2000	2010
Immigrants (000s)	3,178	4,574
Percent		
IT	19	18
Health	12	12
Construction	3	3
Hospitality	1	1
Manufacturing	11	10

Employed in middle-skilled jobs	2000	2010
Immigrants (000s)	3,594	5,051
Percent		
IT	2	2
Health	13	15
Construction	11	12
Hospitality	7	8
Manufacturing	14	9

Employed in low-skilled jobs	2000	2010
Immigrants (000s)	7,144	11,306
Percent		
IT	0	0
Health	6	7
Construction	9	10
Hospitality	14	17
Manufacturing	20	13

Native Workers

All full-time workers	2000	2010
US born (000s)	100,130	103,981
Percent		
IT	3	3
Health	9	12
Construction	7	6
Hospitality	5	6
Manufacturing	14	10

Employed in high-skilled jobs	2000	2010
US born (000s)	26,723	29,366
Percent		
IT	10	9
Health	9	11
Construction	4	4
Hospitality	1	1
Manufacturing	9	8

Employed in middle-skilled jobs	2000	2010
US born (000s)	33,361	33,678
Percent		
IT	2	2
Health	12	15
Construction	10	8
Hospitality	3	3
Manufacturing	13	10

Employed in low-skilled jobs	2000	2010
US born (000s)	40,045	40,936
Percent		
IT	0	0
Health	7	10
Construction	6	5
Hospitality	9	12
Manufacturing	17	12

Source: MPI analysis of data from the 2000 Decennial Census and 2010 ACS.

Appendix B. Educational Attainment of Immigrant and Native Full-Time Workers, by Nativity and Skill Level, Total Economy and Five Sectors (Percent)

Total Economy	Immigrants	Natives
High-skilled	100	100
BA or higher	79	71
AA or some college	13	20
High school/GED	5	8
Less than high school	3	1
Middle-skilled	100	100
BA or higher	29	25
AA or some college	30	44
High school/GED	23	26
Less than high school	18	4
Low-skilled	100	100
BA or higher	9	10
AA or some college	19	38
High school/GED	29	39
Less than high school	42	12

Hospitality	Immigrants	Natives
High-skilled	100	100
BA or higher	45	47
AA or some college	25	34
High school/GED	18	15
Less than high school	11	3
Middle-skilled	100	100
BA or higher	22	21
AA or some college	26	44
High school/GED	29	28
Less than high school	23	7
Low-skilled	100	100
BA or higher	7	9
AA or some college	17	39
High school/GED	31	33
Less than high school	45	19

Health Care	Immigrants	Natives
High-skilled	100	100
BA or higher	86	76
AA or some college	10	18
High school/GED	4	6
Less than high school	1	1
Middle-skilled	100	100
BA or higher	47	30
AA or some college	39	55
High school/GED	11	14
Less than high school	3	1
Low-skilled	100	100
BA or higher	14	9
AA or some college	32	44
High school/GED	31	38
Less than high school	23	9

Information Technology	Immigrants	Natives
High-skilled	100	100
BA or higher	88	65
AA or some college	9	29
High school/GED	2	6
Less than high school	0	0
Middle-skilled	100	100
BA or higher	55	34
AA or some college	33	51
High school/GED	8	14
Less than high school	3	1
Low-skilled	100	100
BA or higher	25	17
AA or some college	39	47
High school/GED	23	32
Less than high school	12	3

Construction	Immigrants	Natives
High-skilled	**100**	**100**
BA or higher	43	36
AA or some college	22	35
High school/GED	19	24
Less than high school	15	5
Middle-skilled	**100**	**100**
BA or higher	8	8
AA or some college	18	36
High school/GED	31	44
Less than high school	43	11
Low-skilled	**100**	**100**
BA or higher	4	6
AA or some college	10	29
High school/GED	28	47
Less than high school	58	18

Manufacturing	Immigrants	Natives
High-skilled	**100**	**100**
BA or higher	78	63
AA or some college	12	25
High school/GED	6	10
Less than high school	3	1
Middle-skilled	**100**	**100**
BA or higher	21	20
AA or some college	26	39
High school/GED	28	35
Less than high school	26	6
Low-skilled	**100**	**100**
BA or higher	7	6
AA or some college	15	31
High school/GED	30	51
Less than high school	49	12

Source: MPI analysis of the pooled 2008-10 ACS data.

Appendix C. Skill Distribution of Full-Time Workers, by Nativity and Job Skill Level, Five Sectors

	Skill Distribution	
	Immigrants (%)	Natives (%)
Information Technology		
Employed workers (000s) in	917	3,382
High-skilled jobs	89	80
Middle-skilled jobs	10	19
Low-skilled jobs	1	1
Health Care		
Employed workers (000s) in	2,077	12,060
High-skilled jobs	27	25
Middle-skilled jobs	36	42
Low-skilled jobs	38	33
Construction		
Employed workers (000s) in	2,069	6,830
High-skilled jobs	7	18
Middle-skilled jobs	32	47
Low-skilled jobs	60	35
Hospitality		
Employed workers (000s) in	2,173	6,224
High-skilled jobs	2	3
Middle-skilled jobs	17	19
Low-skilled jobs	81	79
Manufacturing		
Employed workers (000s) in	2,507	11,128
High-skilled jobs	18	22
Middle-skilled jobs	20	31
Low-skilled jobs	62	48

Source: MPI analysis of the pooled 2008-10 ACS data.

Appendix D. Definitions of Key Terms

Immigrants or foreign born. These terms refer to people residing in the United States who were not US citizens at birth. The foreign-born population includes naturalized citizens, lawful permanent immigrants, refugees and asylees, legal nonimmigrants (including those on student, work, or certain other temporary visas), and persons residing in the country without authorization. By comparison, the term *natives* refers to people residing in the United States who were US citizens in one of these three categories: (a) people born in one of the 50 states or the District of Columbia, (b) people born in United States Insular Areas such as Puerto Rico or Guam, or (c) people who were born abroad to at least one US citizen parent. We use the terms *immigrants* and *foreign born* interchangeably.

Family-sustaining earnings (or incomes). Defined here as $34,000 a year or half of what a dual-earner couple with two young children has to earn annually to cover basic costs such as housing, child care, health care, transportation, savings, and retirement.

Limited English proficient (LEP). LEP workers are those who speak another language at home and report speaking speak English "well," "not well," or "not at all."

Sectors. We define four of our study sectors — health care, construction, manufacturing, and hospitality — based on industry codes in the ACS and Census data, which are based on the 2007 Census Bureau industrial classification system. Because information technology (IT) jobs are spread across many different industries, we rely primarily on occupation codes to define this sector. The occupations examined in this chapter closely map the definition of IT workers developed by the National Research Council (NRC). The NRC definition includes workers who:[33]

- Design, install, upgrade, or maintain and support IT hardware, including computers, switches, routers, and chips with a digital aspect to their operation

- Design, author, adapt, test, implement, maintain, or support software or databases

- Install, configure, support, maintain, or utilize "back-office" systems and applications for use by those who interact directly with these systems for business purposes

---

33   National Research Council, *Building a Workforce for the Information Economy* (Washington, DC: National Academy Press, 2001), www.nap.edu/openbook.php?record_id=9830&page=1.

- Design, develop, document or train on, or implement computer-based business solutions for clients
- Undertake software-based enterprise resource planning or just-in-time inventory control and systems integration
- Write software code for embedded systems such as handheld, palm-top devices or equipment controllers
- Develop design tools, simulation, and IT-intensive systems for the delivery of electronic content
- Are responsible for testing, documentation, or configuration management
- Directly manage IT workers

Accordingly, our analysis focuses on the following "core" IT occupations:

- Computer and information systems managers
- Computer software engineers
- Computer scientists and systems analysts
- Computer programmers
- Network systems and data communication analysts
- Electrical and electronics engineers
- Network and computer systems administrators
- Database administrators
- Computer hardware engineers
- Operations research analysts
- Computer support specialists

In addition we examine the following IT-related occupations that involve the manufacture, installation, repair, or operation of hardware that is critical to the functioning of IT. (These are also included in the NRC definition.) The IT-related occupations are:[34]

- Engineering technicians (except drafters)
- Computer operators
- Computer control programmers and operators
- Data-entry keyers

Finally, we also include high-skilled managers in areas such as computer and information systems, marketing and sales, general operations, and human resources — but only those working in a small group of specific IT industries.[35]

---

34 This is not an exhaustive list of computer-related occupations but the major ones that were available from the ACS. We did not include smaller computer-related occupations such as technical writers or peripheral equipment operators.

35 Daniel E. Hecker, *High-Technology Employment: A NAICS-Based Update* (Washington, DC: BLS, 2005), www.bls.gov/opub/mlr/2005/07/art6full.pdf.

Works Cited

Adler, Patricia and Peter Adler. 2004. *Paradise Laborers: Hotel Work in the Global Economy*. Ithaca, NY: Cornell University Press.

Akresh, Ilana Redstone. 2008. Occupational Trajectories of Legal US Immigrants: Downgrading and Recovery. *Population and Development Review* 34 (3): 435–56.

Batalova, Jeanne and Alicia Lee. 2012. Frequently Requested Statistics on Immigrants and Immigration in the United States. *Migration Information Source,* March 2012. www.migrationinformation.org/USfocus/display.cfm?id=886.

Batalova, Jeanne and Michael Fix with Peter A. Creticos. 2008. *Uneven Progress: The Employment Pathways of Skilled Immigrants in the United States.* Washington, DC: Migration Policy Institute (MPI). www.migrationpolicy.org/pubs/BrainWasteOct08.pdf.

Bernhardt, Annette with Claire McKenna and Mike Evangelist. 2012. *The Low-Wage Recovery and Growing Inequality*. New York, National Employment Law Project. www.nelp.org/page/-/Job_Creation/LowWageRecovery2012.pdf?nocdn=1.

Capps, Randy, Michael Fix, and Serena Yi-Ying Lin. 2010. *Still an Hourglass? Immigrant Workers in Middle-Skill Jobs.* Washington, DC: MPI. www.migrationpolicy.org/pubs/sectoralstudy-Sept2010.pdf.

Carnevale, Anthony, Nicole Smith, and Jeff Strohl. 2010. *Projections of Jobs and Education Requirements through 2018.* Washington, DC: Center on Education and the Workforce. www9.georgetown.edu/grad/gppi/hpi/cew/pdfs/FullReport.pdf.

Chen, Peggy, Leslie Curry, Susannah Bernheim, David Berg, Aysegul Gozu, and Marcella Nunez-Smith. 2011. Professional Challenges of Non-US-Born International Medical Graduates and Recommendations for Support During Residency Training. *Academic Medicine* 86 (11): 1383–8.

Chiswick, Barry and Paul Miller. 2002. Immigrant Earnings: Language Skills, Linguistic Concentrations, and the Business Cycle. *Journal of Population Economics* 15 (1): 31–57.

Creticos, Peter. Forthcoming. *Advanced Manufacturing within the Context of México, El Salvador, Guatemala, Honduras and the United States.* Washington, DC: MPI.

Fernández-Peña, José Ramón. 2012. Integrating Immigrant Health Professionals into the US Health Care Workforce: A Report from the Field. *Journal of Immigrant and Minority Health* 14 (3): 441–8.

Fink, Kenneth, Robert Phillips, George Fryer, and Nerissa Koehn. 2003. International Medical Graduates and the Primary Care Workforce for Rural Underserved Areas. *Health Affairs* 22 (2): 255–62. http://content.healthaffairs.org/content/22/2/255.full.pdf.

Goodin, Janiszewski. 2003. The Nursing Shortage in the United States of America: An Integrative Review of the Literature. *Journal of Advanced Nursing* 43 (4): 335–43.

Hagan, Jacqueline. 2004. Contextualizing Immigrant Labor Market Incorporation: Legal, Demographic, and Economic Dimensions. *Work and Occupations* 31 (4): 407–23.

Hagan, Jacqueline, Nichola Lowe, and Christian Quingla. 2011. Skills on the Move: Rethinking the Relationship between Human Capital and Immigrant Economic Mobility. *Work and Occupations* 38 (2): 149–78.

Hecker, Daniel E. 2005. *High-Technology Employment: A NAICS-Based Update.* Washington, DC: US Bureau of Labor Statistics. www.bls.gov/opub/mlr/2005/07/art6full.pdf.

Iskander, Natasha, Nichola Lowe, and Christine Riordan. 2010. The Rise and Fall of a Micro-Learning Region: Mexican Immigrants and Construction in Center-South Philadelphia. *Environment and Planning A* 42 (7): 1595–612.

Lewin-Epstein, Noah, Moshe Semyonov, and Irena Kogan. 2003. Institutional Structure and Immigrant Integration: A Comparative Study of Immigrants' Labor Market Attainment in Canada and Israel. *International Migration Review* 37 (2): 389–420.

Lowell, Lindsay and Stefka Gerova. 2004. Immigrants and the Healthcare Workforce Profiles and Shortages. *Work and Occupations* 31 (4): 474–98.

Lower-Basch, Elizabeth. 2007. *Opportunity at Work: Improving Job Quality.* Washington, DC: Center for Law and Social Policy. www.clasp.org/admin/site/publications/files/0374.pdf.

National Research Council. 2001. *Building a Workforce for the Information Economy.* Washington, DC: National Academy Press. www.nap.edu/openbook.php?record_id=9830&page=1.

Newman, Katherine. 2006. *Chutes and Ladders: Navigating the Low-Wage Labor Market.* Cambridge, MA: Harvard University Press.

Organization for Economic Cooperation and Development (OECD). 2012. *Better Skills, Better Jobs, Better Lives: A Strategic Approach to Skills Policies.* Paris: OECD. http://skills.oecd.org/documents/oecdskillsstrategy.html.

Orrenius, Pia M. and Madeline Zavodny. 2012. How Immigrants and US Natives Fare During Recessions and Recoveries. In *Immigrants in a Changing Labor Market: Responding to Economic Needs*, eds. Michael Fix, Demetrios G. Papademetriou, and Madeleine Sumption. Washington, DC: MPI.

Papademetriou, Demetrios G., Madeleine Sumption, and Aaron Terrazas with Carola Burkert, Stephen Loyal, and Ruth Ferrero-Turrión. 2010. *Migration and Immigrants Two Years after the Financial Collapse: Where Do We Stand?* Washington, DC: MPI. www.migrationpolicy.org/pubs/MPI-BBCreport-2010.pdf.

Ruggles, Steven, Trent Alexander, Katie Genadek, Ronald Goeken, Matthew Schroeder, and Matthew Sobek. 2012. *Integrated Public Use Microdata Series: Version 5.0 [Machine-Readable Database].* Minneapolis: University of Minnesota. http://usa.ipums.org/usa/index.shtml.

Saxenian, AnnaLee. 1999. *Silicon Valley's New Immigrant Entrepreneurs.* San Francisco, CA: Public Policy Institute of California. www.ppic.org/main/publication.asp?i=102.

Schumacher, Edward. 2011. Foreign-Born Nurses in the US Labor Market. *Health*

Economics 20 (3): 362–78.

Steigleder, Stephen and Louis Soares. 2012. *Let's Get Serious about Our Nation's Human Capital: A Plan to Reform the US Workforce Training System.* Washington, DC: Center for American Progress. www.americanprogress.org/wp-content/uploads/issues/2012/06/pdf/workforce_training.pdf.

Strom, Stephanie. 2012. For Ohio Pottery, a Small Revival. *New York Times,* June 11, 2012. www.nytimes.com/2012/06/12/business/starbucks-turns-to-ohio-not-china-for-coffee-mugs.html?_r=2.

Sumption, Madeleine, Michael Fix, Kristen McCabe, and Jeanne Batalova. Forthcoming. *Immigration and the Health-Care Workforce since the Global Economic Crisis.* Washington, DC: MPI.

The Association of Commercial and Institutional Builders of Massachusetts. 2012. Construction Employment, Spending Drop in Latest Month but Rise from Year Ago. *AGC's Data Digest*, April 2-6, 2012. www.agcmass.org/linkservid/E6FB48E4-D63A-9A68-E115274BA87F9944/showMeta/0/.

The Occupational Information Network (O*NET). www.onetcenter.org/about.html.

The Toronto-Dominion Bank Group (TD Bank Group). 2011. Caught in the Middle: The Polarization of Skills in the US Labor Market. www.td.com/document/PDF/economics/special/td-economics-special-cj0411_polarization.pdf.

US Bureau of Labor Statistics (BLS). 2012. Employment Projections – 2010-20. News Release, February 1, 2012. www.bls.gov/news.release/pdf/ecopro.pdf.

———. Online tables: Employment, Hours, and Earnings from the Current Employment Statistics Survey (National) in Construction, 2000 to 2012. www.bls.gov/CES/.

———. Online tables: Employment, Hours, and Earnings from the Current Employment Statistics Survey (National) in Health Care, 2000 to 2012. www.bls.gov/CES/.

———. Online tables: Employment, Hours, and Earnings from the Current Employment Statistics Survey (National) in Manufacturing, 2000 to 2012. www.bls.gov/CES/.

US Census Bureau, American Community Survey. 2007 and 2008. Online tables: Selected Characteristics of the Native and Foreign-Born Populations. http://factfinder2.census.gov/faces/nav/jsf/pages/index.xhtml.

Wider Opportunities for Women and the Center for Social Development. 2011. *Basic Economic Security Tables.* Washington, DC: Wider Opportunities for Women. www.wowonline.org/documents/BESTIndexforTheUnitedStates2010.pdf.

Yellen, Janet L. 2012 . The Economic Outlook and Monetary Policy. Speech given at the Money Marketeers of New York University, New York, April 11, 2012. www.federalreserve.gov/newsevents/speech/yellen20120411a.htm.

ACKNOWLEDGMENTS

The research in this volume was written for the Migration Policy Institute's (MPI) Labor Markets Initiative to inform its work on the economics of immigration. The thoughts contained in the chapters are the authors' own and do not necessarily represent the views of the Labor Markets Advisory Group or MPI. The editors would like to thank all the members of its Labor Markets Advisory Group, our MPI colleagues, and particularly Michelle Mittelstadt, for help and insightful comments throughout the project.

MPI is grateful for the generous support of funders for its Labor Markets Initiative, including the Ford Foundation, the Open Society Foundations, and the J.M. Kaplan Fund.

The authors would like acknowledge the insight, research assistance, and advice from the following people: Demetrios G. Papademetriou, Elise Brau, Linda Bi, Michael Nicholson, Michael Fix, Marc Rosenblum, Madeleine Sumption, and the participants in the July 2010 meeting of the Labor Markets Advisory Group.

About the Editors

Michael Fix is Senior Vice President and Director of Studies at the Migration Policy Institute (MPI), as well as Co-Director of MPI's National Center on Immigrant Integration Policy. His work focuses on immigrant integration, citizenship policy, immigrant children and families, the education of immigrant students, the effect of welfare reform on immigrants, and the impact of immigrants on the US labor force.

Mr. Fix, who is an attorney, previously was at the Urban Institute, where he directed the Immigration Studies Program (1998-2004). His research there focused on immigrants and integration, regulatory reform, federalism, race, and the measurement of discrimination. He is a Research Fellow with IZA in Bonn, Germany. He served on the National Academy of Sciences' Committee on the Redesign of US Naturalization Tests and was a member of the Advisory Panel to the Foundation for Child Development's Young Scholars Program.

His recent publications include *Young Children of Black Immigrants in America: Changing Flows, Changing Faces* (editor), *Immigrants and Welfare* (editor), *Los Angeles on the Leading Edge: Immigrant Integration Indicators and Their Policy Implications*, *Adult English Language Instruction in the United States: Determining Need and Investing Wisely*, *Measures of Change: The Demography and Literacy of Adolescent English Learners*, and *Securing the Future: US Immigrant Integration Policy, A Reader* (editor). His past research explored the implementation of employer sanctions and other reforms introduced by the *1986 Immigration Reform and Control Act*.

Mr. Fix received a JD from The University of Virginia and BA from Princeton University. He did additional graduate work at the London School of Economics.

Demetrios G. Papademetriou is President and Co-Founder of the Migration Policy Institute (MPI), a Washington-based think tank dedicated exclusively to the study of international migration. He is also the convener of the Transatlantic Council on Migration and its predecessor, the Transatlantic Task Force on Immigration and Integration (co-convened with the Bertelsmann Stiftung). The Council is composed of senior public figures, business leaders, and public intellectuals from Europe, the United States, and Canada.

Dr. Papademetriou is Co-Founder and International Chair Emeritus of *Metropolis: An International Forum for Research and Policy on Migration and Cities*. He has served as Chair of the World Economic Forum's Global Agenda Council on Migration (2009-11); Chair of the Migration Committee of the Organization for Economic Cooperation and Development (OECD); Director for Immigration Policy and Research at the US Department of Labor and Chair of the Secretary of Labor's Immigration

Policy Task Force; and Executive Editor of the *International Migration Review*.

Dr. Papademetriou has published more than 250 books, articles, monographs, and research reports on migration topics and advises senior government and political party officials in more than 20 countries (including numerous European Union Member States while they hold the rotating EU presidency).

His books include *Migration and the Great Recession: The Transatlantic Experience* (co-author and co-editor, 2011); *Immigration Policy in the Federal Republic of Germany: Negotiating Membership and Remaking the Nation* (co-author, 2010); *Gaining from Migration: Towards a New Mobility System, OECD Development Center* (co-author, 2007); *Immigration and America's Future: A New Chapter* (2006, co-author); *Europe and its Immigrants in the 21st Century: A New Deal or a Continuing Dialogue of the Deaf?* (2006, editor and author); *Secure Borders, Open Doors: Visa Procedures in the Post-September 11 Era* (2005, co-author), *NAFTA's Promise and Reality (2003, co-author), America's Challenge: Domestic Security, Civil Liberties, and National Unity after September 11* (2003, co-author); and *Caught in the Middle: Border Communities in an Era of Globalization* (2001, senior editor and co-author).

He holds a PhD in comparative public policy and international relations (1976) and has taught at the universities of Maryland, Duke, American, and New School for Social Research.

Madeleine Sumption is a Senior Policy Analyst at the Migration Policy Institute, where she works on the Labor Markets Initiative and the International Program. Her work focuses on labor migration, the role of immigrants in the labor market, and the impact of immigration policies in Europe, North America, and other Organization for Economic Cooperation and Development (OECD) countries.

Ms. Sumption's publications include *Policies to Curb Illegal Employment, Aligning Temporary Immigration Visas with US Labor Market Needs* (co-author), *Migration and Immigrants Two Years After the Financial Collapse* (co-editor and author), *Immigration and the Labor Market: Theory, Evidence and Policy* (co-author), *Migration and the Economic Downturn: What to Expect in the European Union* (co-author), and *Social Networks and Polish Immigration to the UK*.

Ms. Sumption holds a master's degree with honors from the University of Chicago's school of public policy. She also holds a first class degree in Russian and French from Oxford University.

About the Authors

Jeanne Batalova is a Senior Policy Analyst at the Migration Policy Institute and Manager of the MPI Data Hub, an online resource that provides instant access to the latest facts, stats, and maps covering US and global data on immigration and immigrant integration.

Her areas of expertise include the impacts of immigrants on society and labor markets; social and economic mobility of first- and second-generation youth and young adults; and the policies and practices regulating immigration and integration of highly skilled workers and foreign students in the United States and other countries.

Dr. Batalova has authored *Skilled Immigrant and Native Workers in the United States*, and co-authored *Up for Grabs: The Gains and Prospects of First- and Second-Generation Young Adults; DREAM vs. Reality: An Analysis of Potential DREAM Act Beneficiaries; Uneven Progress: The Employment Pathways of Skilled Immigrants in the United States; Immigration: Data Matters;* and *Measures of Change: The Demography and Literacy of Adolescent English Learners*, among other publications.

She earned her PhD in sociology, with a specialization in demography, from the University of California-Irvine; an MBA from Roosevelt University; and bachelor of the arts in economics from the Academy of Economic Studies, Chisinau, Moldova.

Gordon H. Hanson is Director of the Center on Emerging and Pacific Economies and a Professor of Economics at the University of California, San Diego (UCSD), where he holds faculty positions in the School of International Relations and Pacific Studies and the Department of Economics. Professor Hanson is also a Research Associate at the National Bureau of Economic Research, Co-Editor of the *Review of Economics and Statistics*, and a member of the Council on Foreign Relations. Prior to joining UCSD in 2001, he served on the economics faculties of the University of Michigan and the University of Texas.

Professor Hanson has published extensively in the top academic journals of the economics discipline on issues related to immigration, international trade, and foreign investment. His recent research examines the international migration of skilled labor, the economics of illegal immigration, and the relationship between business cycles and global outsourcing. His most recent book is *Regulating Low Skilled Immigration in the United States* (2010).

Harry J. Holzer is a Professor of Public Policy at Georgetown University and an Institute Fellow at the Urban Institute in Washington, DC. A former Chief Economist for the US Department of Labor and former Professor of Economics at Michigan State University, Dr. Holzer is a Senior Affiliate of the National Poverty Center at the University of Michigan and a Research Affiliate of the Institute for Research on Poverty at the University of Wisconsin-Madison. He is also a Nonresident Senior Fellow with the Brookings Metropolitan Policy Program and a member of the editorial board at the *Journal of Policy Analysis and Management*.

His research has focused primarily on the labor market problems of low-wage workers and other disadvantaged groups. His books include *The Black Youth Employment Crisis* (co-edited with Richard Freeman, 1986); *What Employers Want: Job Prospects for Less-Educated Workers* (1996); *Moving Up or Moving On: Who Advances in the Low-Wage Labor Market* (with Fredrik Andersson and Julia Lane, 2005); *Reconnecting Disadvantaged Young Men* (with Peter Edelman and Paul Offner, 2006); *Reshaping the American Workforce in a Changing Economy* (co-edited with Demetra Nightingale, 2007); and *Where are All the Good Jobs Going? What National and Local Job Quality and Dynamics Mean for U.S. Workers* (with Julia Lane, David Rosenblum and Fredrik Andersson, 2011).

Dr. Holzer received his AB from Harvard in 1978 and his PhD in Economics from Harvard in 1983.

Pia M. Orrenius is Senior Economist and an Assistant Vice President at the Federal Reserve Bank of Dallas and Adjunct Professor at the Hankamer School of Business, Baylor University. Her research focuses on the regional and national labor market impacts of immigration, illegal immigration, and US immigration policy. Her work has been published in the *Journal of Development Economics, Labour Economics, Industrial and Labor Relations Review, and Demography*, among others.

Dr. Orrenius is a Research Fellow at The Tower Center for Political Studies at Southern Methodist University and at the Institute for the Study of Labor (IZA) in Bonn. Dr. Orrenius was Senior Economist on the Council of Economic Advisers in the Executive Office of the President in Washington, DC, from 2004 to 2005. She received her PhD in Economics from the University of California at Los Angeles and BA degrees in Economics and Spanish from the University of Illinois at Urbana-Champaign.

Giovanni Peri is a Professor of Economics at the University of California, Davis, a Research Associate of the National Bureau of Economic Research in Cambridge, Massachusetts, and a Research Fellow at the Institute for the Study of Labor (IZA) in Bonn, Germany. He has done research on human capital, growth, and technological innovation. More recently he has focused and published extensively on the impact of international migration on labor markets and on productivity and on the determinants of international migration.

He recently received a John D. and Catherine T. MacArthur Foundation grant for the study of international migration and its impact in the United States and a World Bank grant for the study of return migration in Europe.

Madeline Zavodny is Professor of Economics at Agnes Scott College in Decatur, Georgia, and a Research Fellow at the Institute for the Study of Labor (IZA) in Bonn, Germany. Her research examines the economic effects of immigration, the effects of minimum-wage laws, and various aspects of economic demography. Dr. Zavodny's work has been published in the *Journal of Labor Economics, Journal of Development Economics, Industrial and Labor Relations Review*, and *Demography*, among others.

She received a PhD in Economics from the Massachusetts Institute of Technology and a BA in Economics from Claremont McKenna College.

About the Migration Policy Institute and its Labor Markets Initiative

The Migration Policy Institute (MPI) is an independent, nonpartisan nonprofit think tank in Washington, DC dedicated to analysis of the movement of people worldwide.

MPI provides analysis, development, and evaluation of migration and refugee policies at the local, national, and international levels. It aims to meet the rising demand for pragmatic and thoughtful responses to the challenges and opportunities that large-scale migration, whether voluntary or forced, presents to communities and institutions in an increasingly integrated world.

Founded in 2001 by Demetrios G. Papademetriou and Kathleen Newland, MPI grew out of the International Migration Policy Program at the Carnegie Endowment for International Peace.

MPI is guided by the philosophy that international migration needs active and intelligent management. When such policies are in place and are responsibly administered, they bring benefits to immigrants and their families, communities of origin and destination, and sending and receiving countries.

For more on the Migration Policy Institute and its research, visit www.MigrationPolicy.org.

The Labor Markets Initiative

The Labor Markets Initiative, a project of the Migration Policy Institute, is a comprehensive, policy-focused review of the role of immigration in the labor market.

The Initiative was tasked with producing detailed policy recommendations on how the United States should rethink its immigration policy in the light of what is known about the economic impact of immigration — bearing in mind the context of the economic crisis, growing income inequality, concerns about the effect of globalization on US competitiveness, the competition for highly skilled migrants, and demographic and technological change.

Within MPI, the project is led by MPI President Demetrios G. Papademetriou and Senior Vice President Michael Fix. The work also is guided by a group of leading experts in labor economics, welfare policy, and immigration. The Initiative's work builds on MPI's Independent Task Force on Immigration and America's Future, while focusing on the labor market impacts of immigration with particular emphasis on low-skilled or low-wage workers.

For more on MPI's Labor Markets Initiative, please visit:
www.migrationpolicy.org/LMI